MW01050518

Emergence of the Modern Mexican Woman

Women and Modern Revolution Series

Series Editors

Jane Slaughter   Richard Stites
University of New Mexico   Georgetown University

EMERGENCE OF THE MODERN MEXICAN WOMAN:
Her Participation in Revolution
and
Struggle for Equality, 1910-1940

by
Shirlene Soto

ARDEN PRESS, INC.
Denver, Colorado
1990

Library of Congress Cataloging-in-Publication Data

Soto, Shirlene Ann.
  Emergence of the modern Mexican woman : her participation in
revolution and struggle for equality, 1910-1940 / by Shirlene Soto.
  199p.   cm. -- (Women and modern revolution series)
  Includes bibliographical references.
  ISBN 0-912869-11-9 : s26.50. -- ISBN 0-912869-12-7 (pbk.) : s16.95
  1. Women in politics--Mexico--History--20th century. 2. Women's
rights--Mexico--History--20th century. 3. Women revolutionists-
-Mexico--Interviews. I. Title. II. Series.
HQ1236.5.M6S67   1990
305.42'0972--dc20   89-77883
                                                             CIP

Typography and design by Van Bogart Graphics, Inc.
Published in the United States of America

Arden Press, Inc.
P.O. Box 418
Denver, Colorado 80201

To E.B.S. for yesterday;
to W.E. for today and tomorrow

Table of Contents

Acknowledgments

I would like to thank the library staffs at the following institutions for their willing assistance, their many courtesies, and their efficient services: the Archivo General de la Nación, the Hemeroteca Nacional de México, and the Biblioteca Nacional (all in Mexico City); the Biblioteca Carrillo Ancona and the Hemeroteca Pino Suárez (both in Mérida, Yucatán); the Research Library at the University of California, Los Angeles (UCLA); the Latin American Collection at the University of Texas in Austin; the Zimmerman Library at the University of New Mexico in Albuquerque; and Oviatt Library at the California State University, Northridge (CSUN).

To those persons who granted personal interviews, often on more than one occasion, I am also grateful. Their insights and contributions added significantly to this study.

I am appreciative also for the funding received from the Institute of American Cultures at UCLA; to Jerome Richfield, Dean of the School of Humanities at CSUN, and to the Research and Grants Committee at CSUN for providing reassigned time to accommodate this project; to Peggy Laird, Director of Photography at CSUN, for preparation of photos; to linguists Solomon Lipp, Sylvia Ehrlich Lipp, and Anita Grillos for responding to my inquiries regarding subtle and difficult translations; to Susan Holte, editor at Arden Press, for the many arduous hours spent editing this manuscript; to Walt Elliott, my husband, for never hesitating to read and reread numerous manuscript drafts; and to those many persons, unnamed because of space limitations, whose support made this book a reality.

Chronology of Events, 1857-1940

Date	Event
1857	New constitution of Mexico proclaimed by Liberals; period of anti-clerical reform laws.
1858-1872	Presidency of Benito Juárez.
1876-1910	Porfiriato begins; Porfirio Díaz president, 1876-1880 and 1884-1910.
1900	Liberal Club "Ponciano Arriaga" organized in San Luis Potosí.
1903	Manifesto by Liberal Club "Ponciano Arriaga" emphasizing socio-economic injustices.
1904	
January	Partido Liberal Mexicano (PLM) meeting in Laredo, Texas.
March	After quarreling with Ricardo Flores Magón, PLM collaborators Acuña, Gutiérrez, Ramírez, Arriaga, and de la Vega leave for San Antonio, Texas.
1906	
June	Cananea mining strike.
July	PLM Program of 1906 issued.
December	Nationwide textile strike begins.
1907	
January	Río Blanco massacre; textile strike ends.
1908	
February	Díaz promises to retire at end of term in 1910.
May	Díaz announces that he will run for another term.

1909	Madero's *La sucesión presidencial en 1910* published.
1910	
November	Date set for nationwide uprising against Díaz (Madero's Plan de San Luis Potosí).
1911	
February	Mexicali, B.C. captured by PLM.
March	Complot de Tacubaya.
May	Díaz resigns and leaves Mexico.
June	A triumphant Madero enters Mexico City.
October	Madero elected president (1911–February 1913).
1912	
July	Casa del Obrero Mundial founded.
1913	
February	Huerta coup d'etat; Madero assassination; Huerta presidency, 1913–July 1914.
March	Plan de Guadalupe (Carranza); civil war between regular army and northern forces led by Carranza, Villa, and Obregón.
1914	Carranza government moves to Veracruz; Villa and Zapata enter Mexico City.
1915	
February	Carranza-Casa del Obrero Mundial alliance; Carrancistas defeat Villistas and Zapatistas.
1916	
December to January 1917	Querétaro Constitutional Convention.
1917-1920	Presidency of Venustiano Carranza.
1919	Emiliano Zapata assassinated.
1920	Carranza assassinated; Obregón ascends to power.
1920-1924	Presidency of Alvaro Obregón.
1924-1928	Presidency of Plutarco Calles.
1926-1929	Cristero Rebellion.
1929	Partido Nacional Revolucionario (PNR) established.
1928-1930	Presidency of Emilio Portes Gil.
1930-1932	Presidency of Pascual Ortiz Rubio.
1932-1934	Presidency of Abelardo Rodríguez.
1934-1940	Presidency of Lázaro Cárdenas.

Editors' Introduction to the Series

The history of the twentieth century has been marked by frequent revolutions and mass popular resistance to oppressive, dictatorial regimes. Few segments of the globe have remained untouched by these conflicts, which have sparked the interest of historians, political scientists, sociologists, and others who seek to understand the unique character of each conflict as well as the themes common to all. An ever-growing body of literature explains the causes or pre-conditions for these mass mobilizations and collective rebellions, examines the role of ideology in the revolutionary process, analyzes leaders and insurgent organizations, and assesses the results of social conflict. The scope of the scholarship on the topic is impressive, but with rare exceptions, until quite recently the actors considered in each drama have been almost exclusively male.

Marie Mullaney, in her recent work *Revolutionary Women*, begins with a review of existing analyses and notes that "the biggest problem with the available literature . . . is neither its unscientific quality nor its reductionist nature, but rather its unstated assumptions regarding the gender of revolutionary participants."[1] The gender bias in revolutionary studies is illustrated in a work by Ted Gurr entitled, appropriately, *Why Men Rebel*, which seeks to determine the specific values that serve as motivation for rebellion. The author points out that among classes of values which drive groups to act, welfare values (material conditions and economic hopes) and power values take precedence over interpersonal values, communality (desire to be useful to others), or an improved sense of social and political responsibility in the community.[2] If women's motivations had been assessed along with those of men, Gurr's conclusions might have been quite different.

Leaders of Revolution, published in 1979, offers a revisionist approach to the subject, criticizing earlier psychoanalytic, psychohistorical, and sociological approaches as speculative, non-empirical, and intuitive. The authors propose a new model defined as the "Situational Approach," which combines a set of personal characteristics with a "particular socio-historical context" to produce a profile of the revolutionary leader. The study statistically analyzes the lives of thirty-two such leaders from around the globe, all of them male.[3] The absence of women from such scholarly endeavors is, of course, not a problem confined to the study of revolution.

In recent years, women's history, the "new" social history, and women's studies in general have recognized and sought to redress imbalances in our historical perspective. We had to begin by naming and locating the women in the past. We now know that there have been female revolutionary leaders and soldiers and women's organizations integrally involved in revolutionary actions. Having discovered this historical material, we are now in a position to move beyond simple description by focusing on gender itself as a category of historical analysis. The implications of this approach were clearly stated by Natalie Zemon Davis in her 1975 address to the Berkshire Conference on Women's History. "Our goal is to understand the significance of the sexes, of gender groups, in the historical past. Our goal is to discover the range in sex roles and sexual symbolism in different societies and periods, to find out what meaning they had and how they functioned to maintain the social order or to promote its change."[4]

Though the focus of history in this series is on women and the female experience, the authors recognize that one gender does not stand alone, but is embedded in relationships with the opposite sex and conditioned by class, ethnicity, and age, among other factors. The sex/gender system as defined by Gayle Rubin is "a set of arrangements by which a society transforms biological sexuality into products of human activity."[5] All societies have such a set of arrangements, but their particular function in social organization and their relative importance in determining the course of human history vary. The multiple and complex set of relationships arising from gender, and the connections among these relationships and other fundamental forces in history, provide the framework for our studies.

Our purpose in this series is twofold. On the one hand we are examining the function of sex/gender systems in the revolutionary process. Our authors will ask the usual questions about revolutions: what are their causes, social components, ideologies, organizations, goals, and results? But in each case they are also asking what is gender-specific about these; do revolutions perhaps mean different things to men and women, and if so, why? We need to know, therefore, what motivates women to become involved in collective rebellions, what women contribute, what their expectations are, and ultimately what happens to women objectively and subjectively as a result of this involvement. Such an analysis of revolutions will add to our more general understanding of the place of sex/gender systems in human history.

The study of revolutions can be informed and improved by asking questions and testing conclusions raised in other works in women's history. The histories of nineteenth-century American female networks and early female volunteer associations, and the development of turn-of-the-century women's suffrage and moral reform organizations, can be used to understand women's motives, mobilization, and goals. Analyses of the more recent entry of women into public politics and the growth of contemporary feminism can shed light on questions of women's perspective, the growth of feminist consciousness, and the ability to effect broader social change.

The volumes in this series are linked by a variety of common themes; among them are the connections between women's culture and women's politics, the ways in which specific gender experience motivates individuals to act and in turn shapes expectations and goals, and, finally, how gender interacts with other historic forces to determine the outcome of a revolutionary movement. It is essential to understand how individual actions and reactions coalesce in movements and organizations with specified goals, but equally important is the analysis of "the political institutions and state structures through which [they] must operate if their agenda is to be realized."[6] On this latter point it is important to understand the relationship of women and their organizations to what Jane Jenson has described as the "universe of political discourse," which

> defines politics, or establishes the parameters of political action, by limiting the following: first, the range of actors who are accorded the status of legitimate participant; second, the range of issues considered to be within the realm of meaningful political debate; third, the policy alternatives considered feasible for implementation; and fourth, the alliance strategies available for achieving change.[7]

Whether women are able to enter this world and challenge its limitations is crucial to assessing the results of any activism.

These common themes are set within the diverse conditions of discrete national histories, and here it is important to emphasize the significance of comparative studies. General questions are addressed in all the volumes of the series, but specific processes and outcomes vary. Comparative studies must consider particular events of national history, different levels of economic development, and characteristic political traditions.[8] Ultimately, by making sense of these differences, we can begin to understand the possibilities and the limitations for women's participation in the world of politics and how such participation may be changing the gender structures of society. Today, as women and men grapple with the complex meanings and values of sameness and difference, we are well advised to seek enlightenment through the study of our common history.

1. Marie Marmo Mullaney, *Revolutionary Women: Gender and the Socialist Revolutionary Role* (New York: Praeger, 1983), p. 3.

2. Ted Robert Gurr, *Why Men Rebel* (Princeton, NJ: Princeton University Press, 1970), pp. 70-71.

3. Mostafa Rejai and Kay Phillips, *Leaders of Revolution* (Beverly Hills, CA: Sage Publications, 1979), pp. 19, 31, 55.

4. Cited in Joan Kelly-Gadol, "The Social Relations of the Sexes," *Signs* 1:4 (Summer 1976), p. 817.

5. Gayle Rubin, "The Traffic in Women," in Rayna R. Reiter (ed.), *Toward an Anthropology of Women* (New York: Monthly Review Press, 1975), p. 159.

6. For these two approaches, see, respectively, Janet Saltzman Chafetz and Anthony Gary Dworkin, *Female Revolt: Women's Movements in World and Historical Perspective* (Totowa, NJ: Rowman and Allanheld, 1986); and Mary F. Katzenstein and Carol M. Mueller (eds.), *The Women's Movements of the U.S. and Western Europe* (Philadelphia, PA: Temple University Press, 1987).

7. Jane Jenson, "Struggling for Identity: The Women's Movement and the State in Western Europe," in Sylvia Bashevkin (ed.), *Women and Politics in Western Europe* (London: Frank Cass and Co., 1985), p. 7.

8. Sharon Wolchik, "Introduction," to Sharon Wolchik and Alfred G. Meyers (eds.), *Women, State and Party in Eastern Europe* (Durham, NC: Duke University Press, 1985), p. 1.

Introduction

Considering that scholars have analyzed the Mexican Revolution from a wide range of perspectives, the paucity of studies dealing specifically with the role of Mexican women in the Revolution is disappointing. The focus of most scholars on political and diplomatic events of the Revolution—events in which the role of women was generally limited—has resulted in little acknowledgment of the significant roles played by women in so many other areas that were fundamental to the Revolution's success. To rectify such historical omissions, this work focuses upon women's participation in the Mexican Revolution (1910-1940) and in the Mexican women's rights movement during this thirty-year period.

The stage was first set for significant changes in the status of Mexican women, and for the emergence of women revolutionary leaders, during the pre-revolutionary Porfiriato period (1876-1910). During these thirty-five years, appreciable numbers of middle-class Mexican women were able to receive a formal education and to enter various professions for the first time. Following the Porfiriato, the revolutionary period served to further catalyze changes for women because of geographical displacement from home regions and wider ranges of occupational opportunities. In addition to filling such traditional roles as nurses, teachers, and office workers, revolutionary women assumed new roles as military commanders, *soldaderas*, union organizers, tradespersons, and writers.

During the early revolutionary period (1910-1920), women succeeded in acquiring additional, though limited, legal rights. Divorce was permitted for the first time, and the 1917 Constitution guaranteed some rights for working

1

women. However, political equality remained elusively outside women's grasp, primarily because of women's traditionally close relationship with the Roman Catholic Church. (Revolutionaries believed church influence had to be destroyed if the Revolution were to succeed.)

Between 1915 and 1924, the most intense struggle for women's rights in Mexico centered in the state of Yucatán. Site of the first two feminist congresses, Yucatán was the scene of the most active social, political, and economic participation by women in Mexico. Yucatán's leadership in the women's movement can be attributed to the support of its two Socialist governors, the progressive ideas and activism of its women leaders, and the economic base derived from its highly profitable henequen crops.

The assassination of the Yucatán governor in 1924 abruptly halted nine successive years of Yucatán social reform. The next administration dissolved women's organizations, removed women from their positions in municipal and state government, cancelled women's suffrage, and halted social programs. Consequently, the momentum of the Mexican women's movement shifted from Yucatán to Mexico City.

Mexican women achieved only limited success in their struggle for equality in the period from 1920 to 1934. After helping to win the Revolution and to carry out many revolutionary reforms, especially in the fields of education and health, women received few immediate benefits.

During the six-year presidency of Lázaro Cárdenas (1934-1940), women continued to work concertedly toward achieving suffrage. They now faced fewer political obstacles than in the past because both the church and the state sought women's allegiance. Women's groups were organized and incorporated into the official state party. In 1936, the official party granted women the right to vote in party primaries, and a few states enacted women's suffrage. In 1938, a national suffrage amendment passed both houses of Congress and was ratified by all twenty-eight states. However, Congress adjourned without completing the ratification process, and the suffrage amendment never became law.

Despite their important contributions to the Revolution, Mexican women leaders remained largely unrecognized during the post-revolutionary period. A few revolutionary women were awarded small pensions, and some were even commissioned with rank, but many of them lived out their lives in poverty and died relatively unknown.

Widespread disillusionment occurred when women realized that they were not to receive their promised share of the Revolution's benefits. The harsh reality was that Mexican women were not to attain national suffrage until 1953, and they were not to vote in a national election until 1958.

* * *

To research the role women played in the Revolution, it is essential to look beyond traditional sources, which tend to be narrow in focus and to reveal little about such groups as the poor, minorities, and women. The few authors who have addressed the subject of women's role in the Revolution have tended to focus on women who were politically moderate and to ignore those who were Socialists or Communists. Accordingly, these historical accounts have suffered from a lack of balance, because a great deal of leadership came from Communists and Socialists.

It is rare to find first-hand accounts by women who participated in the Revolution. Many revolutionary women were illiterate, so their experiences went unrecorded. Further, the disruptive circumstances of violent revolution often precluded literate women from recording their experiences. In addition, very few women are alive today to provide personal accounts of women's roles in revolutionary activities. The author conducted personal interviews with some of the few revolutionary women still living and with deceased revolutionaries' family members and friends, mainly in Mexico City and in Mérida. These interviews proved to be indispensable sources of information.

Preparation of this book also required analysis of a variety of sources. The bulk of information was drawn from a wide assortment of newspapers, magazines, pamphlets, and books, most of which are located in the Hemeroteca Nacional de México and in the Biblioteca Nacional in Mexico City. Information on Yucatán was derived largely from materials located in the Hemeroteca Pino Suárez and the Biblioteca Carrillo Ancona, both located in Mérida, capital of the state of Yucatán. Additional sources were located at the University of Texas and the University of New Mexico.

The only book in English devoted exclusively to the role of women in the Revolution is *The Mexican Woman: A Study of Her Participation in the Revolution, 1910-1940* (1979), which is an unrevised version of this author's doctoral dissertation. There are only two historical monographs in Spanish that are devoted exclusively to the topic: a small volume titled *La mujer en la revolución mexicana* (1961) and, more recently, a monograph titled *Juana Belen Gutiérrez de Mendoza (1875-1942): Extraordinario precursora de la revolución mexicana* (1983), both written by historian María de los Angeles Mendieta Alatorre. The only books in English that include some facets of the Mexican woman's revolutionary struggle are *Woman Suffrage in Mexico* (1962), by Ward M. Morton, which focuses upon the legal aspects of suffrage and concentrates upon the period after the 1930s; and a monograph, *Against All Odds: The Feminist Movement in Mexico to 1940* (1982), by Anna Macías, which focuses upon women's efforts to attain political equality.

This book was written to fill a gap in our knowledge of the history of the Mexican Revolution, to provide specific information about the significant revolutionary contributions of Mexican women, and particularly to provide Mexican and Mexican-American women with a fuller understanding and appreciation of their rich cultural heritage. It introduces readers to the heroic women who participated in a long and difficult struggle for freedom and equality, and who prepared the groundwork for the emergence of the modern Mexican woman.

Yuma

Mexicali

110°W

A R I Z O N A

Tucson

Clifton

Sonoita

Nogales

Nogales

Agua Prieta

Cananea

105°W

N E W   M E X I C O

El Paso

Ciudad
Juárez

30°N

BAJA

Golfo de

I. Tiburón

S O N O R A

Hermosillo

Casas Grandes

CHIHUAHUA

Chihuahua

Rio Yaqui

California

Guaymas

Cabora

Navojoa

Yávaros

Alamos

Rio Mayo

Sierra

Tomochic

Camargo

COAHU

Jiménez

Parral

Pie

25°N

Sinaloa

C A L I F O R N I A

Madre

Culiacán

Gómez Palacio

Ciudad Lerdo

Torreón

D U R A N G O

Durango

ZACATECA

S I N A L O A

Occidental

Rosario

Valparaíso

Zaca

Jérez

P A C I F I C

Islas
Tres Marías

NAYARIT

Colotlán

(A)
Agua

Jalpa

Rio Verd

20°N   O C E A N

Tepic

Guadalajara

Ocotlán

Rio Le

Gu

Zan

J A L I S C O

Colima

Manzanillo

Colima

COLIMA

MICH

| 0 | 100 | 200 | 300 |

| 0 | 100 | 200 |

(A) AGUASCALIENTES

(M) MORELOS

(Q) QUERETARO

(T) TLAXCALA

105°W

95°W · 90°W

MISSISSIPPI

D STATES OF AMERICA   ALABAMA

LOUISIANA

30°N

TEXAS

San Antonio

Laredo

Gulf of Mexico

25°N

nterrey

TAMAULIPAS

MEXICO

Ciudad del Maíz

Ciudad Madero

Tampico

POTOSI

Motul

Mérida   Valladolid

(Q)   Huejutla

HIDALGO

YUCATAN

étaro

andel Río

Papantla

Bahía de

20°N

Mts of Zacapoaxtla

Campeche

1EXICO

Mexico (T)

Jalapa

VERA CRUZ

Campeche

QUINTANA

ROO

luca

City

Puebla

Córdoba

Veracruz

Cuernavaca

(M)

Orizaba

uala

PUEBLA

CAMPECHE

TABASCO

ERO

BR.

ilpancingo

HONDURAS

Oaxaca

San Cristóbal

Tuxtla

OAXACA

Gutiérrez

Tehuantepec

CHIAPAS

GUATEMALA

W   95°W   90°W   HONDURAS

▪ 1 ▪

The Revolution's Antecedents: Women in the Porfiriato, 1876-1910

The thirty-four-year era of Porfirio Díaz (1876-1910), known as the Porfiriato, was one of great modernization and industrial progress for Mexico. Originally from the city of Oaxaca in southwestern Mexico, Díaz first rose to national prominence by virtue of his military prowess and then maintained that prominence by successive election as president of Mexico. Díaz promoted a phenomenal surge in industrial growth and prosperity, during which the nation's railroads, mines, and ports were expanded rapidly and its postal, telegraph, and telephone services were established. Unfortunately, the major benefits of this growth and modernization were reserved for only a relatively small, elite group of Mexicans and for foreign capitalists. Even worse, despite the nation's rapid economic growth, *obreros* and *campesinos* (workers and peasants) sank deeper into poverty, ignorance, and misery. Hunger was common. Disease flourished, making Mexico's death rate one of the highest in the world.

The philosophy that sanctioned this system of plenty for the few was called "positivism." Positivists, known as *"científicos"* by their critics, viewed themselves as naturally selected elites in a Darwinian evolutionary process; and, under Díaz, they took advantage of every opportunity to enrich themselves. Foreign investors were quick to ally themselves with the positivist oligarchy in order to gain economic concessions, and the Catholic Church was just as quick to bless this union of *científicos* and foreigners in order to assure its dominant position in Mexico.

The result of this tripartite union of *científicos*, foreign capitalists, and the church was calamitous for the masses. In addition to economic exploitation

7

and unjust treatment of the masses, the *científicos* ignored the plight of the Indian population (considering Indians to be inferior). They turned their backs on indigenous Mexican cultures while openly emulating European and North American cultural styles.

By 1910, Díaz's three-and-one-half decade rule had resulted in vast differences in personal wealth, a closed political system run by a privileged few, and flagrant favoritism toward foreigners. It had also resulted in the deep alienation of large numbers of Mexican intellectuals, workers, and even some business owners and *hacendados* (owners of ranches and large estates). Thus, by 1910, there was widespread clamor for change, which led ultimately to the overthrow of Díaz and to the Mexican Revolution.

For Mexican women, the transition from the Porfiriato period to the revolutionary period was dramatic. The impetus for the transition increased sharply during the Porfiriato and then became an irresistible force when fanned by the winds of revolution. During the Porfiriato, the clamor for change in the status of Mexican women was led mostly by middle-class women. Although few in number, middle-class women organized an ever-growing wave of protest against the prevailing influence of the Catholic Church, against the traditional social mores that kept women tied solely to home and family, and against the legal code that served to stifle women's political, educational, and economic needs. These middle-class Mexican women, allied with many upper-class Mexican women, were encouraged in their protests by such strong external elements as the philosophy of liberalism, the ideas of sexual equality espoused by Karl Marx and Friedrich Engels, and the international movement for women's rights.

As one might expect of modern political movements, the written word played an important role in the Mexican women's movement. During the early years of the Porfiriato, literate Mexican women were exposed to such journals as *La Internacional*, in which Socialist writers recommended the "emancipation, rehabilitation and integral education of women."[1] Increasingly, Mexican women argued for political equality, drawing upon such feminist sources as Mary Wallstonecraft's *A Vindication of the Rights of Women* (1790), John Stuart Mill's *The Subjection of Women* (1869), and August Bebel's *Women under Socialism* (1883). And, as general dissatisfaction with the Díaz administration grew, Mexican women writers no longer confined themselves to such traditional topics as music and religion, but expanded their subject matter to encompass political and socioeconomic topics, including revolutionary poetry, criticism of the Díaz administration, and reevaluation of women's roles in Mexican society. Of course, this literary effort was restricted almost wholly to a limited number of literate upper-class and middle-class women; the vast majority of Mexican women were still illiterate.

Although more and more middle-class women were studying and pursuing professions during the Porfiriato, unskilled women in lower economic classes had few career choices. Many unskilled women were forced to work for a pittance or to turn to prostitution for survival. Economic mobility for those of the lower class was practically nonexistent; therefore, many of them spent their lives slaving in factories or working as low-paid domestics. By 1895, there were more than 275,000 domestic servants in Mexico, most of them women.[2]

In the early 1900s, North American muckraker John Kenneth Turner, a collaborator of the radical Flores Magón brothers, reported on the working and living conditions of women in the states of Yucatán and Oaxaca. In his widely read exposé *Barbarous Mexico*, Turner sought to expose the alliance of North American business interests with the Díaz administration, government corruption, and Indian slavery, thereby revealing the darker side of "progressive Mexico" under Díaz. Turner recounted how Yaqui Indian women from northwestern Mexico complained constantly of being molested by the *federales* (federal troops), who forcibly transported them to work in the henequen plantations in Yucatán. Upon arrival, women were assigned sexual partners and often forced into marriages, sometimes with Asian workers whom the *hacendados* were trying to placate. On the notorious tobacco plantations in Oaxaca's Valle Nacional, workers were forced to share attractive wives with planters or with bosses. Many of these displaced women were forcibly placed in coeducational dormitories, where at the end of the workday they had to fend for themselves as best they could.

Turner stated that slavery conditions similar to those found in Yucatán and in the Valle Nacional were to be found in nearly every Mexican state, especially in the southern coastal states. Slaves performed the manual labor on the henequen plantations of Campeche; in the lumber and fruit industries of Chiapas and Tabasco; and on the rubber, coffee, sugar cane, tobacco, and fruit plantations of Veracruz, Oaxaca, and Morelos.[3]

As mentioned earlier, during the Porfiriato, prostitution was one of the few economic options available to poor women. In 1899, it was estimated that there were 3,508 prostitutes in Mexico City, of whom only 5 percent could read.[4] In 1905, Luis Lara y Pardo, a physician and student of Mexico's social problems, reported that Mexico City had 11,554 registered prostitutes and that 4,371 unregistered prostitutes were apprehended by authorities during that same year. These numbers appear more revealing when viewed from the perspective that the 15,925 prostitutes reported by the doctor were from a total population of 71,737 Mexico City women between the ages of fifteen and thirty. Because 95 percent of the known prostitutes in Mexico City were in this age group, Dr. Lara y Pardo calculated that at least 22 percent of Mexico City's fifteen-year-old to thirty-year-old women (nearly one out of every four) were prostitutes, a proportion approximately ten times greater than that in Paris.[5]

WOMEN'S LEGAL STATUS

During the Porfiriato, women of all social classes were restricted by laws that were blatantly discriminatory. Articles 40 and 41 of the Mexican Constitution of 1857 defined Mexican citizenship but made no direct reference to citizenship for women, and the Civil Codes of 1870 and 1884 severely limited the rights of women, particularly those of married women. Noted Mexican feminist and Carranza collaborator Hermila Galindo summarized how the Civil Code of 1884 discriminated against married women:

> The wife has no rights whatsoever in the home. [She is] excluded from participating in any public matter [and] she lacks authority to draw up any contract. She cannot dispose of her personal property, or even administer it, and she is legally disqualified to defend herself against her husband's mismanagement of her estate. . . . [A wife] lacks all authority over her children, and she has no right to intervene in their education. . . . She must, as a widow, consult persons designated by her husband before his death; otherwise she can lose her rights to her children.[6]

Once married, a woman was committed permanently to wedlock because divorce was neither legal nor socially acceptable. The Civil Code of 1884 adhered closely to canon law, which proclaimed the indissolubility of marriage. What was known as "divorce" was merely a legalized separation during which remarriage was forbidden. The double standard prevailed. For example, separation was granted unequivocally to a husband whose wife had committed adultery. On the other hand, a wife could charge her husband with adultery only if he committed adultery in the home, kept a mistress, or created a public scandal by mistreating (or permitting his mistress to mistreat) his wife. It was not until 1904 that a bill legalizing divorce was approved by the Chamber of Deputies and sent to the Senate for consideration. President Díaz's wife, Carmen Romero Rubio de Díaz, whose father served in the Díaz cabinet, was a devout Catholic who disapproved of divorce, as did many Catholic conservatives, and the bill was not even discussed when it came before the Senate.[7]

In 1891, one of the most articulate defenders of women's rights in Mexico, Génaro García, in *Apuntes sobre la condición de la mujer* (*Notes on the Status of Women*), emphasized the vast discrepancies between the legal rights of men and women. Stating that "equality is the first condition of liberty," García emphasized that while the Civil Code of 1884 defined a Mexican citizen as anyone twenty-one years or over, no unmarried woman under thirty could legally leave her parental home. Mexican laws also prohibited married women from entering certain professions. The Commercial Code denied women employment in the brokerage field, and the Civil Code prohibited them from serving as trial attorneys or solicitors in trials, except on behalf of their husbands or relatives.[8] Section I of Article 462 prohibited women from tutoring anyone except their husbands and their children, and Article 581 forbade women from acting as legal guardians.

Articles 343 and 345 of the Civil Code prohibited the investigation of paternity but allowed children to trace their matriarchal line. García complained that this constituted "a flagrant violation of all morality and justice, a further impunity for the licentiousness of corrupt men, and a new blow for the already sad condition of women." García concluded by stating that Mexican law "sustains an almost incredible inequality between the conditions of the husband and the wife, restricts in an exaggerated and arbitrary manner those rights due the woman, and . . . erases and nullifies her personality."[9]

WOMEN'S EDUCATIONAL STATUS

Prior to the Porfiriato, a period of rapid growth in general education within Mexico had been initiated by President Benito Juárez. In 1867, President Juárez declared primary education obligatory and laid extensive plans to expand educational facilities nationwide. Under the Juárez Declaration, municipalities and rural *hacendados* were required to establish schools for children.

As a result of the Juárez Declaration, the city council in Mexico City eventually maintained at least twelve tuition-free institutions for boys and an equal number for girls.[10] One school for girls and two schools for boys were opened in Mexico City in 1869. A short time later, professional schools of law, medicine, mining, agriculture, fine arts, commerce, and a school for the deaf opened their doors in Mexico City.

The increase in the number of schools was also substantial nationwide. In 1843, there were only 1,310 officially registered schools in the nation; by 1870, the number had increased to 4,500; and by 1874, the number had grown almost seven-fold to 8,103. Of these schools, about 2,000 were private institutions, though only 117 were supported by the Catholic Church. Fewer than 550 schools were coeducational; of the remainder, the ratio was about four-to-one in favor of schools for boys only.[11]

Due largely to the Juárez Declaration and consequent construction of new schools, illiteracy in Mexico fell from 99.5 percent at the time of independence from Spain (1821) to 78.4 percent in 1910, even though the population of Mexico rose from 6 to 15 million during this same period.[12]

The growth of education during the Porfiriato was even more dramatic than during the Juárez administration. Díaz advocated popular education as one of his general administrative goals. In 1878, to satisfy the new demand for teachers, Mexico City's Escuela Nacional Secondaria de Niñas (later known as the Escuela Normal de Profesoras) rapidly increased its enroll-ment.[13] Art schools for young middle-class women became popular, and at the turn of the century they enrolled more than one thousand students. Dur-ing this same period, the number of vocational schools, whose student bodies included women mainly from working-class families, increased dramatically. (For example, the Escuela Comercial "Miguel Lerdo de Tejada" began instruction for young women in the field of business.)[14]

Rapid growth of educational opportunities for women occurred not only in Mexico City but in the provinces as well. In San Luis Potosí, the Escuela de Artes y Oficios para Mujeres opened in 1881; two years later, in Puebla, the Escuela Mixta de Profesores was expanded to include women; the Escuela Normal de Jalapa admitted women for the first time in 1891; and the Escuela Normal de Jalisco enrolled women in 1894.[15] By 1895, with expanded employment opportunities for teachers provided by the opening of these new schools, over half of the nation's elementary teaching positions were held by women.[16]

While the most popular professions for women during the Porfiriato were teaching, nursing, and clerical work, women did enter other fields.[17] One of the first women to receive a professional degree in Mexico was Margarita Chorné, who graduated in dentistry in 1886. A year later, Matilda P. Montoya became Mexico's first woman physician. Montoya's career choice was considered so unusual that several newspapers announced the time when she was scheduled to take her medical examinations. In 1887, when Montoya received the title "Doctor, the first of her sex in Mexico," Presi-dent Díaz himself presided over the ceremony. Writer and activist María Sandoval de Zarco became Mexico's first woman lawyer in 1889.[18] María Guerrero, the nation's first woman public accountant, completed her studies in 1908. By 1910, the National University in Mexico City had graduated five women medical doctors, two women dentists, a woman lawyer, and a woman chemist.[19]

During the last part of the nineteenth century, a few special schools were established solely for women. In 1897, a school for reformed prostitutes opened in Mexico City. Also, limited educational facilities were made available for the city's orphaned, indigent, and physically handicapped women. In 1888, the capital's asylum for beggars was expanded to include women, and a day care center for Mexico City's working mothers was begun in 1887.[20] Further, a night school for working women was in opera-tion in Mexico City by 1898.[21]

The political demands of the growing number of educated working women incited an ever-widening controversy that touched the very core of a most fundamental social issue in Mexican culture—the role women should play in society. Antifeminists, buoyed by the philosophy of Social Darwinism, argued that women were physically, socially, psychologically, and morally inferior to men, and they attacked feminists as being unchristian and domestic failures. In 1906, the Yucatán writer Ignacio Gamboa penned a widely read antifeminist piece. In *La mujer moderna* (*The Modern Woman*), Gamboa warned that a successful women's movement would be a disaster because, among other problems, it would result in lowered morals. Further, using religious documentation, Gamboa concluded that men were morally and biologically superior to women.[22]

Such journalistic attacks as Gamboa's were countered by prominent feminist authors such as Génaro García, and these responses were published in various magazines, newspapers, and academic theses (theses authored by women students from such institutions as the Instituto Normal del Estado de Puebla). Feminist authors advocated strongly that women should be free to pursue an education and to enter the work force. Although feminist ideas were circulated principally by the print medium, they were also perpetuated through proselytization in the classrooms of feminist professors and feminist public schoolteachers. Shortly after the turn of the century, theses by women in educational institutions reflected the increasingly popular idea that a better-educated woman would be a more efficient homemaker and would help create a better society. Thus, the education of women was perceived by Mexican feminists to be an essential element for a progressive democratic society, and access to education was to become a key goal for women revolutionaries.[23]

WOMEN WORKERS ORGANIZE:
THE TEXTILE AND TOBACCO INDUSTRIES

Between 1895 and 1910, women comprised one-third of all workers employed in manufacturing in Mexico. Many women worked at dressmaking, shoe manufacturing, food and beverage processing, and pottery and glass making, but the greatest numbers were employed in the textile and tobacco industries.[24]

Although women constituted one-third of all the nation's factory workers, the ratio of women to men employed in the textile industry decreased significantly between the 1890s and 1910. Of the ninety-seven textile factories listed for 1893, only two of those factories employing more than ninety-five workers had more women than men.[25] By the end of the century, women constituted only 13 percent of the textile work force.[26] In 1880, "Hercules," an important textile factory located in Querétaro, counted only fifteen women and eight children among its 423 employees. By 1900, Puebla's textile center employed almost no women. And in 1900, "Río Blanco" in Orizaba, by then the nation's largest textile plant and the setting for the massive 1907 strike, employed only 18 percent women. In the north, where labor continued to be scarce and costly, greater numbers of women remained employed, undoubtedly because of their willingness to accept lower wages than those paid to men. "La Estrella," a mill located in the northern state of Coahuila and owned by the Madero family (whose son Francisco would later challenge Díaz for control of Mexico), employed 33⅓ percent women of a total work force of 600.[27]

Deplorable working and living conditions led women textile workers to be the first women to organize in Mexico. The result was a series of strikes. From these strikes emerged some of the principal supporters of the Revolution; and, in many cases, these organizing efforts were forerunners of the nation's women's rights movement.[28]

Women textile workers filled the industry's lowest-paying positions and worked for lower salaries than did men performing the same tasks. Generally, women received roughly one-half to one-third of men's salaries, and children were in a wage class below adults. In 1885, in the "Hercules" factory in Querétaro, women were paid an average of 20 to 25 centavos on a piece-work basis, while operators (usually men) received between 31 and 52 centavos.[29] In "Río Blanco," in 1898, women workers averaged 60 to 80 centavos daily; children, 30 to 50 centavos; and men, 56 centavos to two and one-half pesos. During his trip to Mexico between fall 1908 and spring 1909, North American writer John Kenneth Turner discovered that male textile workers at the Río Blanco mills were paid the equivalent of 37.5 cents U.S. per day; women were paid 25 to 33 cents per day; and children were paid 10 to 25 cents a day.[30]

Julio Sesto, the Spanish author of *El México de Porfirio Díaz*, reported that women in the Federal District (greater Mexico City) were paid as little as 25 centavos a day. However, many of the "women" were no more than children. "To believe it," Sesto remarked, "one has to see the forsaken girls of Mexico spending an embittered adolescence in the shops and factories."[31] In 1906, the Gran Círculo de Obreros Libres (Grand Circle of Free Workers), an anarcho-syndicalist union affiliated with Ricardo Flores Magón's Partido Liberal Mexicano (Mexican Liberal Party [PLM]), urged minimum salaries of 75 centavos per day for male textile workers, 40 centavos per day for women workers, and 30 centavos per day for children.[32] (It is interesting to note that, at this time, Flores Magón apparently did not advocate equal pay for equal work, though later he would demand economic equality for both men and women.)

Low wages were decreased even further by the practice of paying workers partially in *vales* (pay certificates), which had to be redeemed at the over-priced *tienda de raya* (company store) and which were discounted by the company store to about 10 to 12 percent of their face value. Wages also were reduced by deductions for company housing and for fines resulting from machinery breakage. Underpaid, overworked, threatened with replacement by machinery, and often mistreated by male supervisors, women organized to protect themselves against discrimination and miserable working conditions.[33]

As early as 1857, textile workers in the *rebozo* (shawl) factory "El Toril" in Guadalajara, of whom 90 percent were women, demanded salaries equal to those paid in the Federal District. Although unsuccessful in obtaining salary parity, they did receive some salary increases. In 1862, a circular demanding higher wages, shorter hours, and care during pregnancy received wide support among women laborers in Veracruz. In 1867, strikers at "La Fama Montañesa" factory, located in a Mexico City suburb, demanded that the workday be limited to twelve hours to allow more time for domestic duties. When textile workers held their First Permanent Congress in March 1867, improving working conditions for women was part of the platform. The presence of women at this congress, and at future congresses, had a lasting and salubrious effect upon the women's movement; women began to assume more responsibility for organizing congresses and for winning labor contracts that contained protective clauses for women and children. Activist Carmen Huerta, one of two women delegates to the first Mexican National Labor Congress, was elected to preside over the Board of Mutual Benefit Societies of Mexico, a *mutualista* (mutual benefit society) that claimed the right to strike and to seek social justice.[34]

In 1907, textile workers in the Federal District founded the Hijas de Anáhuac (Daughters of Anáhuac), one of the first women's revolutionary organizations. Taking the name Anáhuac from the Indian word for the Valley of Mexico, the Hijas supported the goals of the Partido Liberal Mexicano, which included revolution as the vehicle for social change, resignation of President Díaz, and improved conditions for women. Meeting weekly in the home of sisters María del Carmen and Catalina Frías, the organization grew quickly from a handful to more than three hundred women. Then the Hijas was suppressed by the police, its leaders were subjected to persecution, large meetings of its membership were banned, and clandestine meetings of small groups of members had to be held in fields near the factories. After the Revolution began, members of the Hijas threw their support to political moderate Francisco I. Madero, who would overthrow Díaz and be elected president of Mexico (1911-1913).[35]

Women in the tobacco industry, which employed a higher percentage of women than did the textile industry, were also organizing during the Porfiriato. Tobacco workers demanded higher women's salaries, shorter working hours, and better working conditions. One of the first tobacco workers' strikes took place in the "Moro Muzo" factory in September 1881. The owners wanted to raise the workers' daily quota without an increase in wages.[36] The cigar rollers struck, but hunger eventually forced them back to work without any gains; however, the precedent for the strike as a means of economic protection for women workers had been established. That same year, women cigar rollers struck in protest against unfair wages and poor treatment at the "El César" factory, and in 1884 they struck at the "El Faro" factory. Women did not restrict their acts of protest to the strike, however. In 1884, two hundred women cigar rollers from the "El Borrego" factory, protesting unfit working conditions and low salaries, attacked the "Moro Muzo" factory; and at the "La Niña" factory in 1885, women workers slowed production deliberately as an act of protest.[37]

Throughout the Porfiriato, principally because of low wages and excessive daily quotas, the tobacco industry was plagued by production slowdowns, worker attacks against factories, and numerous strikes. Although many of these strikes were unsuccessful in achieving their immediate goals, chiefly because of the abundance of cheap labor, they laid the groundwork for greater organization of working-class Mexican women.

As a further defense against unfair labor practices and inadequate government protection, workers formed cooperatives and *mutualistas*. *Mutualistas* provided some immediate relief to destitute workers by offering members unemployment benefits, medical care, medicines, and funeral expenses. In 1894, the Workers' Congress recognized fifty-four *mutualistas*, eight of which were exclusively female. Of those eight, seven were located in or near Mexico City. Esperanza y Caridad de Señoras (Women's Hope and Charity), founded in 1874, was representative of nineteenth-century *mutualistas*. This *mutualista* had 124 members, provided medicine and doctors for sick members, and gave 40 pesos in funeral expenses to the family of any member who died.[38]

As noted earlier, the abysmal conditions of women workers provided strong incentives for women to organize to protect their rights; thus, they began increasingly to form societies that could offer protection and call attention to their general plight. The Admiradoras de Juárez (Female Admirers of Juárez) and the Sociedad Protectora de la Mujer (Women's Protective Society) were among the earliest feminist societies in Mexico City.

In 1904, the militant feminist society Admiradoras de Juárez was founded by journalist Laura N. Torres, and was subjected immediately to ridicule by such prominent persons as Justo Sierra, Porfirian Mexico's preeminent intellectual, educator, Supreme Court magistrate, and first rector of the National University. Sierra accused feminists of using the Admiradoras de Juárez as a refuge for old, ugly women who were trying to imitate men and advised them to leave politics to men and to concentrate on creating a more positive social atmosphere for Mexicans.[39] That same year, the Sociedad Protectora de la Mujer was organized by the staff of the magazine *La Mujer Mexicana*. The Sociedad's purpose was to provide vocational training and to find jobs for working-class women. Some of Mexico's most talented women writers and activists were members of the Sociedad, which was chaired first by lawyer María Sandoval de Zarco and later by poet Laura Méndez de Cuenca.

In 1906, the Sociedad de Empleadas de Comercio (Society of Women Business Employees) was established. The Sociedad's principal activities included the formation of two women's academies (one for commerce and one for music), a savings and loan bank, an employment bureau, a library, and a women's journal titled *La Abeja* (*The Bee*).[40]

EARLY POLITICAL STIRRINGS:
TERESA URREA, LA SANTA DE CABORA

During the early 1900s, while women workers were organizing, and while the Partido Liberal Mexicano (Mexican Liberal Party [PLM]) was being organized under the leadership of the Flores Magón brothers, a young Mexican woman named Teresa Urrea (1873-1906) was already exerting tremendous influence in northern Mexico. In fact, had Urrea been more politically motivated, she might have inspired a rebellion twenty years before the Mexican Revolution. The power held by Urrea was mystical, almost spiritual, and was used politically by many of her followers after they grew discontented with the Díaz government.

Urrea was born in 1873 in the west coast area of Sinaloa, the illegitimate daughter of a fourteen-year-old Yaqui Indian woman and a wealthy *hacendado* who supported Díaz's opponent in 1876. In the late fall of 1880, Urrea's father, no longer safe in Sinaloa, moved his family, workers, and servants north to Sonora. At the age of sixteen, while at her father's ranch in Cabora, near Alamos, Urrea began her rise to power as a healer. After she had remained in a trance-like state for three months, Urrea began to practice healing. As the news of her healing powers spread, people began to arrive in ever-larger numbers. In 1891, it was reported that an estimated 10,000 persons sought her services on Christmas day.[41]

Initially, Urrea's father doubted his daughter's special ability but soon resigned himself to the crowds of pilgrims who sought her help. Finally, the father allowed his daughter to receive patients at his home, and then remodeled a separate residence so that Urrea could better serve them. These patients were mainly poor "Christianized" Sonoran Yaquis and Mayos (not to be confused with the Mayas of southeastern Mexico), neighboring Sinaloan Gusaves, and Chihuahuan Tarahumares. To these Indians of the northwest, Urrea became known as "Santa Teresa" or "La Santa de Cabora."

A turning point in Urrea's work occurred on December 26, 1891, when twenty-eight armed men from the village of Tomochic (in the high western Sierras of the state of Chihuahua) arrived at Cabora seeking collaborators in their struggle against the *federales*. Tomochic was in rebellion against the government of Porfirio Díaz and had already routed two federal armies. The villagers of Tomochic had been so impressed by Urrea's healing powers that they elected her to be their saint and adopted "Viva la Santa de Cabora" as their battle cry. The villagers were convinced that Urrea could resuscitate anyone who died in battle.[42] When the tiny village of Tomochic was destroyed by federal troops, it became a symbol of resistance against the Díaz regime. Although Urrea had not encouraged rebellion, the villagers had been inspired by her supernatural powers. A dozen other villages, invoking her aid, took up arms against the government. But the army squelched these movements as well.

Although there was no evidence of Urrea's complicity in any rebellion, the Mexican government, as a precaution (and to the great displeasure of the Yaquis), exiled her and her father to the border city of Nogales in 1892. The Urrea home just north of Nogales became a mecca for pilgrims seeking cures. But more than the sick came. The site developed eventually into a recruitment center for revolutionaries plotting the overthrow of the Díaz government.[43] After three years in the Nogales area, Urrea and her father moved first to eastern Arizona and then to El Paso, Texas.

In August 1896, seventy Yaquis shouting "Viva la Santa Teresa" charged across the border from the American side at Nogales and seized the Mexican customhouse. On the same day, "Teresitas," as the revolutionaries called themselves, captured and held several other Mexican customhouses along the border. These moves, however, failed to incite a general uprising in Mexico. Probably only Urrea, had she been politically motivated, could have initiated and sustained an uprising by her thousands of devoted followers.

Despite the power she wielded, Urrea refused to participate in politics. On September 11, 1896, in a rare note to the El Paso Herald, she disclaimed any responsibility for the uprisings. She affirmed, "I am not the one who encourages such uprisings, nor one who in any way mixes with them. . . ." She called herself a "victim" because of the way in which she had been expelled from her own country.[44]

In spite of Urrea's denials of revolutionary involvement, Díaz administration officials felt threatened having Urrea and her followers so near the border, and the administration repeatedly urged American authorities, who did not consider Urrea to be a political threat, to move her to the interior. Several attempts were made on Urrea's life while she was in El Paso. Although it was never confirmed that these attempts were carried out by Díaz's agents, Urrea's father, refusing to further risk her life, moved his family to Clifton, a remote mining town in southeastern Arizona.

Urrea soon left her father's home in Clifton and toured the United States with a medical company. Later, she married and had two children, but she never returned to Mexico. As Urrea had prophesied, she died on February 12, 1906, at the age of thirty-three. Gradually her fame subsided, and her Yaqui and Mayo followers were captured and shipped forcibly to Yucatán or to Oaxaca, where they were made to serve as slave laborers on henequen and tobacco plantations. No evidence has been found to prove that

Urrea or her father encouraged anti-government rebellions. Rather than a unified revolutionary movement, the rebellions appear to have been a spontaneous resistance to government oppression. Of course, Díaz was alarmed because resistance in one geographical area could quickly spread to another. As memory of Urrea faded following her death, the anti-Díaz mantle shifted from Urrea devotees to the Flores Magón brothers.[45]

WOMEN'S ROLE IN THE PARTIDO LIBERAL MEXICANO (PLM)

Since 1900, Ricardo Flores Magón and his younger brother Enrique Flores Magón had led the Partido Liberal Mexicano (Mexican Liberal Party [PLM]) against the administration of President Porfirio Díaz. The Flores Magón brothers initially worked within Mexico to overthrow the Díaz regime, and then finally from exile in the United States. The Liberal Club "Ponciano Arriaga" (founded in 1900 and named after the nineteenth-century revolutionary leader who helped engineer the overthrow of Santa Anna) was the Flores Magón brothers' organizational and political base; and their newspaper, *Regeneración*, was the PLM mouthpiece.

By 1903, the Flores Magóns were plotting the violent overthrow of Díaz, and were calling for a democratic and popular system of government and an end to clericalism. (Eventually, Ricardo Flores Magón, disillusioned with political democracy, became convinced that only anarchism could free the Mexican people.) Between 1907 and 1918, Ricardo Flores Magón led the Organizing Junta of the Partido Liberal Mexicano in its attempt to overthrow all government in Mexico and to establish a society in which the people would own Mexico's natural and industrial resources. (After 1908, some of the PLM leaders who rejected Ricardo Flores Magón's anarchist philosophy joined the more moderate Francisco Madero cause.)[46]

Women from every social class participated in the PLM's resistance to the Díaz regime. The PLM Liberals espoused the position that women should have equal rights with men. In 1910, PLM leader Praxedis Guerrero stated the following in a speech in Los Angeles, California:

> Equality between the sexes which liberates does not attempt to make *men* out of women; instead, it offers equal opportunity to both for developing their potential without disturbing the natural order between the sexes. Women [and] . . . men must both join the struggle to attain this kind of rational equality. Without it, only a continuation of tyranny in the home and overall social ills will exist.[47]

In 1901, at their first Liberal Party (PLM) convention in San luis Potosí, members of the Liberal Club "Ponciano Arriaga" issued a proclamation

addressing gender equality of salary and work.[48] The comprehensive program, issued by the PLM in July 1906, included provisions for the protection of women and children, the calling of a nationwide eight-hour workday
and a six-day workweek, the granting of rights and privileges to illegitimate
children, and the paying of higher wages for primary school teachers.[49]

Many of the women who supported the Liberal Party movement were the
wives and relatives of male PLM members. These women were often persecuted by the authorities, and many were subjected to imprisonment in
Belén, the notorious prison located in the Federal District, or in San Juan
de Ulúa, the infamous prison located in Veracruz Bay.

Margarita Magón de Flores, the *mestiza* mother of the Flores Magón
brothers and a former member of the nineteenth-century Liberal Party, considered Díaz a usurper who had betrayed Liberal ideals. She lent uncondi-
tional support to the efforts of her sons to establish a new society that
would meet the social and political needs of the poor and indigenous
peoples of Mexico. To provide better educational opportunities for her children, Magón de Flores insisted that the family move from Oaxaca to
Mexico City. Later, it was her suggestion to change the subtitle of the PLM
newspaper *Regeneración* from *Contra la Mala Administración de Justicia*
(*Against the Wrongful Administration of Justice*) to *Periódico Independiente
de Combate* (*Independent Newspaper of Combat*). Magón de Flores supported
and defended her sons' activities, even on her deathbed. When President
Díaz offered to release her sons from prison if she would insist that they
stop their political activities, Magón de Flores replied that she preferred to
die without seeing them than to have them retract what they had said or done.[50]

María Talavera Brousse (1867-1947) was one of the first women to
respond to the call of the Flores Magón brothers' Liberal Party. Talavera
joined the party in 1905, and later became Ricardo Flores Magón's free-
union wife. Although her dedication to the PLM cause resulted in a life of
persecution, poverty, imprisonment, and constant moves, Talavera continued working with the Liberals. Teresa Arteaga de Flores Magón (1880-
1964), wife of Enrique Flores Magón, spent five months in prison for her
Liberal Party work. After Enrique's death, Arteaga died, poor and forgotten, in Baja California. Avelina Villarreal de Arriaga, wife of mining engineer and PLM collaborator Camilo Arriaga, worked for the PLM with her
husband's sister Dolores, and also wrote for *Regeneración*.[51] Crescencia
Garza de Martínez, wife of Liberal journalist Paulino Martínez, and their
daughter Aurora were both imprisoned for their Liberal Party activities.
Garza de Martínez, abducted from her home by *federales* in September
1909, was forced to leave behind her eleven-week-old baby, who died three
months later.[52]

Boston heiress Elizabeth Darling Trowbridge married Liberal leader Manuel Sarabia and donated her entire fortune to the movement, causing her

wealthy family to disinherit her. Socialists Ethel Duffy Turner and her husband, John Kenneth Turner, worked closely with the PLM. With Elizabeth Trowbridge, who provided financial support, Ethel Duffy Turner founded the *Border* and other periodicals dedicated to the defense of Mexican refugees, the exposure of corruption in the Díaz administration, and the defense of the Liberal cause. After retiring to Cuernavaca in 1950, and until her death in 1968, Turner continued to defend the PLM and its leadership.[53]

Outstanding women from all parts of Mexico rallied to the PLM cause.[54] Elisa Acuña y Rossetti (d. 1946), Juana Belén Gutiérrez de Mendoza (1875-1942), Dolores Jiménez y Muro (1848-1925), and Sara Estela Ramírez (1881-1910) must be counted among the most important activists in the Mexican revolutionary movement. All were teachers, organizers, feminists, journalists, and writers. All collaborated with the PLM and all except Ramírez, who died in 1910, became Maderistas and then Zapatistas. In addition, these women leaders founded women's groups and wrote extensively about women's role in Mexican society.

Elisa Acuña y Rossetti and Juana Gutiérrez de Mendoza were among the first women to join the PLM and served as officers.[55] They collaborated on the newspaper *Vésper: Justicia y Libertad*, and they were sent to jail together. Enrique Flores Magón described his first meeting with Acuña in February 1903, when she offered her services at the office of the Liberal newspaper *El Hijo de Ahuizote* in Mexico City: "We invited her to be part of the Center for the Confederation of Liberal Clubs of the Republic 'Ponciano Arriaga' and that is how she came to be a member of the Board of Directors . . . and signed . . . the manifesto written in Mexico City February 27, 1903."[56] Because of Acuña's experience as a teacher and writer, she was drafted immediately by the PLM. Acuña, Gutiérrez, María del Refugio Vélez, and other leading Liberals were signatories of the PLM Manifesto, which denounced social and economic injustices; attacked clericalism, militarism, and capitalism; and stressed the need for radical reform and revolution. After Elisa Acuña left the Liberals, she joined Madero and published *La Guillotina*, a newspaper critical of the administration of Victoriano Huerta (1913-1914). Later she joined the Zapatistas, who were fighting in southwestern Mexico to regain their land from the *hacendados*.[57]

In 1901, Sara Estela Ramírez, at the age of twenty, founded the newspaper *La Corregidora* (named after the Independence movement leader María Josefa Ortiz de Domínguez) to expose the injustices of the Díaz regime. Over the next several years, as Ramírez traveled for the PLM, *La Corregidora* was published from sites in Mexico City, San Antonio, and Laredo. Originally from the border state of Coahuila, Ramírez was a teacher, a labor organizer, a writer, and a revolutionary poet. While in

Laredo, Ramírez served as a contact person between PLM supporters in Mexico and the United States.

Juana Gutiérrez's long career extended throughout the entire thirty-year period of the Revolution. A prolific writer, a Socialist, a teacher, a feminist, and a fearless ideologue, Gutiérrez was imprisoned numerous times during the Revolution. Born in Durango in 1875 to a working-class family, of an Indian mother and a *mestizo* father, Gutiérrez was the daughter and granddaughter of liberals (Gutiérrez's grandfather was executed for his liberal political beliefs during the War of the Reform of 1858-1861). Gutiérrez's closest family tie seems to have been to her father, rather than to her strongly Catholic and conservative mother, whom she considered too intolerant. In 1890, at the age of fifteen, with scant formal education, Gutiérrez left her family, then living near Parral, Chihuahua, to marry Cirilo Mendoza, a miner. The Mendozas soon moved to Palomas Negras, Coahuila. Gutiérrez's career as a revolutionary began when she submitted an article to the Liberal newspaper *El Diario del Hogar* deploring the mining conditions in Coahuila. Upon discovering its authorship, authorities jailed her in Saltillo. Although Gutiérrez was only eighteen at the time, she never forgot the experience of serving three months in prison. From that time on, she no longer confined her criticisms to mining, but expanded them to encompass the Mexican sociopolitical system.

Gutiérrez's first contact with the Liberals came in 1900, soon after they had organized in San Luis Potosí. Impressed, Gutiérrez returned north and founded the Liberal Club "Benito Juárez" in Minas Nuevas, Chihuahua. When the director of the Liberal publication in Guanajuato offered her a position, Gutiérrez accepted, but after making the long trip south, she learned that the newspaper was no longer being printed. Undeterred, Gutiérrez decided to begin her own newspaper and wrote to her husband for money. He quickly sold their only assets—their goats—and on April 5, 1901, when Gutiérrez was twenty-six years old, the bitingly sarcastic anti-Díaz newspaper *Vésper: Justicia y Libertad* was born.[58] In the pages of *Vésper*, Gutiérrez attacked the treatment of miners in Guanajuato, the resurgence of the clergy, and the injustice of the Díaz administration. In 1903, along with other opposition newspapers, *Vésper* was confiscated and its editors and writers jailed. Gutiérrez was threatened with death if she or any of the writers ever tried to publish again. Undaunted, she continued publishing *Vésper*, as well as other newspapers and journals, until her death in the early 1940s.[59]

Prior to 1904, Gutiérrez had worked closely with the Liberals, but this changed as a result of two incidents. The first incident concerned the developing political and personal split between Camilo Arriaga and Ricardo Flores Magón. In February 1904, a Liberal meeting was held at the home of PLM activist Sara Estela Ramírez in Laredo, Texas. Those present were Enrique and Ricardo Flores Magón, Camilo Arriaga, Santiago de la Hoz,

Paulino Martínez, Santiago de la Vega, Sara Estela Ramírez, Elisa Acuña y Rossetti, and Juana Gutiérrez de Mendoza. (PLM members Ramírez, Acuña, and Gutiérrez worked closely together and maintained correspondence during this period.)[60] Assembled under the auspices of the Directorate of the Liberal Club "Ponciano Arriaga," the Liberals made plans to launch the revolution, to reestablish *Regeneración*, and to found a new political party. During discussion of these proposals, serious ideological and personal differences emerged, with factions coalesced around moderate Camilo Arriaga and the more radical Ricardo Flores Magón. Because of the intensity and irreconcilibility of the disagreements, de la Vega, Acuña, Gutiérrez, and Ramírez decided to leave for San Antonio, where they planned to reestablish *Vésper*. Shortly after the meeting, Sara Estela Ramírez, who since 1901 had maintained a warm correspondence with Ricardo, wrote to him explaining her reluctant decision to separate from the group and to continue to work with Arriaga. On March 9, 1904, Ramírez wrote from San Antonio:

> I've become sad and weary, Ricardo, with so many struggles of personal antagonisms. I will tell you frankly, I am disillusioned with everything, absolutely everything. . . . I don't want to analyze the cause of your quarrels with Camilito. I believe you both are right and both to blame.

For Ramírez, the main tragedy was that "we don't know how to forgive one another's shortcomings nor help each other like true human beings. We criticize each other, and tear ourselves apart instead of inspiring one another and mending our fences." Ramírez hoped that "by working in groups apart, separately and in different places, we will get along better and gain a new harmony."[61] Ramírez's aspirations were never realized, however. As the Revolution progressed, PLM unity disintegrated even further.

The other incident leading to Juana Gutiérrez's disenchantment with the Flores Magón leadership was the tragic drowning of Santiago de la Hoz on March 20, 1904, for which she blamed Enrique Flores Magón. The background to the tragedy was that de la Hoz and Flores Magón had been quarreling throughout the Laredo meeting. Their disagreements almost erupted in violence one evening when Enrique Flores Magón pulled a gun and de la Hoz picked up something with which to defend himself. Later, according to Gutiérrez, when de la Hoz was swimming in the nearby Río Bravo (Rio Grande), Flores Magón hit him with a branch and de la Hoz was knocked unconscious and drowned. The only witnesses were children who reportedly were heard screaming, "Don't do it!"[62]

After these two incidents, Gutiérrez refused to work again with the Flores Magón brothers or with the Liberal Party. Gutiérrez's accusations, including the charge that the Liberals wanted to sell Baja California to the United States, were countered by Liberal Party members.[63] On June 15, 1906, in

Regeneración, Juan Sarabia refuted Gutiérrez's criticisms of the Liberal Party Constitution point by point. Also, Ethel Duffy Turner claimed that the split between Camilo Arriaga and Ricardo Flores Magón was not solely the latter's fault. In fact, Turner called Gutiérrez's accusations lies, and stated that she was either a Díaz agent or suffering from hysteria.[64]

Juana Gutiérrez de Mendoza and Dolores Jiménez y Muro collaborated on many revolutionary projects. A Socialist, teacher, poet, writer, and feminist who founded women's rights organizations, Jimènez y Muro was born into a prominent *norteña* (northern Mexico) family in Aguascalientes on July 7, 1848. Jiménez first began writing at an early age, during the French intervention, and spent her formative years in the liberal atmosphere of San Luis Potosí. In 1904 she moved to Mexico City, where she began her career as a writer for anti-Díaz periodicals and in 1905 joined the staff of the feminist monthly *La Mujer Mexicana*. Often imprisoned for expressing her ideas publicly, Jiménez was once released only after staging a hunger strike. She served prison terms with other women revolutionaries and formed close personal relationships with Juana Gutiérrez de Mendoza, Elisa Acuña y Rossetti, Sara Estela Ramírez, and Inés Malváez. After leaving the Liberals, Jiménez joined Madero for a brief time and wrote the "Political and Social Plan" for the Complot de Tacubaya, a revolutionary plan to bring Madero to power by staging a rebellion near the nation's capital. Finally, as did Gutiérrez and Acuña, Jiménez collaborated with the Zapatistas, composing revolutionary plans and undertaking dangerous and sensitive missions.[65]

WOMEN AND THE
PLM-SUPPORTED STRIKES

After the turn of the century, there was a proliferation of strikes in all industries. Known as "the year of the strikes," 1906 was a turning point for labor organizations because of the large number of workers who participated in work stoppages. Most of the strikes took place in the textile, tobacco, mining, and railroad industries.[66] Two major PLM-supported strikes, in the mines at Cananea, Sonora in June 1906 and in the textile mills at Orizaba, Veracruz in January 1907, caused serious repercussions for the Díaz administration.[67] Ironically, they occurred at foreign-owned companies that paid top wages.[68] The strikes resulted from rising living costs, growing bitterness against foreign owners and bosses who paid Mexican workers less than their foreign counterparts performing the same work, mistreatment of employees, lack of educational opportunities for workers and their children, and little or no compensation for job-related injuries.

At the U.S.-owned Cananea copper mine, the 1906 strike ushered in the first important large-scale labor movement in twentieth-century Mexico.

This strike was accompanied by bloodshed and violence, with more than twenty deaths. Dozens of women, most of whom remain anonymous, actively joined their husbands and sons in support of the strike.

Even though the Cananea strike was broken, it focused attention on the Díaz policy of protecting foreigners at the expense of Mexicans (U.S. troops had been allowed to cross into Sonora and kill Mexicans to protect the interests of this American-owned mining company). Moreover, workers demonstrated their willingness to challenge the authority of the Díaz administration.

Women played an even more significant role in the 1907 strike at the French-owned Río Blanco textile mills in Orizaba, where they comprised 18 percent of the work force. Workers were discontented with thirteen-hour days, the deafening roar and din of the factory machinery, the lint-laden air they were forced to breathe, and the salary equivalent of 25 to 37.5 U.S. cents per day. To make matters worse, workers had to pay the equivalent of one American dollar a week for rent of their two-room, dirt-floor shacks. Another major cause for worker discontent was the *vales* (pay certificates) with which workers were paid that were redeemable only at the company store, which charged from 25 to 75 percent more than other stores.[69]

The 1907 Río Blanco strike, one in a long series at that mill, was triggered by labor unrest in the nearby textile mills of Puebla and Tlaxcala, where, because of excessive overtime work, abusive supervisors, censorship of reading materials, overpriced company stores, and child labor (120 children were employed in Río Blanco), the PLM-affiliated Gran Círculo de Obreros Libres (Grand Circle of Free Workers) had ordered a strike. The Río Blanco mill owners responded by imposing a lockout. When mill owners in the adjoining state of Puebla complained of PLM assistance, the proprietors at Orizaba (who also owned the Río Blanco mills) decided to support the Puebla lockout and to close their mills. In a domino-like sequence, a nationwide lockout followed, resulting in 93 of the nation's 150 mills being closed and thirty thousand laborers out of work in twenty states. President Díaz personally directed an investigation of the lockout. In early January 1907, the president ordered that the factories be reopened, that the workers in various mills be paid similar salaries for similar work, that the strikes be halted, and that workers in Puebla, Veracruz, Tlaxcala, Querétaro, Jalisco, and the Federal District return to their jobs by January 7.[70] The only demand that labor won was the abolition of child labor for those under seven years of age, though most children working in the mills were older than seven.

Most workers, suffering from weeks without work, accepted the president's order. However, at daybreak on January 7, 1907, textile workers gathered outside the Río Blanco mill, where a group of men, women, and children blocked the entrance, threw rocks, and shouted anti-government slogans. When the factory whistle blew at 5:30 a.m., few workers attempted to enter. Later, when the women went to purchase food at the company store, they were refused credit and insulted. Frenchman Victor Garcín and Spaniard Manuel Díez, operators of the hated company store, symbolized foreign oppression to the women.[71] The women left the store premises, then returned later with an angry mob (led by Margarita Martínez) who attacked the store and sacked and burned the building. When the *rurales* (rural police force) arrived and faced the workers, Lucretia Toriz, a working woman, stepped forward and asked if the *rurales* wanted to murder unarmed, starving workers. The *rurales* put down their guns. Later that day, other stores and mills were looted and burned by angry workers. When the *federales* were summoned, they opened fire indiscriminately, mowing down men, women, and children. Next, sharpshooters were brought to the scene, and they and the *rurales* were given orders to hunt down fleeing workers. When several of the *rurales* refused, they were shot by the *federales*.[72]

The strike-lockout had turned into a working-class rebellion. In this single bloody massacre, two hundred workers were shot and four hundred were taken prisoner (among them were many women, including Martínez, who was sent to the San Juan de Ulúa prison in Veracruz Bay). At least ten workers were later executed by firing squads for their participation in the strike. The workers' corpses were shipped to Veracruz and dumped in the bay for the sharks.[73]

The PLM, with its leaders factionalized, harassed, and jailed in both Mexico and the United States, was soon eclipsed by other revolutionary organizations. Even though the PLM-supported strikes had not materialized into full-scale insurrections, they did serve to coalesce labor and to severely undermine the credibility of the Díaz regime.

Despite the efforts of Justo Sierra and Francisco Bulnes, high-ranking *científicos* in the Díaz administration, to blame the Río Blanco strike on "infiltrators," the authority of the Díaz administration had been irreparably weakened.[74] By 1907, workers in the mining, textile, and railroad industries of Mexico had forcibly demonstrated their rising consciousness and their growing dissatisfaction with the policies of the Díaz regime. The stage was set for a nationwide revolt.

WOMEN JOURNALISTS

Mexican women were among the first journalists and publishers in the Western Hemisphere. Literary achievement among women in Colonial New Spain was almost exclusively attained by nuns. For example, prolific Sor Juana Inés de la Cruz (1651-1695), a nun, wrote brilliant poetry and plays, and her work epitomized women's early contributions to New World literature. One of the first Mexican women journalists was Independence leader

Leona Vicario, who wrote about the insurgents in the Independence Movement. During the 1860s, a woman's name appeared for the first time as a
member of a Mexican newspaper staff, in *El Búcaro* (*The Jug*), published
in the capital.

The first Mexican periodical devoted exclusively to women's interests, *El
Seminario de las Señoritas Mejicanas* (*The Young Mexican Women's Semi-
nar*), was founded in 1841. The staff of *El Seminario* took the education
of Mexican women seriously and printed articles on literary themes, the
education of women, and historical subjects. In an attempt to maintain intellectual interest, *El Seminario*'s editor excluded recipes, fashions, and jokes,
seeking to fill women's educational void rather than to entertain. The editor
did, however, accept the thesis that women's proper place was in the home as
intellectual companions to their husbands and as teachers to their children.[75]

La Semana de las Señoritas Mejicanas (*The Young Mexican Women's
Weekly*), published from 1851 to 1852, had a less intellectual approach than
El Seminario, but both listed circulations of over one thousand subscribers.
Although the format changed from issue to issue, *La Semana* always contained music, poetry, and short stories. Early issues of *La Semana* featured
historical sketches, while stories and occasional religious pieces filled later
issues. There were regular notes on etiquette and medical advice, as well
as complete instructions for playing parlor games. A frequent section in *La
Semana* was "Economía Doméstica" ("Domestic Economics"), which
included recipes and tips on household management.[76]

During the Porfiriato, more women wrote for more periodicals than ever
before, and, although many women's magazines were short-lived, records
indicate that these authors served an extensive audience. An early feminist
journal titled *El Album de las Señoritas Potosinas* appeared in San Luis
Potosí in 1865, but it was not self-supporting and had a short-lived existence. *La Siempreviva*, published entirely by women in the late 1870s in
Mérida, had a boldly feminist perspective. Appearing in 1880, *La Ilustra-
ción Femenil*, edited by several different women, was a weekly that discussed literature, the arts, and science. *El Album de la Mujer* (1883-1890)
contained poetry by contemporary women writers. *El Correo de las Señoras*
(1883-1893) also featured poetry as well as translations by well-known
women authors. Edited by Laureana Wright de Kleinhans (1847-1896), *Las
Hijas del Anáhuac* (1887-1888) contained works by women who were
prominent socially or literarily. The title of *Las Hijas* was changed to *Violetas del Anáhuac* at the beginning of its second year. Among the contributors to *Violetas del Anáhuac* were Dolores Correa Zapata (1853-1924),
a writer and educator from Tabasco, and Rita Cetina Gutiérrez (1846-1908),
a writer and educator from Yucatán.[77] One of the last periodicals of the century, *El Periódico de las Señoras* (1896), was written and edited exclusively by women in the capital.

Laureana Wright de Kleinhans, a promoter of women's literary efforts, exemplifies the talented women writers who emerged during the Porfiriato. She was born in Taxco, Guerrero in 1846 to an American father and a Mexican mother, and was reared and educated in Mexico. Wright de Kleinhans first proposed the idea of emancipation of women through education in her book *La emancipación de la mujer por medio del estudio* (*Education as Women's Emancipation*). In the periodical *Las Hijas del Anáhuac*, she was one of the first women to call for women's suffrage and for equal opportunities for women. Before her death in 1896, Wright de Kleinhans wrote *Mujeres notables mexicanas* (*Notable Mexican Women*), in which she sketched the history of famous nineteenth-century Mexican women.[78]

In the early twentieth century, many more women's magazines began to address political and social questions. Their audience, however, was limited mainly to upper-class and middle-class women. *Tiempo* (later called *El Tiempo Ilustrado*) and *Arte y Letras* were two general-interest magazines that carried news about women. *Tiempo* presented pieces about famous women; *Arte y Letras* included a section on fashion and the arts. *La Mujer Mexicana* (1904-1908) and *Diario del Hogar* (*Diary of the Home*) were more feminist in their orientation. *La Mujer Mexicana* was published by the Sociedad Protectora de la Mujer, one of the earliest feminist societies, and was edited by three middle-class professional women: Dr. Columba Rivera, a medical doctor; María Sandoval de Zarco, a lawyer; and Dolores Correa Zapata, a teacher. The staff of *La Mujer Mexicana* included some of the most talented women writers and activists of the period, including: Rita Cetina Gutiérrez, Dolores Jiménez y Muro, María Enriqueta, Laureana Wright de Kleinhans, María Arias Bernal, and Matilda P. Montoya.[79] Unfortunately, many of the pieces written by Dolores Jiménez y Muro and by María Enriqueta remain unknown because these women frequently used pseudonyms.[80] *Diario del Hogar*, edited by Filomeno Mata (who had been imprisoned more than twenty times by the Díaz regime), was one of several stars in the anti-Díaz galaxy of magazine publications that carried articles by and about women.[81] Dolores Jiménez y Muro, María Enriqueta, Aurora Colín, and Guadalupe Gutiérrez de Joseph, among others, wrote for *Diario del Hogar*. Jiménez and Enriqueta often contributed poetry; Colín, who had served as a delegate of the Liberal Junta to the First Liberal Congress in 1901, wrote political pieces for *Diario*; and Gutiérrez de Joseph was a contributor to *Diario del Hogar* since the age of fifteen.[82]

In addition to writing and editing magazines, women published and wrote for newspapers. In 1876, *La Comuna*, dedicated to the defense of civil liberty and to the support of the strike as a political weapon, had a circulation of 4,500. *La Comuna* contained a political and economic section, as well as articles for working mothers and articles on equality of the sexes. *La Comuna*'s founders and editors are still unknown.[83]

The boldly anti-Díaz newspaper *Juan Panadero* was published originally in Guadalajara and then in the capital by María Guadalupe Rojo Vda. de Alvarado (1856-1922). When Rojo was sent to the Belén prison in 1904, government orders were issued to poison her, but these orders were never executed for fear of reprisals by her supporters. After the fall of Díaz, Rojo was released and continued her revolutionary activities. For Rojo's extraordinary contribution to the Revolution, President Carranza provided her with a small pension, but she was already elderly and died soon after in 1922.[84]

Sara Estela Ramírez, a leading Liberal and staunch defender of women, founded the newspaper *La Corregidora* to combat the Díaz dictatorship. Carlota Antuna de Borrego founded and directed *El Campo Libre*, a weekly dedicated to the defense of *campesinos*, the common control of land, and the fall of the Díaz government.[85]

After founding the newspaper *Vésper: Justicia y Libertad* in 1901, Juana Gutiérrez de Mendoza collaborated with Elisa Acuña y Rossetti on its publication. *Vésper* usually contained four pages, and had a weekly circulation of 8,000. The outspoken approach of its editors made *Vésper* a prime target for government censorship. In an article written in July 1903, Gutiérrez and Acuña scorned Díaz's fear of them and taunted him as being the first man afraid of women. In the same issue, Gutiérrez published a copy of a note she had sent to the president with the message, "General, retire!" Fearlessly, Gutiérrez signed her name.[86] Gutiérrez's press was confiscated often, and *Vésper*'s writers were hounded constantly by government agents. In 1907, Gutiérrez and Acuña collaborated with Dolores Jiménez and a Mexican Socialist group to publish the anti-Díaz newspaper *Anáhuac*. Government raids on *Anáhuac* resulted in several women being sent to prison.

SUMMARY

As the thirty-four-year Porfiriato period (1876-1910) drew to a close, women had made some gains, mostly in education, in their quest for equal rights. More middle-class women attended schools and universities than ever before, and many entered the labor market as teachers, nurses, and government employees. Also, women joined labor organizations and participated in demonstrations in unprecedented numbers. Politically, women had begun to organize to protect themselves and to actively participate in the anti-Díaz movement. More women than ever were writing and publishing in books, magazines, and newspapers. But despite the significant progress made during the Porfiriato, Mexican women still experienced widespread discrimination and were far from enjoying equal rights with men.

▪ 2 ▪

Igniting the Flames of Revolution: The First Phase, 1910-1920

BREAKING THE CHAINS OF TRADITION

In the spring of 1911, the *New York Times* proclaimed that Mexican women were playing "a spectacular part" in the Revolution.[1] Women from all socioeconomic backgrounds were joining resistance groups; publishing revolutionary newspapers and magazines; serving as teachers and nurses; founding hospitals and health organizations; purchasing, smuggling, and selling arms; fighting on the battlefields; and collaborating in the planning and drafting of revolutionary documents. This widespread participation in the Revolution thrust Mexican women into many roles that traditionally had been reserved for men (for example, train dispatchers, telegraphers, and engineers). North American author Frederick Turner stated that the Revolution helped to equalize relations between men and women because "men saw themselves united in a new relationship with the woman, now that she assumed a totally unfamiliar role as partner and equal. For the first time in the history of Mexico, she developed her abilities . . . and gained recognition as companion, consort, and equal."[2] Thus, for many women, the Revolution created unique opportunities to break the chains of tradition.

Prior to the Revolution, Mexican women lived in virtual seclusion. Only 8.82 percent of Mexican women were gainfully employed in 1910; marriage, family life, and the Catholic Church dominated their existence.[3] In the early 1910s, Mrs. E. Alex Tweedie, a British visitor, noted that "the life of a Mexican woman is not a jovial one; she marries straight from the

31

convent or school, and her home is her horizon. Very ideal no doubt, but rather dull."[4]

Because the historically restrictive social mores that controlled pre-revolutionary Mexican women were altered so radically, the lives of women in all social classes were changed dramatically. Upper-class women generally served the Revolution by donating their time to such health organizations as the Red Cross or White Cross;[5] middle-class women served the revolutionary cause by working in a broad range of skilled and semi-skilled capacities; and thousands of lower-class women worked at unskilled jobs heretofore closed to them. Some women even followed their men into battle, serving the cause as *soldaderas*. In addition to their being thrust into nontraditional roles and trades, the geographical isolation of Mexican women was altered in an unprecedented way because the Revolution drove women from their native regions. Further, many of the women who remained at home were forced to survive without their husbands' salaries and thus sought employment for the first time. Pressured by lack of spousal income and by food shortages, large numbers of women, particularly those of the lower socioeconomic class, resorted to prostitution to survive.

In the constant milieu of separation, uncertainty, and death, family life was disrupted on an unprecedented scale.[6] "Press-gangs" from both federal and revolutionary armies swept through villages and city streets conscripting men for military service and women to cook and to work in powder mills. In addition to conscription, many women were kidnapped, transported to distant geographical areas, and then sold into peonage or prostitution.[7] Edith O'Shaughnessy, author and wife of the U.S. Chargé d'Affaires to Mexico, described one such tragic incident that occurred during the Huerta administration (1913-1914). The government seized three hundred *campesinas* (women peasants) from Morelos and sent them to Quintana Roo, an inhospitable region south of Yucatán, intending to establish a colony with men who earlier had been deported to the area. After the women's arrival, competition for them led to such fighting that officials shipped them to Veracruz and then dumped them on the beach. Almost every woman was pregnant and later bore a child. Characteristic of the times, no one in authority claimed responsibility for these uprooted women or their children, and they were left stranded in Veracruz hundreds of miles from their homes and families.[8] O'Shaughnessy also reported on a family of five who were left abandoned on the streets of Mexico City after the father had been kidnapped by a "press-gang." After giving the young mother money and her blessing, O'Shaughnessy remarked: "When I put my hand on her head I felt the tears come to my eyes. I suddenly saw in *one* woman all the misfortunes of the women of this land, separation, destitution, ravishments— all the horrors flesh is heir to."[9]

Confronted by such deleterious conditions, women were forced to organize to protect themselves and to work to change discriminatory laws. The early feminist organizations, such as Admiradoras de Juárez (1904), Sociedad Protectora de la Mujer (1904), Hijas de Anáhuac (1907), Hijas de Cuauhtémoc (Daughters of Cuauhtémoc) (1910), Amigas del Pueblo (Female Friends of the People) (1911), and Regeneración y Concordia (Regeneration and Consensus) (1911), demanded an end to sexual discrimination and to repressive government.

Women Organize Against the Díaz Administration

Astute observers sensed that the splendor of Mexico's centennial celebration in September 1910 was a charade that concealed the real spirit of the Mexican people. It was becoming increasingly evident that although President Porfirio Díaz was utilizing powerful methods to crush political opposition, his efforts were not generally effective and Mexico was being engulfed in ever-widening turmoil and dissension.

In early 1908, in an interview with North American reporter James Creelman, Díaz announced his plans to retire, to not seek reelection, and to allow democratic elections. Francisco I. Madero, a relatively unknown political figure from Coahuila and member of a powerful and wealthy *hacendado* family, vowed to hold Díaz to his word. In his book *La sucesión presidencial en 1910* (*The Presidential Succession in 1910*), Madero condemned the Porfirian political system, called for free elections, and declared himself a candidate for the presidency. As Madero's criticisms touched an increasingly responsive cord in the Mexican people, the situation grew grimmer for Díaz. As a further challenge to Díaz, the Partido Liberal Mexicano (PLM), which had been at war with the Díaz administration since 1900, organized anti-reelectionist clubs throughout Mexico to prevent Díaz from seeking reelection.

In early May 1910, the Liga Feminina Anti-reelectionista "Josefa Ortiz de Domínguez" (Feminist Anti-Reelection League "Josefa Ortiz de Domínguez"), named after the Independence heroine, called for the formation of a national anti-reelection club. Fiery Dolores Jiménez y Muro, a former PLM member and a Liga Femenina leader, summarized the need for a change of political leadership: " . . . [E]quality before the law does not exist in general, since we have . . . those who are privileged by fortune, position, or influence, to whom everything is allowed."[10] After Díaz reneged on his pledge to retire and had himself reelected president, members of the Liga Femenina mounted a protest demonstration in the most conspicuous place possible—under the Columbus statue on Avenida Reforma in the capital.

Jiménez y Muro also served as president of the Hijas de Cuauhtémoc, a feminist organization that took its name from the Aztec emperor tortured by Hernán Cortés. Hijas members included Julia Nava de Ruisánchez, Inés Malváez, and Juana Gutiérrez de Mendoza. The Hijas de Cuauhtémoc demanded the resignation of President Díaz, staged protest marches, circulated anti-Díaz petitions, and generally focused public attention on the growing political crisis. On September 11, 1910, the Hijas de Cuauhtémoc sponsored a huge march in Mexico City to protest the policies of the Díaz regime, declaring that it was time for Mexican women to recognize that their "rights and obligations go much farther than just the home." And the Hijas de Cuauhtémoc drafted a manifesto that called for political enfranchisement of Mexican women in their "economic, physical, intellectual and moral struggles." For her role in organizing the September 11 demonstration, Dolores Jiménez y Muro was jailed.[11]

While unrest grew in the capital, revolutionaries along the U.S.-Mexico border were planning to ignite further the flames of revolution spreading across Mexico. In San Antonio, Texas, Francisco Madero and his collaborators formulated their revolutionary plans for Mexico's future, and on October 5, 1910, they issued the Plan de San Luis Potosí, which, like *La sucesión presidential en 1910* before it, focused on political solutions to Mexico's problems. This plan proclaimed the recent Díaz election victory fraudulent and named Madero as provisional president until free elections could be held. The plan also contained instructions for a nationwide uprising to begin on November 20. Because Madero was under surveillance and his mail was monitored closely, it was difficult for the Madero revolutionaries to distribute copies of the plan throughout Mexico. Mary Petre de Fernández, a United States citizen who was married to a Madero agent and lawyer, volunteered to carry the plan across the border for distribution within Mexico. When both Madero and her husband objected because of the potential danger, Petre de Fernández reminded them that as a United States citizen she would not be suspect. She took along her nine-year-old daughter and hid the documents in the girl's doll. When she and her daughter arrived at the border at Nuevo Laredo, Petre de Fernández stated that tourism was the object of their trip. The doll containing the documents was examined carefully by a customs official, who admired it so much that he offered to buy it. Finally, after the young girl began to cry for her doll, mother and daughter were permitted to cross the border with the doll.[12] The Plan de San Luis Potosí was subsequently distributed from Nuevo Laredo to sites throughout the republic.

Aquiles Serdán, anti-reelectionist leader in Puebla, working with his brother Maximo and his sister Carmen (1873-1948), had built a sizable anti-Díaz organization that consisted of an anti-reelectionist club and a workers' club named "Luz y Progreso" with its own publication, titled "No Re-election." Carmen Serdán, the three Narváez sisters (Guadalupe, Rosa, and María), and several women teachers had organized a women's network to carry out anti-Díaz activities. This network coordinated the Puebla anti-Díaz operation, printed political pamphlets, and manufactured and distributed arms to revolutionaries. Because of the dangerous nature of their work, these women often used pseudonyms: Carmen was known as "Marcos Serratos," Guadalupe as "María Gómez," and Rosa as "Rosa Nervo."[13]

Madero's Plan de San Luis Potosí called for the Puebla uprising to occur simultaneously with uprisings in other Mexican cities, thereby triggering a nationwide revolt. The distribution of arms to Puebla revolutionaries was to take place on November 18, 1910, and the insurrection was to occur two days later. However, at 7:30 on the morning of the day arms were to be distributed, Mexican Army Colonel Miguel Cabrera and his troops appeared unexpectedly at the Serdán home on Calle Santa Clara (Puebla) to investigate a reported cache of arms. A struggle ensued between the federal troops and the revolutionaries. After shooting erupted, Carmen Serdán stepped onto the balcony and, clutching a rifle in her raised hand, urged the townspeople to join in the battle.[14] When no one responded, the small revolutionary group, led by Aquiles Serdán, continued to battle the troops but was overwhelmed eventually by the greater odds. Carmen Serdán was wounded in the back, and Aquiles was killed. Of the surviving insurrectionists, all were taken prisoner, including Carmen, her mother Carmen Alatriste, and Filomena del Valle (Aquiles's pregnant wife).

Tried by the Díaz government, Carmen Serdán was condemned to death, but was offered liberty if she would divulge the names of other conspirators. Serdán refused and consequently spent seven months in prison before she was liberated by Madero's revolutionary followers. After her release, Serdán continued to work for Madero. Both Francisco Madero and his wife Sara Pérez de Madero personally expressed their gratitude to her. A photograph taken on the day of her release from prison shows Carmen Serdán, Sara Pérez de Madero, Filomena del Valle, Carmen Alatriste, the three Narváez sisters, and six other women gathered to commemorate the occasion.[15] As part of the ceremonies, attended by more than 50,000 persons, the women placed a wreath on the tomb of Aquiles Serdán.[16]

After the assassination of Francisco Madero in February 1913, Carmen Serdán continued her revolutionary activities. With the Narváez sisters, she organized a revolutionary junta that operated in Puebla, Tlaxcala, parts of Veracruz, and other parts of Mexico. The junta's main functions were to provide arms for the revolutionaries, to recruit troops, and to distribute revolutionary information. Serdán, under her alias "Marcos Serratos," served as junta president.[17] Later, she joined the Carrancistas (supporters of revolutionary leader Venustiano Carranza). As a trusted collaborator, Serdán was commissioned by Carranza to carry messages to Emiliano Zapata[18] (who five years later would die in an ambush ordered by President Carranza). When Carranza visited Puebla in November 1914, Serdán and the Narváez sisters were among the few women present at a banquet held in his honor. Photographs show the group assembled with members of the revolutionary junta in the Hotel del Pasaje.[19] One of Serdán's last revolutionary acts was to organize a group of volunteer nurses to help with war casualties and epidemics.[20]

Despite her significant contributions to the Revolution, Carmen Serdán received very little recognition. She did receive some compensation in 1920, when Congress awarded her a pension of 10 pesos daily. In 1945, her small pension was increased to 20 pesos.[21]

Women and the Madero Movement

In early 1911, members of the Díaz government reached an accord with Francisco Madero when it became obvious that the only way to avert a full-scale civil war was for President Díaz to resign and to be succeeded by his Minister of Foreign Relations Francisco de la Barra. Following Díaz's resignation and de la Barra's succession, elections were scheduled for late 1911, at which time Francisco Madero was elected president of Mexico.

The women of the Madero family (Francisco's wife Sara, his mother Mercedes González de Madero, his sisters Mercedes and Angela, and his brothers' wives) were committed supporters of the Revolution. To support the cause, these women traveled to revolutionary camps, nursed the wounded, pawned their jewelry to buy arms and ammunition, and sacrificed considerable personal comforts.

Francisco Madero's wife, Sara Pérez de Madero, was a remarkable woman. Born in Querétaro in 1872 to a distinguished family, she followed upper-class tradition by pursuing her studies abroad at St. Mary's College in California. She met Francisco while he was taking courses at the University of California at Berkeley. Theirs was a close relationship, and they were rarely apart after their marriage in 1903.[22] As soon as revolutionary fighting erupted, Pérez de Madero took personal charge of caring for the wounded, organizing nursing brigades, and supervising sanitation crews. Because of her strong dedication to the cause, she was held in high esteem by Madero supporters. On May 10, 1911, when Ciudad Juárez fell to the Maderistas, a *New York Times* reporder described Pérez de Madero riding behind the Mexican national colors: "Her face was beaming with joy, her black dress covered with dust. She spurred her horse to her husband's side.

The shouting increased as the two embraced and entered the municipal building, now the Madero Headquarters."[23]

The wife of the U.S. Chargé d' Affaires, Edith O'Shaughnessy, described Sara Pérez de Madero as "a dark type of New England woman," small and thin, with "a sort of determination in the cut of her face." O'Shaughnessy commented on one of Pérez de Madero's first proposed projects as first lady, that of organizing the lace and embroidery industry. Pérez de Madero told O'Shaughnessy that one hundred thousand women in Puerto Rico had been organized and that she wanted to do the same in Mexico.[24] However, Pérez de Madero was unable to undertake this ambitious project because of her husband's assassination in early 1913.

When General Huerta staged a coup and arrested President Madero and his vice-president on February 19, 1913, family members, friends, and many foreign diplomats attempted to intercede to save the captives' lives. President Madero's parents contacted United States Ambassador Henry Lane Wilson asking for his intervention. On February 21, 1913, Sara Pérez de Madero, accompanied by her sister-in-law Mercedes, visited the United States Embassy to speak personally with Wilson. Later, in 1916, Pérez de Madero recounted this visit to North American journalist Robert Hammond Murray. She stated that when she pleaded with Wilson to exert his influence to protect the president and vice-president, he responded, "That is a responsibility that I do not care to undertake, either for myself, or my government. You know, Madam," Wilson continued, "your husband had peculiar ideas." Pérez de Madero retorted, "Mr. Ambassador, my husband had not peculiar ideas, but high ideals." Wilson admitted that when General Huerta asked his opinion about what to do with the prisoners, he advised him to do "what was best for the interests of the country." Mercedes protested that without the ambassador's intervention Francisco would be killed, and Pérez de Madero asked only that her husband and his followers be allowed to leave Mexico peacefully.[25]

Two days later, on February 23, 1913, the president and vice-president were executed. Ambassador Wilson revealed his predisposed bias when he attempted immediately to have the Huerta government recognized by the United States. Newly inaugurated President Woodrow Wilson refused, and Ambassador Wilson was replaced in mid-July. Huerta's government fell a year later, in July 1914.

In addition to the Madero women, several other distinguished women collaborated with the Maderistas. Inés Malváez, a schoolteacher and one of the most prominent women in the Madero movement, began her revolutionary career in 1909. As did Juana Gutiérrez de Mendoza and Dolores Jiménez y Muro, Malváez worked mainly as a propagandist, and she eventually achieved the rank of colonel in the revolutionary forces. Malváez conducted her work principally in Puebla, where she was persecuted by the *federales* and imprisoned many times. When Carranza triumphed, Malváez joined his forces in Veracruz.[26]

Another distinguished Maderista collaborator was Lidia Calderón, a member of the Club Femenil Revolucionario Lealtad (Feminine Revolutionary Loyalty Club). Calderón printed copies of the Plan de San Luis Potosí in the basement of her home and was jailed and persecuted for her revolutionary activities.[27] Paulina Maraver Cortés, a professor and Maderista who worked in Puebla with the Serdáns, was also imprisoned for her anti-Díaz activities. Like many former Maderistas, Maraver later joined the Zapatistas, for whom she directed the agrarian reform program in the state of Puebla.[28]

Carmen Parra Vda. de Alaniz organized an uprising in Casas Grandes, Chihuahua, and later led three hundred men in the capture of Ciudad Juárez. After fighting in northern Mexico, Parra traveled south to the state of Guerrero to join Emiliano Zapata, where she was captured and imprisoned by *federales*.[29] Soledad González was a personal secretary to President Madero, and later to presidents Obregón and Calles, each of whom she continually urged to improve conditions for women. Adopted by Madero as a child, González traveled with him to Mexico City and continued her revolutionary activities there following Madero's assassination.[30]

One of the best known of the Maderistas spies was Josefina Ranzeta. Daughter of a wealthy planter in the Laguna district on the Coahuila-Durango border, and educated in a Washington, D.C. boarding school, Ranzeta was a friend of Madero and devoted to the revolutionary cause. In the spring of 1912, when General Huerta, before betraying President Madero, moved north with the federal army to squelch the revolt of former Madero supporter Pascual Orozco, Ranzeta volunteered her services. Her mission was to learn Orozco's war plans and troop strength. Disguised as a peasant and accompanied by a ragged, aged servant, Ranzeta set out on the 150-mile trip to Orozco's camp. Because the railroad lines had been destroyed, the two traveled on donkeys. After reaching Orozco's headquarters, Ranzeta slowly and cautiously made friends with the women there. Disguised as a servant, Ranzeta was able to enter Orozco's tent, gain access to valuable information, and steal important letters and documents. She barely avoided being caught on her return trip to Huerta's camp.[31]

The Early Struggle for Equality

In the early 1910s, Mexican women, encouraged by the worldwide struggle for women's equality, began to press increasingly for equal political rights. On May 29, 1911, Edith O'Shaughnessy wrote, "I saw some

Mexican suffragettes the other day whom I wish their American sisters could have gazed upon. They were armed with bandoliers full of ammunition crossed over their breasts, and it did look like bullets rather than ballots among the sisterhood here."[32] The need for change in the status of Mexican women was addressed by O'Shaughnessy:

> . . . How can a nation advance when the greater part of the women pass their lives grinding corn, making tortillas, and bearing children? There is no time or strength left to sketch in the merest outline of home-making, let alone a personal life, or any of the rudiments of citizenship.[33]

From her prison cell shortly after the Revolution began, Dolores Jiménez y Muro (president of the Hijas de Cuauhtémoc) founded a women's rights organization called Regeneración y Concordia (Regeneration and Consensus). As did the Hijas de Cuauhtémoc, Regeneración y Concordia combined feminist demands for equality with issues of political reform. The organization's leaders, consisting mainly of teachers and writers, included Julia Nava de Ruisánchez, María Arias Bernal, Dolores Sotomayor, María Gómez Vda. de Bacmaister, and Inés Malváez.[34] The goals of Regeneración y Concordia were to improve the lot of the indigenous races, the *campesinos*, and the *obreros*; to unify all revolutionary forces; and to elevate women economically, morally, and intellectually.

In March 1911, several former PLM members joined Camilo Arriaga (now a Maderista) in a revolutionary plot to bring Madero to power. Known as the Complot de Tacubaya, this plan called for rebellion in the San Diego army barracks in the District of Tacubaya, in the western part of Mexico City. With only slight modifications, the Complot's "Political and Social Plan" contained many of the far-reaching social and economic principles established by the PLM Program of 1906; namely, to protect indigenous peoples, to reform agrarian laws, to establish a maximum work day, to improve education, to ensure that a certain percentage of workers be Mexican, and to improve both wages and working conditions for rural and urban workers. The Complot de Tacubaya was composed under the direction of Arriaga's San Luis Potosí colleague, poet Dolores Jiménez y Muro. The plan carried her feminist imprint in such demands as raising the wages of rural and urban workers of both sexes. Jiménez y Muro and Juana Gutiérrez de Mendoza, along with more than twenty men and a militant group of medical students, signed the plan. However, the goals of the plan were never realized because members of the movement (possibly more than 10,000 in six states) were betrayed and arrested on March 27, 1911. With the failure of the Complot de Tacubaya, Arriaga was jailed, but he was released months later when Madero triumphed in May 1911.[35] After Madero's death in 1913, Jiménez, then sixty-five years of age, joined Zapata in Morelos and worked with him until his death in 1919.

In May 1911, more than one thousand women signed a petition demanding that Díaz resign. Even Díaz's wife, Carmen Romero Rubio de Díaz, concerned for his health and safety, advised his withdrawal.[36]

In June, the *Mexican Herald* reported that feminists had demanded their rights in the coming election via a petition sent to the Minister of the Interior. Members of the Amigas del Pueblo (Female Friends of the People), organized by Juana Gutiérrez de Mendoza and other prominent feminist activists, also were advocating women's suffrage. In June 1911, members of the Amigas del Pueblo sent a letter signed by several hundred women to interim president de la Barra demanding that suffrage be granted to women. This demand was based upon a section of the Constitution of 1857, which they argued gave women an equal right to the vote. In this letter, members of the Amigas del Pueblo stated that they hoped they would not be forced to take the extreme measures of their sisters in other countries and that the Mexican government would take advantage of the opportunity to demonstrate the extent of its political awareness.[37] In this same month, nine persons were reported killed and many wounded at a suffrage demonstration in Santa Julia, one of the poorest districts of Mexico City.

In October, even though women could not vote, they demonstrated in the capital in favor of Madero's election.[38] This demonstration typified the increased political activity of Mexican women in 1911.

In addition to sending political messages and promoting local demonstrations, women picketed the Congress in a further effort to call attention to their plight. Dubbed *"mujeres sandwiches"* ("women sandwiches"), they were ridiculed by congressional deputies and by male reporters because they appeared to be sandwiched between the large signs they carried.[39]

Women of all political persuasions joined in these ever-widening efforts to organize. In 1912, the Unión Femenina Católica Mexicana (Feminine Catholic Mexican Union) was founded in Mexico City, ostensibly to encourage development of the home and the community but actually to unify Catholic women to combat the growing political influence of feminist groups. About this same time, the Liga Femenil Latino Americana (Feminine Latin American League) was founded. The Liga Femenil's goals were basically apolitical: to work for the moral, social, and intellectual perfection of Latin American women; to secure women for the teaching staffs of primary and secondary schools; to abstain from "direct or indirect connection with politics" in any foreign country; and to avoid questions "which refer to religious beliefs."[40]

During General Huerta's administration (1913-1914), María Arias Bernal, Dolores Sotomayor, Inés Malváez, and Eulalia Guzmán organized the feminist Club Lealtad (Loyalty Club). The club protested strongly against the brutality of the Huerta administration and even organized an anti-administration demonstration in front of Madero's tomb.[41]

María Hernández Zarco (1889-1976) and María Arias Bernal (1884-1923) are noteworthy for their revolutionary activity during the Huerta administration. María Hernández Zarco, a dedicated feminist, a labor activist at the Casa del Obrero Mundial (Home of the Worldwide Worker), and a typesetter by trade, established her reputation for courage in 1913 by printing almost one thousand copies of Chiapas Senator Belisario Domínguez's highly critical anti-Huerta speech, for which Domínguez was assassinated two weeks later. After Domínguez's death, Hernández further defied the administration by publishing *Palabras de un Muerto* (*Words of the Dead*). Unlike most women revolutionaries, Hernández did eventually receive some national recognition when, in 1976, the Mexican Senate honored her posthumously with its highest civilian tribute, the Gold Medallion "Dr. Belisario Domínguez."[42]

Although schoolteacher María Arias Bernal is noted here for her revolutionary activity during the Huerta administration, her personal history was one of life-long struggle for freedom and equality. Born in the capital in 1884 to a poor family, she was remembered by a classmate as the poorest but brightest young woman in the teachers training college. When Arias's father died, her mother made great sacrifices to educate her children. After receiving her teaching certificate in 1904, Arias first joined the Madero revolutionaries and then later the Carranza forces. When Carranza triumphed, Arias was designated director of the Escuela Normal para Maestros (Teachers Training College).

María Arias Bernal received national attention for her revolutionary contributions when she was presented with a special commendation by General Alvaro Obregón. When General Obregón spoke at the martyred Madero's grave, he praised Arias for her revolutionary actions and presented her with a pistol, representative of the many personal risks she had taken. Obregón chided the men who were present for their apathy: "Since I admire valor, I cede my pistol to Señorita Arias, who is the only one worthy of bearing it."[43] Henceforth, Arias was known by the nickname "María Pistolas." However, her revolutionary fame was only fleeting. Arias died in obscurity on November 6, 1923 after a three-year bout with tuberculosis.[44]

Women and the PLM Movement

As in the rest of the nation, northern Mexico was absorbed in the turmoil that followed the February 1913 assassinations of President Madero and Vice-President Pino Suárez and the subsequent presidential takeover by General Victoriano Huerta. Fighting between supporters of the Constitutionalist Party (formed by Coahuila Governor Venustiano Carranza, who refused to recognize the Huerta takeover) and General Huerta's troops engulfed northern Mexico in widespread conflict.

During this period, the PLM was in control of vast areas of northern Mexico. In Baja California, PLM victories were largely the work of a woman named Margarita Ortega, whom Ricardo Flores Magón called "a great anarchist." Beginning in 1911, Ortega served the PLM in several capacities, including liaison, nurse, and smuggler. A weapons expert, Ortega traveled across enemy lines carrying arms, ammunition, and dynamite, often accompanied by her daughter, Rosaura Gortari. When the Maderistas triumphed, Ortega and Gortari were expelled from Mexicali by military officer Rudolfo Gallegos, who ordered them to march out of town on foot under the hot desert sun, without water or food. Both managed finally to reach Yuma, Arizona, where Ortega was arrested by U.S. immigration officials. Later, Ortega escaped, joined her daughter, and fled to Phoenix, where they assumed the aliases "María Valdés" and "Josefina." Gortari, seriously weakened by the long desert trip, died shortly after they arrived in Phoenix, but Ortega continued working with the PLM after her daughter's death, eventually collaborating with Natividad Cortés.

Together, Ortega and Cortés reorganized the Sonora PLM movement, working out of the small border town of Sonoita. On October 13, 1913, both were caught off guard by the forces of Rudolfo Gallegos, who had now become a Carrancista. Gallegos ordered Cortés shot at once, and Ortega was taken to Baja California, where she was left for the Huertistas to punish. While attempting to elude the Huertistas, Ortega was discovered near Mexicali on November 20, 1913. Jailed and tortured, Ortega was forced to stand continuously in the center of a room without touching the walls. After four days, she was taken out and shot.[45]

PLM leader Ricardo Flores Magón, in his famous essay "A la mujer" (1910), pointed out that women's lowly position in society and in world history had been enforced "by law . . . and by custom." Flores Magón especially condemned Christianity for the damage it had done to women:

> Humiliated, degraded, bound by the chains of tradition to an irrational inferiority, indoctrinated in the affairs of heaven by clerics, but totally ignorant of world problems, [the woman] is suddenly caught in the whirlwind of industrial production which above all requires cheap labor to sustain the competition created by the voracious "princes of capital" who exploit her circumstances. She is not prepared as men for the industrial struggle, nor is she organized with the women of her class to fight alongside her brother workers against the rapacity of capitalism.[46]

Despite Ricardo Flores Magón's statements to the contrary, the PLM leadership ignored the feminists' call for suffrage because they considered it politically unrealistic. As Flores Magón explained, women could secure true emancipation only through anarchist principles of economic freedom, rather than through the exercise of political rights. In Flores Magón's analysis, it was capitalism, not male chauvinism, that was the root of women's problems. Flores Magón added that to demand equal participation for women in a corrupt system was retrogressive because such a demand detracted from the paramount economic struggle. His response to the landmark First Feminist Congress, held in Mérida, Yucatán in January 1916, was one of futility: "What good the lovely and talented Yucatecans would have done for humanity, if in a moment of sane aspiration, they would have set democracy aside, and in its place adopted the Anarchist principles. . . . "[47]

Even though Liberals generally held Ricardo Flores Magón's views about the misdirection of much of the women's movement, they recognized women as a powerful revolutionary force capable of inciting and inspiring the people, and they openly expressed their admiration for women revolutionaries. Ricardo Flores Magón's brother, Enrique, reserved his highest praise for "nuestras revolucionarias" ("our women revolutionaries"). Speaking of their invaluable services, he expressed pride in women's ability to smuggle arms, munitions, pamphlets, and subversive materials. Enrique remarked that he had seen women with skills that "exceed many men's." Reflecting the kind of tribute to Mexican women contained in Enrique's praise for PLM women, and in Ricardo's praise for Margarita Ortega, PLM collaborator Camilo Arriaga wrote admiringly of the work of Aurora Martínez and her mother Crescencia Garza de Martínez, both of whom would continue the struggle after PLM leader Paulino Martínez was exiled to Havana by Huerta.[48]

Even with such devoted, capable partisans as Margarita Ortega, Aurora Martínez, and Crescencia Garza de Martínez, the PLM suffered numerous defeats during this period. The party's problems were both external and internal—most of its leaders were eventually killed or imprisoned, and the remaining members were divided ideologically over revolutionary goals. For example, the PLM's failures in Baja California and in Chihuahua were a direct result of internal struggles between PLM anarchists and PLM Socialists. These struggles were exacerbated by the activities of an assortment of filibusters, mainly from the United States.[49] Because of severe internecine quarreling among PLM members, almost as soon as revolutionary violence erupted in 1910 many members left the party to join Madero in the hope that he could consolidate revolutionary factions and achieve the rapid socioeconomic reform they felt was essential to the goals of the Revolution.

Soldaderas

Soldaderas, or *galletas* ("*cookies*"), as they were often called, traveled with the revolutionary armies.[50] These women fought, foraged for food, cooked meals, nursed the wounded, washed clothes, collected the soldiers' salaries, and performed a multitude of services not provided by the Mexican military. Most of the *soldaderas* were Indians or poor *mestizas* (women of mixed European and American Indian ancestry). When their men were conscripted or kidnapped by the army, these women took their children and joined the march. *Soldaderas* endured miserable living conditions, malnutrition, and even childbearing in inhospitable surroundings. Traveling constantly, they often bore their babies in the fields and then returned immediately to their work.[51] Observer Edith O'Shaughnessy lamented that "a thick and heartbreaking book could be written upon the *soldadera.*" Tito F. Foppa, a reporter for an Argentinian review, considered the *soldaderas* to be the real martyrs of the Revolution. Foppa predicted so very accurately that while their heroism was well known at the time, it would be forgotten quickly when the *soldaderas'* services were no longer needed.[52]

A description by Francisco Ramírez Plancarte of the federal army's withdrawal from Mexico City on August 15, 1914 reveals the *soldaderas'* arduous everyday living conditions:

> At the rear, singly or in groups, walked the soldaderas, burdened with
> a profusion of shoddy cooking implements and large bundles of
> clothes, and most of them with two or three children. They were fol-
> lowing their husbands, whom they had not left since they had been
> carried off from home. Suffering had erased all graceful softness of
> line from their faces and all expressions of sweetness from their eyes,
> leaving in their place the august marks of grief and the sublimity of
> resignation. They were just starting the march and they already showed
> a marked feeling of fatigue and tiredness. It was a sad caravan of suf-
> fering. The women were miserably dressed; some went barefoot, most
> wore sandals and very few had rough, worn-out shoes. The children
> were half-naked, barefoot, filthy, dressed in rags, many of them with
> nothing to cover their heads, their little faces numb with cold and
> emaciated by repeated fasts. Their look was inexpressive, like that of
> an idiot. Many of them wept in a heartrending manner.[53]

Corridos (ballads) helped to establish and to maintain the fame of the *soldadera*. "La Chinita Maderista," "La Adelita," "La Valentina," and "La Reilera" were popular *corridos* during the Revolution. Some of the words of "La Chinita Maderista" are: "If you love me as I love you, let us both go to fight for Madero."[54] Two heroines of the Revolution, Adelita and Valentina, were considered "the essence of Mexican femininity," and the *corridos* written to honor them had widespread popularity. The song "La Adelita" drew its inspiration from a Durangan woman who had joined the Maderista movement at an early age.[55] Among Francisco (Pancho) Villa's soldiers, "La Adelita" served as a battle hymn:

If Carranza would only marry Villa,
And Zapata marry Obregón,
If Adelita would only marry me,
Revolution would be dead as a stone.[56]

"La Valentina" was a *corrido* based upon the life of Valentina Gatica, a *soldadera* from Sinaloa who followed Obregón's troops; the *corrido* achieved widespread popularity after the year 1914. Valentina attracted particular attention with her military dress—two cartridge belts slung across her chest and a rifle hanging from her shoulder. In the *corrido*, a love-sick suitor portrayed Valentina in these lyrics:

A passion dominates me.
It's what brought me here.
Valentina, Valentina,
I wish to tell you so.

They say because of your love
A bad turn will be done to me.
I don't care if they're the devil,
I too know how to die.[57]

While most *soldaderas* remained virtually anonymous, a few achieved some recognition. Several *soldaderas* established reputations for their fighting prowess. One of the most famous was Margarita Neri, from southern Mexico. Many stories surround Neri's life, making it almost impossible to separate myth from reality. Neri rapidly became a high-ranking revolutionary officer, assuming command over large numbers of Indians.[58] Neri, supposedly a Dutch-Maya from Quintana Roo, was noted for her dancing as well as her fighting. She was alleged to have been the mistress of a member of the Díaz cabinet.[59] In 1910, Neri led one thousand men north through Tabasco and Chiapas, vowing to decapitate Díaz with her own hands. It is reported that when the governor of Guerrero heard that Neri was approaching, he had himself shipped from the state in a packing crate. Upon being informed that Neri had reached the Río Balsas, Don Porfirio [Díaz] growled, "Guerrero, that's the state in which a woman like her started the pinto by cohabitating with a crocodile!" So many legends surround Neri that she is portrayed as both commanding Zapatistas in Morelos and as cutting off the ears of Zapatistas sent to recruit her.[60] Despite the mass of contradictory accounts, it seems that Margarita Neri was a capable and respected guerrilla commander.

Margarita Mata, María Aguirre, and María Luisa Escobar were prominent *soldaderas* also. Margarita Mata was a rebel leader and a commander in the state of San Luis Potosí; María Aguirre fought on the Costa Chica in the state of Oaxaca; and, although María Luisa Escobar never attained military rank, she achieved prominence for her propaganda and dynamiting skills. Like many *soldaderas*, Escobar died fighting.[61]

The Revolution Becomes a Civil War: Women and the Villistas and Zapatistas

Even before President Huerta's removal from power in 1914, serious splits had begun to develop between revolutionary leaders over the direction the Revolution should take. While Zapata continued his struggle against federal troops in southern Mexico, Francisco (Pancho) Villa and Venustiano Carranza fought against each other in northern Mexico. *Soldaderas* accompanied all these armies, although Villa's troops, because of their swift cavalry movements, had fewer *soldaderas* than did the other armies.[62]

Zapatista guerrillas had many women among them. The services of *curandera* (healer) Apolinaria Flores were especially valuable to Zapata. Because of his enormous faith in her healing ability, Zapata had the wounded brought to Flores by night from the mountains and then returned to their camps by light of day to continue the fight.[63] Historian John Womack in *Zapata and the Mexican Revolution* describes the activities of a famous Zapatista *soldadera*, "La China," in a small village in southwestern Guerrero:

> In Puente de Ixtla the widows, wives, daughters, and sisters of rebels formed their own battalion and revolted "to avenge the dead." Under the command of a husky ex-tortilla maker called La China, they raided wildly through Tetecala district. Some in rags, some in plundered finery, wearing silk stockings and dresses, sandals, straw hats, and gun belts, these women became the terrors of the region. Even de la O [a seasoned Zapatista commander] treated La China with respect.[64]

Soldaderas participated actively in numerous Zapatista offensive forays. In the early summer of 1913, four hundred Zapatistas attacked railroad workers in Michoacán, and at least twenty women were seen among the attacking forces.[65]

In addition to attracting *soldaderas* from southwestern Mexico, Zapata's movement drew the support of women from all social classes and from all parts of Mexico. Paulina Maraver Cortés, a professor and former Maderista, with Nachita Vázquez, initiated the agrarian movement in the state of Puebla. As with most female revolutionary leaders, Maraver died poor and forgotten.[66] Aurelia Rodríguez, after working for various women's revolutionary groups, also joined Zapata. Although pregnant at the time, Rodríguez worked on dangerous and sensitive assignments. She gave birth while jailed in Puebla, but the infant died in prison because Rodríguez was not allowed to nurse him. Rodríguez sacrificed all her worldly possessions for the success of the Revolution, but she, too, died penniless and forgotten.[67]

Rebecca Bobadilla, a colonel from Morelos, regularly performed hazardous tasks, often in the midst of spies. After being captured and tortured, Bobadilla was dramatically rescued by Zapatistas. Carlota Bravo Vda. del Gral. Cándido Navarro, who accompanied Zapata during his military campaigns, was persecuted by the *federales* and imprisoned in Guanajuato.[68] Colonel Carmen Amelia Robles, who dressed as a man, fought in the Federal District, in Morelos, and in Guerrero. Mexican author Antonio Uroz, in his book *Hombres y mujeres de México* (*Men and Women of Mexico*), complains that Robles's significant contributions to the fighting have been completely overlooked by historians and that she remains virtually unknown. Uroz concludes that "it is inexcusable that women in our country have not been recognized for . . . what they've done for the Revolution, as much in war as in peace."[69]

In addition to spying, smuggling, and fighting, women contributed significantly to delineating revolutionary ideology. Revolutionary ideologists Elisa Acuña y Rossetti, Dolores Jiménez y Muro, and Juana Gutiérrez de Mendoza were important in the PLM movement and later collaborated with the Zapatistas. Elisa Acuña published an anti-Huerta newspaper, *La Guillotina* (*The Guillotine*), financing it with her own money. She eventually was forced to leave Mexico, but later returned to join the Zapatistas. Acuña's activities centered in the Puebla area, where she was also active in feminist organizations. A member of the Pan American Women's League, in 1923 Acuña helped to organize the Primer Congreso Feminista de la Liga Pan Americana de Mujeres (First Feminist Congress of the Pan American Women's League). Throughout this period, she earned her living by working at the National Library.[70]

Dolores Jiménez and Juana Gutiérrez both held the rank of colonel in Zapata's army. Jiménez, in her sixties when the Revolution began, had a long revolutionary career with the PLM, the Maderistas, and the Zapatistas. She had been president of the Hijas de Cuauhtémoc and the founder of Regeneración y Concordia. In the Zapatista camp, Jiménez worked closely with Emiliano Zapata and Gildardo Magaña, a prominent Zapatista general.

Dolores Jiménez is well remembered for the introduction she wrote to the Plan de Ayala (1911), which delineated the Zapatistas's basic agrarian reform plan.[71] In addition to writing parts of the Plan de Ayala, Jiménez undertook dangerous and sensitive missions for Zapata, even carrying messages from him to Obregón. When she was sixty-five years old, Jiménez was imprisoned for thirteen months by the Huerta administration. After Zapata's assassination in April 1919, when she was nearly seventy, Jiménez retired. As with so many other women revolutionaries, she received no awards and scant recognition for her long years of service. On October 15,

1925, a few months before she died, Jiménez was awarded a small pension from Secretary of Education José Vasconcelos.[72]

Juana Gutiérrez de Mendoza was one of the most extraordinary women of the Revolution. From 1910 to 1920, Gutiérrez participated in several revolutionary organizations, published newspapers, directed the feminist club Amigas del Pueblo, which she founded in 1909, and fought with the Zapatistas in southwestern Mexico. After briefly collaborating with the Maderistas and participating in the Complot de Tacubaya in 1911, she joined the Zapatistas. In 1914, Gutiérrez served as a colonel in the regiment "Victoria," which she organized and commanded even while she continued editing *Vésper* in the Sierra Madre del Sur.[73]

In 1914 in Chilpancingo, Guerrero, Gutiérrez founded *La Reforma*, a publication to revindicate the indigenous peoples of Mexico. *La Reforma* was subtitled "por la tierra y por la raza" ("for the land and for the people"). The following year, publication of *La Reforma* was discontinued because its editor, Santiago Orozco, was killed in a battle over Indian lands and Gutiérrez was apprehended by the Constitutionalist Army and imprisoned in the Federal District.[74] In the same year as her imprisonment, 1914, Gutiérrez founded the study group Labradores Mexicanos Instituto Popular (People's Institute of Mexican Workers) in the capital; Laura Mendoza, Gutiérrez's elder daughter, served as a leader in the study group.[75]

After Zapata's assassination in 1919, Gutiérrez resumed her organizing activities in Mexico City and published the weekly newspaper *El Desmonte*, which had the same theme as *La Reforma*—"por la tierra y por la raza." In the first issue of *El Desmonte* (June 15, 1919), Gutiérrez portrayed a revolution that fell short of fulfilling its promises. Gutiérrez stated that the people were exhausted from years of fighting and anxious for social and economic justice that the Revolution failed to accomplish. The leadership provided by the labor movement and by political parties was dismal and Carranza and the Constitutionalists offered no hope. However, Gutiérrez did not despair; in fact, she reaffirmed her commitment to continue the revolutionary struggle. She always urged *obreros* and *campesinos* to participate in the electoral process, "not to integrate power, but to disintegrate it, as a means of forming, not a new oligarchy, but of transforming the oligarchies into truly public administrations." It is noteworthy that the initial issue of *El Desmonte* contained an article by Professor Elena Torres, a representative from the Partido Socialista de Yucatán (Yucatán Socialist Party [PSY]), an indication that women revolutionaries from different parts of Mexico maintained contact with one another.[76]

Juana Gutiérrez also served as president of the Consejo Nacional de Mujeres Mexicanas (National Council of Mexican Women), founded on May 20, 1919. The Consejo's purposes were to raise the general level of women's consciousness, to develop women's character, to aid miners and youths, and to work toward the emancipation of the general populace. Consejo members included Secretary General Julia Mendoza (Gutiérrez's younger daughter), Socialist Elena Torres, and Laura Mendoza.[77]

Gutiérrez's accomplishments were extraordinary. She participated extensively in the Revolution for many years, reared her family by herself (her husband had died when their three children were only babies), adopted and reared additional children, and authored numerous articles and books as well as poetry. Despite her active life, Gutiérrez maintained a warm relationship with her children. Her son Santiago died when he was quite young, but Julia and Laura participated fully in their mother's projects.[78] For her extensive participation in the Revolution, Gutiérrez received only a small pension from Carranza. She was unable to support her family adequately on the meager pension and lived in poverty until her death in 1942.[79]

WOMEN AND THE CARRANZA ADMINISTRATION

In February 1913, Coahuila Governor Venustiano Carranza, an enthusiastic Madero supporter, refused to recognize the Huerta administration and organized the opposition Constitutionalist Party. Within weeks, Carranza won support in Chihuahua, where Pancho Villa assumed military leadership of the anti-Huerta movement, and in Sonora, where Alvaro Obregón took charge of the movement. These northern revolutionaries proclaimed the Plan de Guadalupe, which named Carranza as "First Chief" of the Constitutionalist Army and provided that he, or his designee, occupy the interim presidency upon Huerta's defeat. It should be noted that Carranza's Plan de Guadalupe was strictly a political document that focused on the method of presidential succession rather than on social reform.

Shortly after the Plan de Guadalupe was announced, its supporters disagreed over the direction the Revolution should take and civil war erupted. Villa fought against Carranza in northern Mexico, while Zapata challenged Carranza in the south. The ensuing civil war was brought to a halt by Carranza's military triumphs and his subsequent election to the presidency in 1917.

Venustiano Carranza was the first revolutionary leader to appeal directly to women for their political support, and his Constitutionalist Party attracted thousands of women from all socioeconomic classes.[80] For example, working-class Artemisa Sáenz Royo, wealthy Margarita Robles de Mendoza, middle-class Hermila Galindo de Topete, and *soldaderas* from the poorest classes joined the Constitutionalists.

Feminist Artemisa Sáenz Royo, or "Xóchitl," as she preferred to be known, became an avid Carranza supporter. Born in the state of Veracruz in the 1890s, Sáenz was the prolific author of sixteen books and twelve pamphlets. A member of the Red Battalions of the Casa del Obrero Mundial, which fought for the Constitutionalist cause, Sáenz was twice wounded and by 1920 had achieved the rank of colonel. In 1916 Sáenz visited Havana on a special mission for Carranza, and the same year she attended the Second Feminist Congress in Mérida.[81] In 1919 Sáenz served as chairperson of the Consejo de Trabajadores de la Región Veracruzana (Council of Workers of the Veracruz Region), where she led demands for political and social equality for women. She was also a labor organizer for the first nationwide union, the Confederación Regional Obrera Mexicana (Regional Confederation of Mexican Workers [CROM]), during the early 1920s, working mainly in her native state of Veracruz.[82]

Feminist professor Margarita Robles de Mendoza (1896-1953), though born into wealth, spent much of her life trying to improve conditions for the poor. Robles became interested in education and in women's liberation early in her life. In 1914, when she was eighteen, she accompanied Carranza to Veracruz as an official of the Secretariat of Agriculture. Later, she campaigned against prostitution and agitated for women's suffrage. In 1917, Robles taught English and French at the Universidad Nacional Autónoma de México (UNAM). As with Sáenz, Robles's period of most intense activity was during the 1920s and 1930s when she was a leader in the suffrage movement and served as director of the Acción Femenina section (Feminine Action) of the Partido Nacional Revolucionario (PNR) and as the Mexican delegate to the Inter-American Commission on Women in Washington.[83]

Hermila Galindo de Topete (1896-1954) was Carranza's most visible female collaborator. Born in Ciudad Lerdo, Durango, on May 29, 1896, and reared by her father and her aunt (after the death of her mother), Galindo attended school in Durango, Chihuahua, and Torreón. She studied English and had become an accomplished stenographer and typist by the time she was fifteen.[84] Galindo's father planned to send her to the United States to study chemistry, but because of his death she was forced to work to support herself and her aunt.[85]

Galindo received her first exposure to politics in Torreón in 1909, in an incident that marked the beginning of her close association with the Constitutionalist movement. In the course of her training in typing, English, and shorthand, Galindo transcribed an anti-Díaz speech delivered by Francisco Martínez Ortiz, a lawyer from Coahuila. When the municipal president learned of the existence of the anti-Díaz speech, he had all copies collected to prevent its publication. Unknown to the municipal president, Galindo retained her copy.

Later that year, at a commemoration honoring former President Benito Juárez, a group of anti-Porfiristas arrived in the city, among them Benito Juárez Maza, son of the former president. When Juárez learned that

Galindo had a copy of the Martínez speech, he requested it, had copies made, and distributed them widely. In 1909, Galindo returned to Durango. Then, in 1911, when she was fifteen, she relocated to Mexico City and joined the Liberal Club "Abraham González," which led to her subsequent involvement in the Constitutionalist movement.[86]

In 1914, as a representative of the Liberal Club "Abraham González," Galindo gave a welcoming speech to Carranza upon his arrival in the capital. In the address, Galindo compared Carranza with Benito Juárez and evidently impressed him greatly with her speaking ability. In fact, Carranza was so moved that he requested that Galindo accompany him as his private secretary. During the politically chaotic years of 1914 and 1915, when Carranza moved his government to Veracruz, Galindo served as Carranza's secretary and traveled throughout Mexico organizing revolutionary clubs and propagandizing for the Constitutionalist cause. Then, because of her success in public oratory, Carranza persuaded Galindo to carry the Constitutionalist message abroad.[87]

Galindo had developed a strong position on women's rights, although the Mexican women's movement had not yet acquired widespread support. In September 1915, with Artemisa Sáenz Royo and several others, she began the feminist magazine *La Mujer Moderna* (*The Modern Woman*) in Mexico City, and was still serving as editor when the magazine ceased publication in 1919.[88] Galindo's perspective on women's rights created a furor at the First Feminist Congress held in Mérida in January 1916, where she demanded women's complete equality, including sexual equality. Despite the controversy her message created, Galindo was invited to speak at the Second Congress (which met in Mérida ten months later), where her earlier position was reiterated in a paper (see pages 79-80).

In September 1916, Galindo traveled to Havana to deliver a series of speeches defending the Constitutionalist revolution. She argued that the only hope for future progress in Latin America lay in collective resistance to any attempted political or economic domination by the United States. Galindo cited American intervention in the Mexican Revolution as an indication of the future role that North Americans would play in Latin American affairs unless Latin American countries formed a united front against the "Colossus of the North."[89] In addition to her plea for Pan-Americanism, Galindo stressed the need to develop a strong sense of nationalism to combat the aggression of capitalist countries.

After returning from Cuba, Galindo devoted her full attention to the struggle for Mexican women's rights, and in December 1916, she campaigned unsuccessfully for women's suffrage at the Querétaro Constitutional Congress. Despite this setback, Galindo continued her feminist activities. In 1917, she ran for deputy from the Fifth Electoral District in Mexico City. Galindo stated that, though she had no hope of being elected, she felt compelled to bring to the nation's attention the large number of women who wanted the right to vote and to run for office, and to establish a precedent for Mexican women of the next generation.[90] Following her election, Galindo appeared before the Electoral College of the Chamber of Deputies to claim her seat. However, the Chamber of Deputies refused to seat her because she was a woman. Had she been seated, Galindo would have been the first woman to serve in the Chamber of Deputies.[91]

Galindo's journalistic career was a particularly productive one. In addition to writing numerous articles and to co-founding the feminist journal *La Mujer Moderna*, Galindo published at least five books on the Mexican Revolution and a biography of Carranza. In 1919, in *La doctrina Carranza y el acercamiento indolatino* (*The Carranza Doctrine and the Indo-Latin Approach*), she used Mexico as an example of a country where women had worked profitably and fought valiantly side by side with men. Galindo's second book, *Un presidenciable. El General Pablo González*, was a laudatory biography of General Pablo González, who directed the government campaign against the Zapatistas in Morelos. The biography was written in support of González's presidential campaign in the 1920 election.[92]

After Carranza's assassination in May 1920 and Obregón's succession to the presidency, Galindo retired from public life, though she continued writing. In 1923, she married and moved to the United States, where she wrote, painted, and reared her two daughters. Later, Galindo returned to Mexico but did not maintain her activist profile. She died in Mexico City on August 19, 1954.[93]

As noted earlier, the thousands of women who supported Carranza's movement represented a broad cross-section of women in Mexico. Ana María Ruiz Reyes, a nurse and diplomat for Carranza, collaborated with the clandestine anti-government press to produce *El Renovador* (*The Renovator*). A former leader in a revolutionary women's organization, Ruiz aided the Constitutionalists by working with the Cruz Blanca Neutral (Neutral White Cross).[94] Leonor Villegas de Magón, born in Nuevo Laredo, founded the Cruz Blanca Constitutionalista (Constitutionalist White Cross) on May 18, 1913, and spent her family inheritance on the Constitutionalist cause. "La Capitana," known also as "La Chata" (pug nose), was a poor, illiterate *campesina* from Sonora who rose to fame in Oaxaca for her military prowess.[95] María Gómez Vda. de Bacmaister, from Sonora, a charter member of the feminist revolutionary organization Regeneración y Concordia, was active in several feminist groups, including the exclusive Brigade "Supreme Command" created by Carranza. In 1918, Gómez retired and was decorated for her services to the nation.[96]

Ramona Flores, known as "Güera Carrasco" because of her light complexion, came from a wealthy family in the U.S. border area of Piedras Negras, Coahuila. Although she led revolutionary forces in northern

Mexico, information about her is so contradictory that it is difficult to draw a clear picture of her personal life or her revolutionary activities.[97] However, Flores did attain the rank of chief-of-staff in the Constitutionalist Army. Flores's husband was rumored to have been killed while serving as a Maderista officer, and to have bequeathed to Flores a gold mine, which she used to finance a regiment. Even after retirement, Flores retained her title "colonel."[98]

The critical support that *soldaderas* provided to the Constitutionalists is exemplified by the following incident, during which the Constitutionalist Army captured Tampico from federal forces in 1913. Four of the ablest Constitutionalist generals launched an attack on part of the city of Tampico, but the *federales* were well armed and had superior numbers. For seven days and nights, the rebel ranks were diminished by shelling and machine-gun fire. At week's end, the rebels had failed to advance beyond the city's outlying swamps, and were exhausted from the prolonged fighting. Suddenly, one of the *soldaderas* grabbed a banner, raised it above her head, and cried, "We've got to enter Tampico, no matter how. All of you who've got the nerve, follow me!" When she rushed toward the city, everyone followed. The rebel losses were great, but no more so than they had been during the preceding week, and Tampico was finally liberated. As was often the case with the *soldaderas*, today no one even knows the name of that courageous woman.[99]

Although Carranza's movement attracted large numbers of women, there were many who questioned not only Carranza's political views but also his personal attitude toward women. This questioning resulted mainly from the manner in which Carranza responded to the needs of the disenfranchised— the *obreros*, *campesinos*, and women; he had a record of acceding to their demands only when he needed their support.

Hermila Galindo was one of the women who questioned Carranza's views, but she was allowed considerable latitude in her criticism because she had proven to be so valuable a Constitutionalist publicist.[100] In her newspaper *El Desmonte*, Juana Gutiérrez de Mendoza described Carranza's Constitutionalist program as a "cadaver" that had produced nothing but "impurities, monstrosities, and bastardies." Another important woman revolutionary leader who questioned Carranza's views was María del Refugio García, who remained steadfast in her refusal to support Carranza. Known by her nickname "Cuca," García was born sometime between 1898 and 1900 in Uruapan, Michoacán. Little is known about her background, but it appears that García was from the middle class because her father was the town doctor. As García matured, she became such a well-known revolutionary speaker that her friends, concerned about her safety, felt it necessary to transport her from state to state. In 1913, García became a representative of the Michoacán Revolutionary Movement in Mexico City and dedicated her life to protecting the rights of *campesinos*.[101] García's disappointment in Carranza stemmed from her view that he was too mildly reformist and unwilling to undertake fundamental societal change.[102]

Women's Rights at the Constitutional Congress, 1917

Against the backdrop of a civil war, in which Carranza was succeeding against both Zapata and Villa, and in the midst of the economic chaos and widespread famine that plagued Mexico after so many years of fighting, President Carranza convened a constitutional congress in Querétaro in December 1916. While Carranza did not specifically exclude women from voting in congressional elections, or from membership in the Congress, only those persons who were eligible to run for deputy under the Constitution of 1857 were allowed to be congressional candidates. Thus, women could neither vote nor stand as candidates for congressional seats.

Mexican feminists closely monitored the proceedings of the Constitutional Congress in Querétaro, especially watchful of the formulation of those constitutional articles that established requirements for citizenship, suffrage, and office-holding. Generally, feminists were optimistic because extending suffrage to women would fulfill one of the Revolution's basic promises of equality. Also, they were aware of the attention that women's issues were receiving worldwide and felt that these struggles for women's rights would work to their advantage in Mexico. By 1916, several states in the United States had granted suffrage, European women were breaking down the political barriers that had restricted them, and women in the Far East were fighting for suffrage. A few weeks before the Constitutional Congress convened, Mexican women had met at the Second Feminist Congress in Mérida to advocate suffrage.

The constitutional delegates who assembled in Querétaro received three significant messages concerning women's suffrage. Hermila Galindo's message, read on December 12 amid sporadic applause, called for the right of women to vote for representatives to the lower house of Congress. Galindo expressed particular concern over how citizenship was to be defined for women, how voter qualifications would impact women's suffrage, and how women would be qualified to hold office. In earlier writings, Galindo had pointed out that working women paid the same taxes as did men; that women contributed equally to society; that they were required to obey the law equally; and that if women broke the law, they were subject to the same penalties as men. Attempting to appeal to the male delegates' "sense of justice as popular representatives," Galindo reminded them that women had participated fully in the Revolution, adding that she hoped the Mexican woman would not be "excluded from the political part [of the Revolution] and, consequently, will achieve from the new situation, rights, which, even though incipient, will put her on the path toward her own advancement. . . . " Galindo concluded that there were no rational grounds for denying women suffrage, or for denying women the right to hold public office.[103] Three days later, a second proposal to improve the status of women was presented by General Salvador González Torres, a delegate from Oaxaca. González recommended that women be granted more rights, including suffrage. The third proposal, presented on December 16, was a counterproposal from Inés Malváez, who had earlier supported suffrage but now recommended against it.[104]

The First Committee on Constitutional Reforms, which debated constitutional articles 34 and 35 (citizenship, suffrage, and the holding of public office), was chaired by thirty-two-year-old General Francisco Múgica of Michoacán. Múgica, an eloquent speaker well known for his radical views, soon emerged as spokesperson for the radicals. Luis G. Monzón, deputy from Sonora, presented the articles to the Congress for consideration. Monzón, a thirty-four-year-old primary school teacher originally from San Luis Potosí, had collaborated earlier with the Flores Magón brothers. Monzón reported the Constitutional Reforms Committee's conclusions: Mexican women had been restricted traditionally to home and family, had developed no separate political consciousness, and "do not understand the necessity of participating in public affairs, which is demonstrated by their lack of any collective movement for this purpose."[105]

The discussion might have ended with this report by Monzón had it not been for objections from conservatives. In the afternoon of January 26, a lively exchange ensued between the radical Luis G. Monzón and the conservative Félix F. Palavicini, founder of the Mexico City daily El Universal, representative from Tabasco, and Carranza's education director. Monzón, speaking for the committee in the absence of its chairperson, opposed women's suffrage, while Palavicini championed women's right to vote. Palavicini demanded to know why the committee had not considered the recommendations of Hermila Galindo and General González in support of suffrage. Monzón responded that several delegates had approached the committee requesting that the question of women's suffrage not be considered, and that the committee members had assumed the traditional position that women should not participate in politics. Palavicini countered that "the Article provides that all citizens have the right to vote" without gender distinctions and insisted upon clarification of the committee's position. But Monzón replied simply, "We did not take this into consideration." Ironically, Monzón, who had advocated previously for unrestricted suffrage for the masses, appealed to the delegates' "truly democratic impulses" and to their "revolutionary soul" for support against women suffrage. In January 1917, the articles defining citizenship and political rights were passed by the delegates exactly as Carranza had submitted them and as the committee had recommended, with citizenship and political rights granted only to men.[106]

Thus, while women in other parts of the world were achieving basic political rights, Mexican women were still being denied theirs. Despite the many promises of adherence to democratic principles espoused during the Constitutional Congress, the delegates imposed gender limitations on suffrage. The delegates' message was clear—the full benefits of the Revolution would not be shared with women. The delegates' lack of concern over women's rights was not out of character but rather reflected the traditional Mexican value of male dominance. In 1916, Francisco Bulnes, a historian and old *científico*, characterized these attitudes when he wrote:

> It is well known that in Latin countries it is only the unattractive women, despairing widows, and indigent spinsters, when they are susceptible to hysterical emotion, who consecrate themselves to the social cause. A woman . . . is a great social peril if her energies are not diverted into religious and charitable channels.[107]

The question of women's suffrage in Mexico, however, reached far deeper than male chauvinism or male indifference. Political power hung in the balance. Many of the leftist delegates, fearing the influence that the Catholic Church exerted on women, refused women the right to vote as a means of thwarting church power. The conservatives, on the other hand, supported women's suffrage because they believed that women would vote in support of their cause and would provide them with a wider political power base. Accordingly, neither the radical nor the conservative politicians were particularly concerned with granting women the vote as an exercise in democracy, or as a way of fulfilling the goals of the Revolution; rather, both leftist and conservative politicians were concerned primarily with political control. It is no wonder that author Ernest Gruening, reflecting on the period, commented that the Revolution had done little toward the emancipation of women.[108]

Years later, some of the male politicians present at the Constitutional Congress admitted openly that issues concerning women were of scant importance in their deliberations over suffrage. In the 1920s, well-known feminist Elvia Carrillo Puerto asked Luis Monzón, then a senator from San Luis Potosí, why the issue of women's suffrage had not been debated, especially since considerable support for suffrage existed at the time. Monzón, who had presented the articles to the Constitutional Congress and who was considered one of the radical deputies at the Congress, replied: "I tell you compañerita, when that question [of women's suffrage] came up, we had been on such a tremendous *parranda* [spree] and I was so drunk that we really did not know what we were doing."[109]

Even though delegates to the Constitutional Congress did not seriously consider political rights for women in general, they did grant important rights to working women. Article 123 entitled working women to childbirth benefits, protection against night work and certain types of heavy and dangerous labor, a minimum wage, and limitations on the number of hours they could work per day. Also, maternity legislation was passed that provided for a period of compulsory absence of eight days from work just prior to childbirth, a compulsory absence of one month following childbirth, and an additional absence in case of childbirth-related illness. Additionally, women were to receive full pay during pregnancy absences, and they were to retain the right to assume their former positions upon returning to work. Further, when women returned to work, they were to be allowed a half-hour rest twice daily while nursing, and every establishment employing more than fifty women was to provide a nursery.[110]

In many ways, passage of Article 123 represented a significant legal step forward for Mexican women. However, although Article 123 established a minimum wage for workers without regard to gender, no provision was made for equal employment opportunities for women. And, although it forbade unhealthy and dangerous occupations and overtime work for women and for children under sixteen years of age, the article was not enforced consistently. As a consequence, many women were forced to continue to work during evening hours, under dangerous conditions, and in unhealthy environments. Even worse, there were times that the article was knowingly misinterpreted and then enforced to prevent women from earning a decent living by excluding them from higher paying jobs.[111]

Efforts To Change Women's Legal Status

In the "Additions" to the Plan de Guadalupe, published in Veracruz on December 12, 1914, Carranza included a "revision of the laws relating to matrimony and the civil status of persons." On December 29, 1914, Carranza issued a decree that legalized divorce (prior to this decree, only legal separation had existed), alimony, and the right of women to manage and to own property. In January 1915, Carranza ordered the Civil Code of the Federal District and the Territories to be amended to correspond to this decree.[112]

Carranza issued the decree because he believed that it offered the most effective means for reducing quickly the large number of free unions and consequent illegitimate children. He argued that free union was universal among the poor in Mexico not so much because weddings were expensive but because legal marriage was indissoluble. Further, Carranza felt that the decree would also benefit both upper-class and middle-class women, for whom legal separation was seldom a satisfactory solution to an unhappy marriage. He further reasoned that because of custom and limited education, most women could not support themselves. If a marriage failed, the wife, unable to support herself or to remarry, became her husband's victim and was, by Carranza's definition, a virtual slave. Carranza summarized, " . . . [I]n the middle classes the woman, due to special conditions of education and custom, is incapacitated for successful participation in the economic struggle." In addition, Carranza stated that the decree would give the woman of the lower class "the opportunity for her own uplift and for her emancipation from the slavery in which she finds herself."[113]

Generally feminists were enthusiastic over the divorce decree. Hermila Galindo endorsed it, stating that divorce would have "a moralizing effect" in Mexico.[114] Mexico's first woman lawyer, María Sandoval de Zarco, affirmed Galindo's stance by declaring that "divorce is not only an advancement but an absolute necessity" to replace "the farce that existed."[115] Some feminists, however, opposed the decree because they believed it would benefit only men. Indeed, it was not women who pressured Carranza to issue the decree, but Carranza's male colleagues.[116]

Several of the decree's provisions discriminated blatantly against women. For example, it considered a wife's one-night absence to be abandonment, while the husband was considered to have legally abandoned his wife only after an absence of thirty days. A woman was required to wait 300 days after a final divorce decree before she could remarry, to ensure she was not pregnant with her former husband's child. A man had no required waiting period for remarriage.[117]

Although the new law made divorce legal, a divorced woman faced many obstacles, including nonenforcement of both alimony and child support payments, limited employment opportunities, and social ostracism. These obstacles stemmed largely from a lack of enforcement legislation to ensure improvement of women's general living and working conditions. The decree did not require employers to hire more women, improve women's educational opportunities, or initiate other measures to encourage women's economic opportunities or self-sufficiency. Further, social custom and Catholic tradition conspired against women who filed for divorce, to the extent that divorcees frequently were treated with scorn and contempt. A woman's family usually preferred that she avoid scandal by remaining married, regardless of the circumstances. Consequently, women rarely took advantage of the divorce provisions of the decree, because they were generally dependent economically upon their husbands and because divorce was considered a social disgrace.[118]

On April 9, 1917, Carranza issued the Law of Family Relations, to complement the divorce decree. This law guaranteed married women equal guardianship and child custody rights, the right to participate in legal suits, and the right to draw up contracts. Not only were women finally afforded a legal voice in their children's education and in the expenditure of family funds, but the Law of Family Relations also permitted paternity suits and allowed fathers to acknowledge illegitimate children.[119] While this law removed some of the legal discrimination against women, many legal inequities remained. A woman still could not engage in any profession or business without the consent of her husband. Equally restrictive for single women was the provision that prohibited an unmarried woman under the age of thirty from leaving her parents' home without their consent, except to marry.[120] Hence, even under the new laws, the sexual double standard was still firmly entrenched and institutionalized in Mexico.

Women and Organized Labor

Mexican presidents of the revolutionary period had varied reactions to labor's efforts to organize. Madero was fairly supportive of labor and established the national Department of Labor, Huerta was not supportive of labor and closed down the Casa del Obrero Mundial, and Carranza was ambivalent toward labor. Carranza's unwillingness to support labor consistently was not due to an unbending philosophical stance, such as that of the Porfiristas, but to his practice of courting labor's support only when he needed it to survive politically. Thus, while Carranza's government presented itself as a champion of the rights of workers to build independent labor unions, in reality it manipulated labor to secure political support for itself.[121]

Carranza's political balancing act on the labor issue was rewarded in 1915 when labor backed him during the civil war, in which he was pitted against both Villa and Zapata. The largest single labor recruitment by the Carrancistas occurred when industrial workers from the Casa del Obrero Mundial pledged their support to Carranza, tipping the scales of political power in Carranza's favor.

During the first part of March 1915, members of the Casa del Obrero Mundial formed six "Red Battalions" and left the capital to join Carranza's forces in Orizaba, Veracruz. Between 7,000 and 10,000 persons, including many members' wives and children, comprised the six Red Battalions that left Mexico City in this great exodus. Under the Casa del Obrero Mundial-Carranza agreement, "female workers who perform service in aiding or attending the wounded, or other similar service will be known . . . as red."[122] Thus, to be designated as a member of a Red Battalion was considered an honor. Many women prominent in the Casa were also prominent in the battalions, for example, María Del Carmen Frías and her sister Catalina, both labor organizers and founders of one of the first revolutionary women's organizations, the Hijas de Anáhuac; teacher and writer Soledad Orozco Avila; and attorney María Hernández Zarco. In addition to the six Red Battalions, the Grupo Sanitario Acrata was formed in Mexico City on February 14, 1915. The Grupo was composed of women from various industries, and its purpose was to provide a nursing corps to serve in combat zones.[123]

Shortly after the Carrancistas triumphed militarily over both the Zapatistas and the Villistas, in battles that the Casa's Red Battalions and the Grupo Sanitario Acrata helped to win, Carranza's provisional government began to suppress the labor unions. Carranza's patience had been worn thin by workers who, suffering from a wage-price crush, depreciation of the peso, and constant food shortages, called an increasing number of strikes that severely impeded the ability of his administration to function.[124] When a general strike was planned in the Federal District during July 1916, Carranza demanded that the strike committee, composed of Angelita Inclán, Esther Torres, and seven men, rescind the strike orders. When the committee refused, Carranza ordered the Casa del Obrero Mundial closed and members of the strike committee and other labor leaders arrested. Tension mounted even further in August, when Carranza invoked an 1862 anti-revolutionist law to control striking labor leaders. Because the 1862 law provided the death penalty for anyone "disturbing the public order," when Carranza extended its application to strikers, many workers felt that the Casa had betrayed them by supporting Carranza. It was in this atmosphere of mistrust that General Obregón's disagreement with "First Chief" Carranza over the harassment of strikers won Obregón the support of the union movement that was later critical to his political success.[125]

Esther Torres, a member of the 1916 strike committee, had a long history of labor activity. The daughter of a miner, she was born in Guanajuato on September 27, 1896, and moved with her family to Mexico City in 1910. In her youth, Torres worked first in a cigar factory and later became a seamstress. She joined the Casa in 1915 and later organized the Primer Sindicato de Costureras (First Trade Union of Seamstresses). In February 1916, during the formation of the First Federal Council of the Federation of Trade Union Workers of the Federal District, Torres represented the Sindicato de Costureras. Later she served on the Casa's general strike committee. When Carranza exempted women on the committee from arrest, Torres objected, explaining that "women have the same . . . responsibility in the strike as our comrades." Carranza immediately changed his orders and charges were brought against the women. They were all arrested but were later released.[126]

Toward the end of the Carranza period, women helped to establish two major labor unions: the Confederación Regional Obrera Mexicana (CROM), in 1918; and the Confederación General de Trabajadoras (CGT), in 1921. In addition, women participated actively in the Mexican Communist Party (founded in 1919), which was struggling to gain a foothold in the labor movement. All three of these organizations demanded equality for women as part of their political platforms.[127] Over the next decade, however, women leaders in CROM and CGT were eventually displaced by men because the government succeeded in co-opting the labor movement and establishing its own male-dominated leadership. As a consequence, during the 1920-1930 period there were no strong labor leaders who lobbied for women's rights or for women's representation on labor union committees. However, for the sake of political appearances, CROM and CGT did continue to include women's rights measures in their platforms.

Women, the Catholic Church, and the Revolution

The Catholic Church was important in the course of revolutionary events because of the strong link it had established and fostered with Mexican women. The church's response to the events of the Revolution, including the feminist movement, was to found its own socially oriented organizations and its own women's movement. For these reasons, when the Constitutionalists began to enforce anti-church laws, many women rushed to the church's defense.

As mentioned previously, male delegates meeting at the Constitutional Congress in Querétaro used women's traditional alliance with the church as part of their justification for denying suffrage to women. Paradoxically, this church-vs.-state conflict resulted in conservatives supporting women's suffrage and radicals objecting to it. The radicals believed that women's support of the church would result in their voting for church-sponsored candidates and that this support could mean the end of hard-fought revolutionary gains.

The church-state conflict had erupted openly in the mid-nineteenth century when anti-clerical reforms were instituted by Benito Juárez. But, during the Porfiriato, the Catholic Church regained much of its lost political influence because Díaz, due in part to the influence of his devoutly Catholic wife, permitted anti-clerical statutes to remain unenforced. In this atmosphere, it was reported that women could openly practice their faith "to the point of fanaticism," and this concerned the radicals greatly.[128]

Before the fall of Díaz, the Catholic Church had introduced programs to compete with those of the revolutionaries. To this end, a series of church conferences was held on various social issues, beginning in Puebla in February 1903 and continuing throughout the revolutionary period. Catholic Social Action, a reform program to organize the working class into unions, was activated when the Revolution began. Further, the church supported those presidential candidates it felt were most likely to maintain the church's position in Mexican society. Initially, the church supported the revolutionary Madero, principally because it believed he was the candidate who would win the presidency. But after finding Madero's vice-presidential choice unacceptable, the church switched its support to de la Barra. Finally, after Huerta's fall in 1914, the church refused to assist any revolutionaries, supported only conservatives, and consequently suffered severe political losses.[129]

The violence of the Revolution increasingly affected the Catholic Church, which suffered numerous indecencies perpetrated by the revolutionaries. An exiled nun described a scene she had witnessed involving Villistas and Obregónistas. She stated in disgust, "I have seen the chasubles [sleeveless outer garments worn by priests at Mass], scarfs, maniples, cordons, pluvial-capes, and altar cloths used for protecting the horses, while women wore the copes and albs and used the corporals as handkerchiefs."[130]

Revolutionaries even attacked nuns, desecrated churches, and turned convents into brothels. Rebels tried to discredit priests by dressing soldiers in Mass vestments and then photographing them standing with nude women. A common practice was for a prostitute to dress in nun's attire and then go into the streets to preach against Catholicism. Observer Edith O'Shaughnessy wrote of nuns being outraged in the March 1914 sacking of Tamaulipas, and she worried about future generations of children who had witnessed such violence: "What kind of adults will develop out of the children to whom the desecration of churches and the outraging of women are ordinary sights; who, in tender years, see the streets red with blood, and property arbitrarily passing into the hands of those momentarily in power?"[131]

During the early revolutionary years, the church was weakened considerably, but it managed to survive the revolutionary attacks directed against it. Then, in January 1915, General Alvaro Obregón launched his anti-clerical campaign. After capturing Mexico City, Obregón summoned priests to the National Palace, where the vicar-general and 167 priests were taken prisoner and held for ransom. On Sunday, February 21, Catholic women in Mexico City organized a demonstration to protest Obregón's actions; workers from the Casa del Obrero Mundial countered by organizing their own pro-Obregón demonstration. When demonstrators from the two movements clashed, many were injured and two were killed. Finally, in March, Carranza ordered the priests released.[132] However, the stage was set for further conflict, and similar church-state confrontations occurred over and over again during the course of the Revolution.

The church's opposition to the 1917 Constitution and the government's enforcement of anti-clerical provisions, which stripped the church of its power over education, its property, and its control over religious ceremonies, brought the church-state crisis to a head during the next decade. The new constitution prohibited clerics from political participation and from criticism of government laws, forbade clerical periodicals to address political matters, and denied clerics the right to bequeath property. Many women rallied to defend the church. During the Constitutional Congress, delegates debating the issue of church-controlled education received a message from women in Monterrey protesting anti-clerical measures as "oppressive of God and our holy religion." The delegates hooted and roared with laughter when the message was read. On December 25, 1917, Catholics in the states of Mexico, Puebla, and Michoacán published a signed pamphlet opposing the attacks against freedom of church-controlled education; significantly, more than 80 percent of the signatories were women.[133]

The willingness of so many women to defend the church served to convince Mexican revolutionaries that Catholic women constituted an important reactionary force that, if not curbed, would compromise the goals of the Revolution. This conviction made granting suffrage to women politically unacceptable. By 1920, the church and state were locked in bitter disagreement, and during the next decade these differences would erupt into more bloodshed. The violent struggles between the church and the state caught women in the middle and boded ill for the political advancement of Mexican women.

Women Journalists

Women journalists wrote prolifically during the Revolution and founded several women's magazines. Magazine readership was aimed at literate Mexican women, the vast majority of whom were from the middle and upper classes. In September 1913, Emilia Enríquez de Rivera began the monthly magazine *El Hogar*. An orphan whose writing skills were self-taught, Enríquez pioneered in the field of journalism. Initially working alone with an old hand press, Enríquez's magazine grew from a single sheet to one of fifty pages. Not only was Enríquez responsible for printing *El Hogar* but, under the pen name "Obdulia," contributed regularly to its contents.[134]

La Mujer Moderna, founded by feminists Artemisa Sáenz Royo and Hermila Galindo de Topete in September 1915, printed progressive articles by Mexican women in an effort to elevate "the feminine spirit to the level . . . it deserved." During its four-year existence, *La Mujer Moderna* featured subjects ranging from politics to face cream formulas. The few issues that still exist reveal the editors' strong interest in the international women's movement. The late-October 1915 issue of *La Mujer Moderna* informed its readers of a women's conference in Toluca (to be addressed by Hermila Galindo); carried a news brief informing readers that Candelaria Ruz Patrón had ordered the magazine for the Liga Feminista "Rita Cetina Gutiérrez" ("Rita Cetina Gutiérrez" Feminist League) in Yucatán; and contained an article in support of women's suffrage.[135]

La Semana Ilustrada provided extensive coverage of women's organizations and contained numerous photographs.[136] For example, the January 6, 1911 issue carried a photograph of María Gómez de Bacmaister performing her duties as president of the Sociedad Protectora de la Niñez Escolar (School Children's Protective Society). In the May 18 issue, White Cross members were pictured as they departed to treat the wounded; the June 2 issue showed women working for the Red Cross in Chihuahua, with guns and bandoliers strapped to their chests.[137] As depicted by photographs in *La Semana Ilustrada*, the Anti-Alcoholic League headquartered in Mexico City was active and had many women members.[138] Also, *La Semana Ilustrada* published a photograph of the legendary "Valentina." Valentina was photographed just prior to the attack on Culiacán, wearing long pants, toting a rifle, carrying a pistol, and draped with bandoliers.[139] The Zapata brothers, Emiliano and Eufemio, and their *compañeras* were pictured in the June 10, 1913 issue. A month later, there appeared photographs of women Zapatistas, with their children, following their capture in Morelos.[140]

Women who were active in politics and education also received extensive coverage. The members of a women's political club in Culiacán were pictured in September 1911, as were the delegates to the National Congress of Primary Education. On September 11, 1912, a photograph of Spanish free-thinker Belem de Sárraga appeared in *La Semana Ilustrada*, taken during her visit to Mexico.[141] Like many feminists, Sárraga equated progress in women's rights with a lessening of church influence. Catholics, objecting to Sárraga's strong anti-clerical views, tried unsuccessfully to prevent her from speaking. Sárraga advised her audience that to be free and to be equal, women must develop their minds. She stated: "No country can be fully assured of its liberty and tranquility as long as its women do not take an intelligent interest in the affairs of the nation."[142]

El Tiempo Ilustrado, *El Universal Ilustrado*, and *Arte y Letras* occasionally carried news about women. The May 28, 1911 issue of *El Tiempo Ilustrado* pictured eighteen arrested members of the anti-reelectionist club Hijas de Cuauhtémoc. It also contained a photograph of Elena Arizmendi de Mejía and a short report about her work in organizing the Cruz Blanca (White Cross).[143] *El Universal Ilustrado* and *Arte y Letras*, two general-interest magazines, covered women's suffrage, though not as thoroughly as *El Tiempo Ilustrado* or *La Revista de Revistas: El Seminario Nacional*. *El Universal Ilustrado* published a photograph of the board of directors of the Mexican Committee of the Pan American Association, in which Esperanza Velázquez Bringas was shown serving as secretary. Originally from Orizaba, Veracruz, Velázquez was a Socialist, a lawyer, the director of the National Library in Mexico City, and a prolific writer.[144]

Newspapers, another principal source of information on women's activities, reached many middle-class and upper-class Mexican women. Many of the articles were written by women journalists. *El Voto, El Diario del Hogar*, and the *Mexican Herald* (an English-language newspaper) regularly carried news items about women. On May 1, 1913, *El Voto* printed an article by members of the Amigas del Pueblo, in which they made a plea for women to unite to create a better world, to abandon their indifference, and to work for human betterment by "separating themselves from old traditions" and by "stripping away prejudices," thereby setting an example for the world. This proclamation was signed by several women, including Juana Gutiérrez de Mendoza, her sister, and her elder daughter.[145]

Other noteworthy women also used the print medium to promote their political viewpoints. Inés Malváez, Dolores Jiménez y Muro, and Aurora Martínez conducted an anti-Huerta campaign in the pages of the Cuernavaca newspaper *La Voz de Juárez*. Juana Gutiérrez de Mendoza wrote about injustice in the pages of *Vésper*. In the May 8, 1910 edition of *Vésper*, she supported Madero, though later she became disillusioned with his slow, legalistic approach to solving societal problems. Toward the end of the period, Esperanza Veláquez Bringas published widely in the capital's newspapers and magazines. Sara Estela Ramírez, the revolutionary poet, writer, and founder of *La Corregidora*, pursued her journalistic and writing career until her early death in 1910 at the age of twenty-nine.[146]

SUMMARY

As the violent phase of the Revolution came to a close, Mexican women found themselves scarcely better off than during the Porfiriato. Women had gained constitutional protection in the workplace, but this legal protection was rarely enforced. They had gained valuable political and economic experiences, and had assumed new positions and new responsibilities, but they had not acquired concomitant political rights. Further, the long-lasting negative effects of the Revolution on women were devastating: rape, pillage, death of loved ones, and break-up of the family had taken a severe toll. As a consequence, women were forced to organize even further in their efforts to combat sexist injustices and to secure equal rights.

The focus of the women's rights movement in the period from 1915 to 1924 was in the state of Yucatán, where two Socialist governors encouraged women to play a far greater societal role than they had ever assumed in Mexican history. It was in Yucatán that Mexican women took their first significant steps toward achievement of political equality.

▪ 3 ▪

The Women's Movement in Yucatán, 1915-1924

THE WOMEN'S MOVEMENT AND
GOVERNOR SALVADOR ALVARADO, 1915-1918

Between 1915 and 1924, the state of Yucatán (located in the far southeastern corner of Mexico and bordered on the north by the Gulf of Mexico) was the lodestar of the women's rights movement. Yucatán was the site of the first two feminist congresses in Mexico, as well as the scene of extensive political and social participation by Mexican women. Yucatán's leadership in the women's movement was due to the active support of two Socialist governors, Salvador Alvarado (1915-1918) and Felipe Carrillo Puerto (1922-1924), the economic wealth Yucatán derived from henequen, and the progressive ideas and spirited leadership of its women.

In 1870, one of the earliest feminist societies, La Siempreviva, was founded by Cristina Farfán de García Montero in Mérida, the Yucatán capital. In collaboration with Yucatán's well-known teacher and poet, Rita Cetina Gutiérrez (1846-1908), Farfán and other Yucatecas published a women's periodical, also named *La Siempreviva*, that encouraged women to pursue educational goals.[1]

Yucatán was one of the first Mexican states to provide education for women. The Instituto Literario de Niñas (Literary Institute for Girls) was established in Mérida in 1877 under the direction of an American, Enriqueta Dorchester. Dorchester was succeeded by Rita Cetina Gutiérrez, who devoted her life to improving women's education.[2] Cetina and her staff at the Instituto Literario de Niñas educated almost all the women who were hired as public schoolteachers in Yucatán. Among the Instituto's graduates were educators Consuelo Zavala y Castillo and Domingo Canto, both organizers of the First Feminist Congress in Mexico.[3] The strong interest in the status of women was reflected by the large number of law students in Yucatán who chose women's topics for their theses during the period between 1900 and 1915.[4]

It is ironic that the state of Yucatán should be known both for holding the first two feminist congresses in Mexico and for its enslavement of Mayas, Yaquis, and other Indians. North American author John Kenneth Turner, posing as a wealthy investor, visited the Yucatán Peninsula during the last years of the Díaz administration and publicized the sordid conditions of workers in his widely read *Barbarous Mexico*. Turner stated:

> I was told that I could buy a man or a woman, a boy or a girl, or a
> thousand of any of them, to do with them exactly as I wished, that the
> police would protect me in my possession of those, my fellow beings.
> Slaves are not only used in henequen plantations, but in the city, as
> personal servants, as laborers, as household drudges, and as
> prostitutes.[5]

Two British visitors touring Yucatán during the same period confirmed Turner's findings. Their remarks on women are especially illuminating. The horrendous working conditions of the *campesinas* and the "sexual excesses" of the *hacendados* and their sons appalled them. These visitors described wealthy Yucatecas as being extremely lazy, leading "empty and vapid" existences. After completing their brief tour of the Peninsula, the visitors concluded that the suffrage question, burning at the time in Britain, had not yet reached Yucatán.[6]

In contrast to other Mexican states during the pre-revolutionary period, wherein government programs benefited only the few, social reform to benefit the masses in Yucatán reached its apex between 1915 and 1918 under the governorship of General Salvador Alvarado. Women's issues played an important part in the general's reform proposals. Alvarado summarized his reasons for focusing so much attention on women's roles in society:

> The women of our country, no matter her social level, is more of a
> slave than a laborer; she cannot do or resolve anything on her own.
> The society itself is criminal in the subtlety of justice for women, and
> ought to be more liberal, more consistent, more tolerant. She has the
> duty to make herself free, to enter in the tournament of progress. . . .
> The strong woman is the aspiration of the moment. Elevate woman![7]

Unlike many Mexican revolutionaries, the general considered women's emancipation to be integral to the overall revolutionary goals of elevating Mexico's oppressed peoples.

A *norteño* born in Sinaloa in 1880, General Alvarado spent the formative years of his life in the U.S.-Mexico border state of Sonora. He spoke English well, authored several books, and was an avid reader of social and economic history. The general's political career dated from his involvement in the Cananea mining strike of 1906. After the strike, Alvarado joined Francisco Madero's Anti-Reelectionist Party and took part in the subsequent uprising against the federal government in 1910. During the course of the Mexican Revolution, Alvarado rose from the rank of captain to the rank of general by 1915.[8] As newly appointed governor and military commander, Alvarado arrived in Yucatán in early 1915 with orders from President Carranza to bring the state under Constitutionalist control. After a decisive military victory in March, the general set out to establish civil order, to organize a government, and to begin reconstruction.[9] Although his appointed term as governor lasted only three years, Alvarado effected radical socioeconomic changes by redistributing income, expanding educational reforms, and broadening the Constitutionalists' political base to include unorganized labor, *campesinos*, and women.

The main vehicles employed by the general to effect such rapid and radical changes were a sympathetic press; a new political party, the Partido Socialista de Yucatán (Socialist Party of Yucatán [PSY]); and the use of local leadership. The Mérida newspaper *La Voz de la Revolución* (*Voice of the Revolution*) became the semi-official organ for the Constitutionalists, and Alvarado's proclamations and speeches were given full coverage within its pages. Felipe Carrillo Puerto, who eventually headed the Partido Socialista de Yucatán and later served as Yucatán's governor, exemplified the kind of capable local talent that the general cultivated.[10]

In addition to being an idealistic Socialist reformer, Alvarado had an advantage that few visionaries have—money. By the early revolutionary period, henequen revenues had made Yucatán the richest state in Mexico. Yucatán's economic windfall was fanned by World War I, which produced an insatiable demand by American farmers for binder twine and, at the same time, eliminated competition from more distant twine producers. Besides funding Alvarado's reform programs, henequen revenues provided funds for President Carranza's Constitutionalist armies, which at that time were fighting Pancho Villa's troops in northern Mexico and Emiliano Zapata's troops in southern Mexico.

Education and Labor

Governor Alvarado's social programs were designed to alter radically the Yucatán economic, political, and social structure through the education of the disenfranchised *campesinos*, Mayas, and women. The Rural Education

Law of May 1915 provided that elementary schooling be free, secular, and compulsory; and it shifted educational responsibility from the *hacendados* to the state government. *Henequeneros*, many of whom had opposed rural education, were required by the new law to furnish school buildings, equipment, and money for teachers' salaries and other educational expenses. Those *henequeneros* who did not comply were fined, and some were imprisoned. In addition, Alvarado encouraged parents to participate in their children's education. For example, the governor ordered educational councils, composed of students' mothers, to be established in all rural areas.[11]

Alvarado promoted vigorously the education of women as preparation for active roles in social, occupational, and political life; encouraged women to enter professional schools; and urged those with intellectual interests to join cultural centers.[12] One of Alvarado's first official acts as governor was to increase the number of schools for girls and to open these to students of all economic backgrounds. The Escuela Vocaciónal de Artes Domésticas (Vocational School of Domestic Arts), one of the most important new institutions for young women, enrolled 230 students who studied subjects ranging from home economics to telegraphy. The school's staff was predominantly female.[13]

Alvarado used education to implant new ideas which he felt were essential for the success of the new system and to attack those he felt were weaknesses inherited from the old system. One of his primary goals was to free women from the influence of the Catholic Church. For example, the archbishop's house in Mérida was expropriated and converted into a school, and women instructors were commissioned to hold public meetings to warn against religious fanaticism. In addition to attacking the hold of the clergy, classrooms were used to educate students about such social problems as gambling, drinking, drugs, and bullfighting.[14]

To publicize and win support for his educational programs, the governor called Mexico's First Pedagogical Congress in September 1915. More than 600 teachers attended, mostly women whose expenses were paid by the state. Several of the delegates at this 1915 congress later provided essential leadership in Mexico's first and second feminist congresses, held in January and November 1916. It was the consensus of the delegates at the First Pedagogical Congress that coeducational and rationalist (Socialist) programs should be instituted in public schools. Support for these nonreligious programs was reaffirmed at the Second Pedagogical Congress, held in August of the following year.[15]

Rational education, which Alvarado promoted vigorously, was defined by Colonel J. D. Ramírez Garrido, Alvarado's director of public education, as "nothing more than selective teaching, integrated with the political program of the socialist state government generated by the revolution."[16] Educators espousing rational education were brought from central Mexico to Yucatán to help establish this system in the state's public schools. For example, Porfiria Avila de Rosado, a strong proponent of the new education, arrived in Mérida in late 1916 to begin the first rationalist school in Yucatán. Professor Elena Torres worked closely with both Governor Salvador Alvarado and Governor Felipe Carrillo Puerto. She attended the Second Feminist Congress in Yucatán in 1916 and in 1923 was instrumental in calling the first international women's congress in Mexico. In Yucatán, she was invited to work with local educational leaders to establish rationalist primary schools, and in September 1917, she opened the state's first Montessori school in Mérida. Torres favored the rationalist approach so strongly that she spoke of older methods as being part of a "prison system" and called for suppression of the "disgraceful practices that have been considered good up to now, and which consist of examinations, rewards, and punishments, diplomas, and titles obtained by these means." "Aptitudes," Torres informed, "will be measured only by the competence which students demonstrate in practice [and knowledge will be acquired] in the fields, in the shops, and in the experimental rooms of the school itself."[17] After Alvarado left Yucatán, Torres continued her efforts to elevate the lot of the Mexican people, particularly through educational activities. In 1918, Torres, political leader Felipe Carrillo Puerto, and others organized the Latin American Bureau of the Third International, a Socialist organization whose primary purpose was to create solidarity between the Mexican and Russian working classes.[18]

As noted earlier, improving working conditions for women was central to Governor Alvarado's goal of remolding the social structure of Yucatán. One of his first acts was to send a circular to all military commanders and heads of public offices in which he instructed:

> The best way to emancipate woman is to enable her to support herself so that she will not be compelled by isolation or misery into forced marriages or illicit unions; and this is so much more urgent to accomplish . . . since until today she was considered an object of luxury and an article of social dissipation.[19]

In December 1915, the general signed a progressive labor law that benefited working women specifically. This law defined the rights and obligations of employers and employees, including maximum working hours, minimum wages, working conditions for women and children, and health standards. It also authorized the right of workers to strike and to bargain collectively, and it established a department of labor. The law further required guaranteed days off for pregnancy, rest periods for nursing mothers, and a safe place for children to stay while their mothers worked.

Alvarado also encouraged working women's participation in the Socialist movement by forming special cooperatives for women, by founding the

Ligas Femeniles Socialistas (Feminine Socialist Leagues) in 1915, and by encouraging women employed in specific industries to form unions. The Sindicato de Señoritas de las Fábricas de Cigarros (Young Women's Cigar Factory Trade Union), for example, was organized in March 1915, only four months after the general arrived in Yucatán.[20]

Several of Alvarado's labor reforms were directed specifically at women at the lower end of the economic scale. For instance, the governor issued a decree aimed at improving the conditions of domestic servants, who consisted mainly of Mayan women and children. Aware of the deplorable situation in which servants existed, Alvarado stated:

> I believe that if we do not improve the condition of woman it will not be possible to build [our] nation. Our efforts ought to be directed to emancipate and dignify her. Sadly, I found in Yucatán that there were thousands in the countryside as well as thousands of poor women in the cities, degraded in domestic servitude in such a way that, with the risk of being paternalistic [it] was in fact real slavery.

The general attempted specifically to correct egregious wage inequities by decreeing minimum wages and maximum hours for servants. In addition, because *henequeneros* often obtained their servants by first "adopting orphans" and then retaining them as domestics, Alvarado prohibited adoptions of this type.[21]

Another series of reforms directly affecting poor women were new laws that regulated prostitution. In an attempt to halt the widespread exploitation of women by brothel owners and police, Alvarado issued a decree that eliminated bordellos (but not prostitution), required prostitutes to undergo periodic physical inspection, and made it an offense for men with venereal disease to patronize prostitutes. To ensure the decree's implementation, physical examinations were administered by the Sanitation Department, which was not under the jurisdiction of the Police Department.[22]

It was through reforms in labor laws, implementation of special social and educational programs, and constant personal encouragement that Alvarado succeeded in opening employment opportunities for women in Yucatán. Concurrently, many women were hired in government offices as cashiers, secretaries, and clerks. Within an amazingly short time, Alvarado's reforms of working conditions and his provisions for expanded educational opportunities had altered dramatically the traditional role women had played in Yucatán society.

The First Feminist Congress: January 1916

Alvarado's boldest political move during his three-year administration was to convoke the first feminist congress in Mexico's history. In late

October 1915, the general announced in *La Voz de la Revolución* that a women's congress would convene in Mérida for three days, beginning on January 13, 1916. Four basic themes were to be considered: 1) freeing women from the yoke of tradition, 2) the role of primary education in the re-vindication of women, 3) arts and occupations to prepare women for the dynamic life of modern society, and 4) women's participation in public life as a means for women to achieve a guiding role in society.[23]

Extensive preparation and widespread publicity preceded the inauguration of the congress. Throughout November and December, Alvarado continually issued orders. For instance, on Christmas Day, the governor issued Order #410, which encouraged the Women's Organizing Committee in Mérida to intensify its efforts. It went into great detail about the obligations of congressional officials, carried several arrangement details, and was signed personally by General Alvarado. In the months before the congress, *La Voz de la Revolución* printed articles and advertisements about the upcoming meeting, encouraging women to attend. The basic criteria for congressional attendance were that delegates possess an "honest reputation" and at least a grade-school education. Organizing committees and publicity agents notified women in even the most isolated rural areas.[24]

The chairperson of the Central Organizing Committee for the First Feminist Congress was schoolteacher Consuelo Zavala y Castillo, who directed a private laical school; Dominga Canto served as vice-president. Secretaries, a treasurer, committee members, and publicity agents comprised the remainder of the committee. Special commissions were named, each composed of five women, to prepare resolutions relative to each of the four congressional themes. Two weeks before the congress convened, chairperson Consuelo Zavala, in an interview in *La Voz de la Revolución*, stressed her optimism about the upcoming congress. Asked about her position on women's roles, Zavala replied, "Oh, yes! I am a grand feminist!" and added, "I believe that modern woman has the right to struggle."[25]

After months of extensive preparations, the congress convened at 9:00 a.m. on January 13, 1916, in the Peón Contreras Theatre in downtown Mérida. More than seven hundred delegates, primarily from the state of Yucatán, packed the theater; most of the delegates were teachers, whose expenses were paid by the state.

Although mainly from the middle class, the delegates held widely different views on the role of women. After selection of officers, these ideological differences surfaced quickly during the afternoon session when a speech written by feminist Hermila Galindo was read to the assembly.[26] One of Mexico's most prominent feminists and Constitutionalists, Galindo had been invited to participate in the congress by the Department of Public Education. Unable to attend, she sent a paper to be read entitled "La mujer en el porvenir" ("Women in the Future"). In her paper, Galindo defended adamantly the view that women were the intellectual equals of men; therefore, they should be included equally in the revolutionary ranks. The most shocking part of her message, however, was Galindo's demand that women should have the same sexual freedom as men. Galindo insisted that women needed to understand their sexuality, and that schools should include study of the human reproductive system in a required biology course. Galindo reiterated her earlier position on the relationship between women and the Catholic Church, stating that "religion has wanted woman to ignore her sexuality in order to always keep her in ignorance and in order to exploit her."[27] Also, Galindo recommended the establishment of rehabilitative programs for "wayward" women. Galindo's plea for recognition of female sexuality and the need for sex education in the public schools received less than enthusiastic support.[28] (Sex education in public schools did not become part of the Mexican educational system until the Cárdenas presidency in the 1930s).

Hermila Galindo's speech upset and divided the delegates. The reaction of the delegates was understandable because to most Mexican women public discussion of such topics as abortion, prostitution, and sexuality was unthinkable. Even though it was agreed that Galindo's work should not be published by the congress, the Catholic conservative faction, led by teachers Isolina Pérez and Evelia Marrufo, did not even want her ideas discussed. The Pérez partisans dismissed Galindo's message as "immoral." A faction opposing the conservatives, led by Encarnación Rosado Avila and Candelaria Ruz Patrón, took the position that Galindo had addressed key issues which they thought should be discussed. Consequently, from the dialogue generated by both factions, Galindo's viewpoints received a thorough airing. Later, Galindo defended her position in the magazine *La Mujer Moderna*, which she helped to found, and in a statement sent to the Second Feminist Congress.[29]

Three basic ideological positions emerged from the First Feminist Congress: 1) the Catholic conservative position, 2) the moderate position, and 3) the radical position. The Catholic conservatives were concerned primarily with maintaining women in their traditional roles of wife and mother, and fought any proposals that threatened this status quo. Catholic conservative delegates also feared that too much education and experience would make women unattractive to the opposite sex. Francisca García Ortíz articulated this apprehension when she commented that "women don't need as much education" as men and declared that "women teachers don't marry" and, even sadder, "encyclopedic knowledge seems to be an obstacle to happiness."[30]

Such arguments as those articulated by García were totally unacceptable to women at the other end of the ideological spectrum. The radicals considered women the equals of men in every sense, and they concurred with the perspective of the Socialist government that women should take an active role in society by voting and by running for office. In the radical's opinion, it was the government's duty to stop gender injustices by opening economic, political, and social opportunities to competent women.

Other congressional delegates held strongly to the moderate middle-of-the-road viewpoint. The moderates supported education for women, especially laical and rationalist programs, and viewed education as a way of loosening the shackles that had bound women. Also, the moderates argued that women should receive a practical education that would help them be better wives and mothers. Although the moderates supported women's participation in civic affairs, they addressed the issue of suffrage more cautiously than did the radicals. This moderate element, represented by delegates such as Consuelo Zavala, argued that political rights should be exercised only by men until women were prepared adequately to exercise those same rights.[31]

Moderates and radicals did concur on the need to reform the old Civil Code of 1884, which blatantly discriminated against women. Sections of the code recommended for revision included those on guardianship, matrimony, inheritance, and freedom for single women after the age of twenty-one.

Regarding the congressional theme of releasing women from the yoke of tradition, several points were agreed upon, including the following:

1. In the primary schools, children should be informed of the real origin of humankind and religions.

2. The state should institute university extension classes or public lectures for women and young ladies for the purpose of implementing point 1, above.

3. Women should be instructed about their [physical] nature, and this instruction should be provided by the school system whenever it is clear that a woman acquires or has acquired the ability to conceive.

4. The government should be petitioned for modification of the Civil Code, granting greater liberty and rights to women, so that with this freedom they might scale the heights of new aspirations.

The second and third congressional themes addressed primarily education, the arts, and occupational training for women. After heated discussion, the delegates agreed to support laical education, primary school reforms as passed by the First Pedagogical Congress, new curricula, and the establishment of art academies.[32]

The consensus on the fourth congressional topic, the public functions and duties of women, was as follows:

1. All fields of employment should be open to women.
2. Women of the future could fulfill any civic charges which did not demand a vigorous physical constitution: because there were no differences in the intellectual status of women and men, the former were equally capable of being a guiding element in society.[33]

The most important political proposal passed by the congress concerned suffrage. During the final session, on the afternoon of January 16, a petition on women's suffrage was initiated, signed by over thirty of the most radical women, and submitted to the delegates for consideration. The petition called for the state to assume leadership in altering the national constitution to allow women to vote in municipal elections. The petition also called for revision of the state constitution to allow women twenty-one and over to vote in statewide municipal elections and to run for statewide municipal offices. The petition was passed unanimously by a group of exhausted delegates at the close of the session.[34]

While Mexico's First Feminist Congress was a landmark in the women's struggle, its immediate effects were limited. The congress did not produce a women's organization, nor were its two major proposals, revision of the Civil Code of 1884 and municipal suffrage, acted upon immediately. However, by April 1917, President Carranza's Law of Family Relations corrected many of the faults of the outdated Civil Code, and the municipal and state vote was granted to women in Yucatán in the early 1920s under the governorship of Felipe Carrillo Puerto. By contrast, women in most other Mexican states had to wait until 1946 to vote even in municipal elections.

Perhaps the most outstanding accomplishment of the First Congress was that it brought women together to debate vital issues publicly for the first time, laid the groundwork for collective action on a wider scale, and encouraged women to continue demanding reform. General Alvarado was both pleased and troubled by the First Feminist Congress. Extensive coverage of the meetings in the official newspaper, *La Voz de la Revolución*, and a telegram he sent to President Carranza in Mexico City on January 15 (after the congress had met for two days) indicated the deep satisfaction Alvarado felt. With obvious pride Alvarado reported to the president:

> The audience discussed in a vehement manner the most adequate
> ways for making women less religiously fanatic and improving their
> social conditions. Vibrant speeches were given with grand enthusiasm.
> Permit me to express to you that this is a new triumph for the revolu-
> tion. A year ago, when I arrived, there were few women seen alone in
> public.[35]

General Alvarado, however, had hoped for a clearer mandate from the delegates. In a further attempt to win support for his programs, he announced that a second feminist congress would convene in Mérida in November.[36]

The Second Feminist Congress: November 1916

Held eleven months after the First Feminist Congress, the Second Feminist Congress attracted many of the same delegates, although the total number was reduced. Again, the delegates were mostly middle-class school-teachers from the state of Yucatán.[37] The tone of the second meeting was more pragmatic and more circumscribed than the first, perhaps because of the extended length of the November congress (November 23 to December 2) and because of the widespread congressional support garnered by the moderate faction. Topics of discussion paralleled those of the First Congress and included primary school education, marriage, rights of divorced parents and their offspring, and women's suffrage and office-holding. As in the first meeting, several heated debates and protests took place, especially over the roles women should assume in society.

The Second Congress was convened at the Escuela Vocaciónal de Artes Domésticas in Mérida at 4:00 p.m. on November 23, 1916. As in the previous congress, the first session was devoted to electing nine members to the executive board. Porfiria Avila de Rosado, a radical who had been a candidate for president of the First Congress, served as president of the Organizing Committee and as presiding officer for the Second Congress. Matilde Acevedo de Paullada, director of the Escuela Vocaciónal de Artes Domésticas, who had served as vice-president for the First Congress, was elected president of the Second Congress.[38]

On the first day, strongly feminist speeches were delivered by Professor Mercedes Betancourt de Albertos and by Candelaria Ruz Patrón. Both speakers emphasized the need for women to have equality under the law. Betancourt pointed to the contradiction between the ideals of equality, as stressed by the leaders of the Mexican Revolution, and the current exclusion of women from the benefits of the Revolution, noting that "nothing would be served by so much sacrifice [on the part of women]" if men did not comply with the promises of the Revolution. As a reminder to Mexican revolutionaries, Betancourt quoted writer and feminist Emilia Pardo Bazán: "For woman to advance, it would be necessary, in the first place, that she want to, and second, that she find some ground prepared, [and] some help from man too." For Yucatecas, this statement was optimistically close to the reality of their situation; it was obvious that many women wanted changes and that Salvador Alvarado was certainly cooperative. Both speakers ended their speeches by proclaiming that, under the circumstances, emancipation was accessible if the women present would put all their souls into it. Betancourt concluded dramatically by exclaiming, "Let us unite into a heroic phalanx and struggle until we win the inalienable rights of our sex!"³⁹

After this auspicious beginning, the congress became mired in disagreements and bickering. The delegates did agree to support women's apprenticeship programs and practical training at the elementary level. However, discussions over marriage, suffrage, and office-holding brought a sharp divergence of opinion. As with the First Congress, the November meeting was filled with protests and petitions. There were numerous objections to the way the president conducted sessions, but an attempt by radical elements to censure her failed. There were also protests over both the selection of discussion topics and their priority on the agenda. One of Mexico's leading feminists, Artemisa Sáenz Royo, representing Oaxaca and Chiapas, lodged a strong protest, accused some delegates of purposefully delaying discussions, and refused to attend any more meetings.⁴⁰

As in the First Congress, the issue of suffrage particularly divided the delegates. The Suffrage Committee reported that "what is important in suffrage is not that women have the obligation to vote but the right to do it because that signifies the fruition of liberty." The committee stated further that women were sufficiently intelligent and sufficiently motivated to participate in community activities at the municipal level. While the committee acknowledged that the delegates should proceed cautiously, it emphasized that "what is important, is to have the right [to vote]." The committee's concluding recommendation was that literate women over twenty-one be allowed to vote in municipal elections, but not to run for office.

Several objections to the Suffrage Committee's recommendations were voiced. Lucrecia Vadillo, who served on the committee, argued that women's mission should be one of "sweetness and peace." Women in the future should vote, Vadillo conceded, but not at present because they were unprepared. Besides, Vadillo said, suffrage "is the element that will destroy conjugal peace, wives' happiness, and family life." Vadillo concluded her speech by recommending that women neither vote nor run for municipal office.⁴¹

After the Suffrage Committee members completed their presentations, the suffrage question was opened to the floor for debate. Mercedes Betancourt, among others, spoke in favor of the committee's recommendations. Evelia Marrufo, who had led the conservative faction in the first congress, was representative of the opposition. To the outspoken Marrufo, women's participation in civic affairs presented a direct threat to home life. Betancourt countered that exercising the right to vote hardly meant abandoning the home.[42] The debate became so lengthy and so bitter that it spilled over into Monday's business, with Betancourt and Marrufo continuing to spar. In exasperation, Betancourt finally reminded her audience that this was a feminist congress and that women were only asking for the right to vote. No one, Betancourt continued, would be obligated to vote if she preferred not to exercise that right. At the end of the discussion, the delegates approved women's suffrage on the municipal level (147-87), but rejected the right of women to seek office in municipal elections (60-30).[43]

Another intense debate occurred during the Wednesday afternoon session, which *La Voz de la Revolución* called the most exciting of the congress. The topic of discussion was how women could best be freed from the yoke of tradition and converted into agents of change to disseminate scientific knowledge and to further the principles of liberty. The committee in charge stressed freedom of life choices, the merits of secular education, and the benefits to be derived from science. Because most of the delegates were dissatisfied with the committee's work, which they considered too lofty and too abstract, a new committee was selected to address women's freedom. The new committee's more pragmatic focus on elementary education and participation in civic affairs received approval just before the delegates adjourned.[44]

The gaiety of the late afternoon closing session was in sharp contrast to the acrimonious debate of previous days. Governor Alvarado, along with many other dignitaries, attended the ceremonies. The congress came to a close with a poetry reading, speeches, and much praise for the delegates and their work.[45]

Impact of the Feminist Congresses

In retrospect, the accomplishments of the First Feminist Congress, where delegates passed motions supporting both municipal suffrage and the right of women to run for municipal office, were more substantial than those of the Second Feminist Congress. While the issues of suffrage and the right to run for office were debated hotly at the Second Congress, only a municipal suffrage resolution passed. Controversial feminist Hermila Galindo, unable to attend because of illness, sent her speech to be delivered by Guanajuato delegate Elena Torres, a professor and writer who held ideas similar to those of Galindo. Galindo's speech, a defense and reaffirmation of the ideas she had presented in January to the First Congress, was printed and distributed in Mérida. Galindo began by clarifying her work as a serious study. Ironically, she explained, the sections considered most scandalous had been copied literally from the works of famous sociologists. She contended that to condemn those works was either not to have understood them fully or to have analyzed them inadequately. The heart of Galindo's message was that a major responsibility of women's efforts should be to correct society's injustices and to improve the treatment given "fallen women." On the question of how women could be freed from traditional bondage, Galindo had two recommendations: 1) women must be given the necessary weapons to struggle with life, and 2) a way must be found to redeem "fallen women." A major area upon which Galindo focused was suffrage. She explained that "women need the vote for the same reasons that men do . . . to defend their interests, especially the interests of their children, the interests of the home and of humanity." These interests "cannot be separated" from those of men. Most importantly, women must vote for "moral reasons." In a democracy, only by voting can women struggle against alcoholism, prostitution, juvenile delinquency, pornography, and the demoralization of children.[46]

While neither the first nor second feminist congress reached the accord for which Alvarado had hoped, the congresses provided an important forum in which women could discuss their goals and aspirations. The congresses also revealed the deep divisions between radical feminists, who sought equality on all levels, and the conservative faction, who strove to improve women's lot only as it related to the roles of wife and mother. These political and ideological differences ran deep and created critical dissension in the Mexican women's movement. Nevertheless, the first and second congresses, viewed in the context of the times, served to keep women's issues before the public and represented a significant leap forward for the women's movement in Mexico.

Of course, the controversy over the place of women in society did not end with the publication of Hermila Galindo's speech or with the close of the Second Feminist Congress. *La Voz de la Revolución* continued to print articles, editorials, and news items on the status of women. On March 29, 1917, an editorial signed "Demófilo" reaffirmed that "the rights of women, in our days, constitute one of the most important problems of nations" and "they are going to be resolved everywhere" in a positive way. A month later another editorial, signed by the same author, linked the issue of women's emancipation with the goals of the Revolution and concluded on the favorable note that "the future belongs to women!"[47] In addition, many theses and pamphlets addressing women's issues continued to be written by law students in the state capital.[48]

Alvarado's director of public education, J. D. Ramírez Garrido, who had carried the suggestion for a feminist congress to the governor, helped to keep the women's movement alive with the 1918 publication of his staunchly feminist tract *Al margen del feminismo* (*Concerning Feminism*). Tracing the historical roots of the women's movement, Ramírez praised the efforts of Governor Alvarado and encouraged women to remain active at all levels of society.[49]

The loss of momentum for continued reforms in the Yucatán began with the passage of a bill at Mexico's Constitutional Congress in Querétaro in December 1916. This bill disqualified Salvador Alvarado from running for reelection as governor of Yucatán because he had neither been born there nor resided there for five years.[50] The loss of Alvarado's leadership, a renewed outbreak of political violence over Mexico's presidential succession in 1920, and the economic squeeze caused by falling henequen prices caused social reforms to slow dramatically in Yucatán. Under such adverse circumstances, few gains for women were possible. However, General Salvador Alvarado and the women of the first and second feminist congresses had prepared the groundwork for an enduring Mexican women's movement. The Yucatán movement was not to flower again until the early 1920s under the leadership of Socialist Governor Felipe Carrillo Puerto and his sister Elvia.

THE WOMEN'S MOVEMENT AND
GOVERNOR FELIPE CARRILLO PUERTO, 1922-1924

The reform programs initiated by General Salvador Alvarado were continued under Socialist Felipe Carrillo Puerto while he was president of the Partido Socialista de Yucatán (Socialist Party of Yucatán [PSY]) and later during his tenure as governor of Yucatán (February 1922 to January 1924). Under Carrillo, women were granted suffrage and the opportunity to run for office, provided access to birth control information, and encouraged to join Socialist Leagues.

Felipe Carrillo Puerto is a difficult figure to assess because of the strong reactions he evoked from contemporary observers. Writer Ernest Gruening likened Carrillo to Moses, describing him as "a god among his countrymen . . . , a cosmic figure" whose "leadership was almost unknown in this day and belonging to a rather legendary age."[51] A.G.B. Hart, a North American reporter, also compared Carrillo to Moses, and stated that he was a god to his Indian followers.[52]

Carrillo was born in Motul, a hamlet north of the state capital, on November 8, 1874. His father had been a civic leader with a distinguished military career; his mother was a housewife who raised fourteen children.[53] Carrillo worked at a variety of occupations, including butcher, railroad conductor, teamster, founder of the newspaper *El Heraldo de Motul* (1906), and correspondent for the prominent publication *Revista de Mérida*. He also established himself in the business of hauling machinery and supplies from the railroad to the haciendas. As a businessman, Carrillo was exposed firsthand to the horrible conditions of the Mayas. *Hacendados* owned their Indian slaves "body and soul" and used their women at will. Carrillo, who claimed to be of Mayan descent, began to inform the Indians of their rights.[54] He explained his ideological position as follows:

> I stand first, last and always for Socialism. My ideas are above all Socialistic. My ideals are centered in the welfare of the Indian who is my blood brother. . . . I shall continue to put into that side of the balance the weight of my influence till I die.[55]

Carrillo translated the federal constitution into the Mayan language and became known for his defense of the Mayas. For these activities, he was imprisoned in Yucatán on five different occasions, and at one point a price was placed upon his head.[56]

The association between Felipe Carrillo and General Alvarado had begun soon after the general arrived in Yucatán. Impressed by Carrillo after only a brief meeting, Alvarado appointed him head of the Motul Agrarian Committee.[57] After that, Carrillo organized the Ligas de Resistencia (Leagues of Resistance), which he built into a personal power base. In 1917, Carrillo was Alvarado's frequent companion on trips throughout the state, and in 1918 Carrillo assumed the presidency of the Partido Socialista de Yucatán. The Ligas de Resistencia formed the backbone of this politically powerful organization. Through reorganization and a massive membership drive, Carrillo provided the Ligas with an even larger membership and broader jurisdictional authority.[58]

In 1918, Carrillo established *Tierra*, the official Liga publication, and convened a workers' congress in Motul. This congress, which met in March, addressed organization of the Liga, social welfare issues, and economic problems. Liga membership was open to women, who after holding membership for one year could pay half-dues, vote in Liga elections, and run for office.[59]

When Alvarado's power waned, the *hacendados* launched an all-out attack against the Socialist Ligas de Resistencia, and in 1918 Carrillo barely escaped with his life. Subsequent internal political fighting and declining henequen prices resulted in a period of stagnation for social programs in Yucatán. Finally, the military victory of General Obregón stemmed the internal violence. With the support of Obregón and Manuel Berzunza (who was appointed temporary governor of Yucatán in February 1921), Carrillo and the Partido Socialista de Yucatán, now renamed the Partido Socialista del Sureste (Socialist Party of the Southwest [PSS]), reemerged stronger than ever.[60]

When Carrillo ran for governor of Yucatán in 1921, he called a series of meetings to marshall support for his programs. Especially significant was the workers' congress that met at Izamal (central Yucatán) in mid-August 1921. Here it was decided that Carrillo would serve as president of both the Liga Central (Central League), which coordinated all Liga activity, and the PSS. The delegates pledged their support for rational education, for the organization of Ligas Feministas (Feminist Leagues), and for the expansion of the Partido to include the entire southeastern part of Mexico.[61]

For reasons that remain vague, the relationship between Alvarado and Carrillo began to cool. Alvarado, under heavy criticism from the PSS, left Yucatán, refusing to support Carrillo in his bid for the governorship. In early September, Alvarado returned to Yucatán to try to prevent Carrillo's election. However, realizing that the PSS was completely entrenched, Alvarado left Yucatán for good at the end of September.[62]

On November 6, 1921, at the age of forty-seven, Carrillo was elected governor of Yucatán by a wide margin, and the entire Socialist ticket of fifteen representatives triumphed with him.[63] Immediately Carrillo began to eliminate other political parties and to clear the way for his reform programs. Major changes were then effected in education, labor, and women's roles. In addition, Carrillo extended state control over the henequen industry, increased progressive taxes, redistributed land, and constructed new roads.

The Ligas de Resistencia were the heart of Governor Carrillo's reform program. Local Ligas were grouped administratively under the direction of the Liga Central in Mérida, which met regularly on Monday evenings (known as Red Mondays). Purposely constructed to usurp functions formerly performed by the Catholic Church, the Ligas operated night schools, led discussion groups on economic and social problems, and sponsored athletic contests. In a short time, the Ligas became the social, economic, and political centers of Yucatán communities. In accordance with Carrillo's desire to instill civic responsibility and to encourage participation, each Liga maintained its own baseball team and band.[64]

In addition to the Ligas, Carrillo relied upon another important source of support—the media. *Tierra* and *El Popular* (a daily directed by Socialist Miguel Cantón) publicized political issues. Consistent coverage was given to women's activities, both on a local and an international level. Such issues as birth control, education for women, and the new divorce law were explained and discussed thoroughly.[65] Women writers were among the regular contributors. *Tierra* and *El Popular* carried articles by such women leaders as Susana Betancourt; the governor's younger sister and collaborator, Elvia Carrillo Puerto; Nelly Aznar Gutiérrez, the director of the magazine *Rebeldía*; Socialist Esperanza Velázquez Bringas; and Communist María del Refugio García. Alma Reed, a North American writer and the governor's fiancée, graced the September 30, 1923 cover of *Tierra*.[66]

Education

Education was the cornerstone of Governor Carrillo's reform program. The governor considered education so important that the first decree he issued, on February 6, 1922, was "The Instruction Law of the Rationalist School." It was Carrillo's hope that the law would result in all Yucatecos becoming literate. Each Liga appointed a three-person commission to conduct a literacy census. Those Yucatecos who could read and write were to instruct those who could not, and anyone failing this obligation was declared a "bad Socialist" and could neither run for office nor be employed in public services. Those Yucatecos who passed the reading and writing examination were rewarded by exemption from paying Liga dues for one year. After a Liga acquired 100 literate members, it was entitled to be designated "Liga de Previsión y Resistencia" ("League of Prevention and Resistance").[67]

Carrillo was determined further to rid Yucatán of religious influences. To keep his campaign pledge of not resting until he had "eradicated ignorance, superstition and priestcraft" and "driven them disgraced from my country," Carrillo began immediately to increase both the numbers and the types of available schools, or, as he stated, to "take the schools to the children and not drag the child to the schools."[68] Under Carrillo, the state and the federal government jointly supported 209 elementary schools, 2 secondary institutions, 28 night schools, and 180 rural schools. Among the new types of schools established were an agrarian school, a school for abandoned and orphaned children, and the University of the Southeast (the present-day University of Yucatán).[69]

In addition to their vital role in supporting an increase in the number of schools and in extending literacy, the Ligas functioned as community learning centers. Teachers, mostly women, were organized into the Liga de Maestros Racionalistas (League of Rationalist Teachers), which sponsored conferences to promote the coeducational, rationalist system of education that Carrillo considered essential to implementation of his ideology.[70] Yucatán teachers received particular indoctrination in the teaching of rational education and were required to attend a special month-long training program devoted to Marxism, the history of labor, the socialization process, and the land and labor reforms incorporated into the 1917 Constitution.[71] Carrillo's long-range goal was to use education as the principal tool to shift emphasis from an individual to a collective consciousness.

Women in the Labor Force

To improve the lot of the working man and woman, Governor Carrillo held numerous congresses and initiated several pro-labor bills. His major reform program was built upon laws passed in 1918 by the Twenty-fifth Congress of Yucatán. These laws set forth the obligations of employers and workers, the structure and role of labor organizations, personal debt limitations, working hours, salaries (fixed by local Ligas under the jurisdiction of the Liga Central), occupational health and hygiene requirements, industrial and worker protection, arbitration, and the requirement that a certain percentage of workers be Mexican. Section nine of the Labor Code addressed specifically the employment of women and children. Pregnant women were to be allotted two months of rest prior to confinement, and two months of rest at full pay immediately following birth. After returning to work, women were to be allowed two one-hour periods per day to nurse their children.[72]

As did General Alvarado, Carrillo felt compelled to address the problem of the large number of prostitutes in Yucatán. Lamenting the situation, the governor stated, "We cannot abolish it [prostitution] by decree. I believe it wholly unnecessary and that in time with the economic emancipation of women it can be wiped out." Carrillo attempted to open other work opportunities to women, to enforce compulsory medical inspection of prostitutes, and to require prophylaxis of both the men who patronized prostitutes and the women who remained in the profession.[73]

In the workers' congresses sponsored by the PSS, Carrillo attempted to include women. At the Motul meeting in 1918, however, it appears that fiery Elena Torres, representing Mérida and the Liga Central de Resistencia, was the sole woman to participate. Nevertheless, Torres was vocal and spoke strongly in favor of the rationalist system of education and against the power wielded by the Catholic Church.[74]

At the Second Workers' Congress, held at Izamal in 1921, Elvia Carrillo Puerto (the governor's sister), schoolteacher Rosa Torres C. González, and a few other women were in attendance.[75] Elvia Carrillo and Rosa Torres demanded that women be allowed to attend the workers' congresses, to speak at the congresses, and to vote "to defend their rights." Although the women conceded that the majority of schoolteachers in the state were still under the influence of the church, they felt confident that the situation would improve by the time of the next congress. These feminists recommended that those Ligas Feministas members who were free from religious and social prejudice be admitted to Workers' Congress meetings. A member of the Congress Board of Directors, Miguel Cantón, agreed, and he urged that the men's Ligas work closely with the Ligas Feministas so that both might better accomplish their goals. In the end, the Congress Board agreed to admit delegates of the Ligas Feministas as soon as they shed their religious and social prejudices.[76]

Elvia Carrillo Puerto and the Ligas Feministas

Elvia Carrillo Puerto, the sixth daughter born to the Carrillo Puerto family, collaborated with her brother Felipe during his governorship by directing women's activities in the state. Strikingly good-looking, with a vivacious personality, Elvia Carrillo organized the Ligas Feministas; was elected to the state legislature at the age of twenty-eight; and represented Yucatán as well as the republic of Mexico at numerous state, national, and international feminist congresses. After the governor's death in 1924, Elvia Carrillo continued her feminist and Socialist activities in San Luis Potosí and Mexico City.

Elvia Carrillo's adolescence was unremarkable for early twentieth-century rural Mexico. She married Vicente Pérez Mendiburo in 1909 at the age of thirteen, had two children (one died shortly after birth), and was widowed by the time she was twenty-one. Carrillo's second marriage to Francisco Barroso (whom both her brother and her sister called a "brute" and "ignorant") was short-lived, and she supported herself subsequently by working as a rural schoolteacher in Yucatán.[77]

Elvia Carrillo expressed an interest in women's issues as early as 1912, founding the first feminist organization for *campesinas*, and in 1919 she organized the Liga Feminista "Rita Cetina Gutiérrez." But the period of her most active participation in the women's movement corresponded with her brother's governorship. Carrillo recalled that her brother once comforted her with the words, "Don't be afraid, sister. You help me. You work with the women, and I with the men." In 1922 Carrillo led the Yucatán delegation to the Pan American Conference of Women in Baltimore; the following year she represented Yucatán at the first international women's congress held in Mexico City; and in 1923 she was elected, along with two other women, as a state representative for the Fifth District in Yucatán.[78]

Building on the programs begun by General Alvarado, Governor Carrillo and Elvia Carrillo attempted to include women in all spheres of government. The Ligas Feministas, under the direction of Elvia Carrillo, were central to these activities. The basic purpose of the Ligas Feministas was to raise women's consciousness so that they could participate more fully in all phases of community life. The Ligas Feministas launched campaigns against illiteracy, superstition, alcoholism, poor hygiene, and improper child care practices.

An important function of the Ligas Feministas was to encourage women to participate in social and political activities. Governor Carriool, aware of the pitiful condition under which women and children existed, sought to alleviate these conditions. Carrillo's program for illegitimate children, for example, gave the "natural born" child its father's name and the right to "share equally in all rights and privileges with the so-called legitimate children."[79] One of the Liga's responsibilities was to explain these provisions of the laws to women, assuring that they understood their rights.

Another prime activity of the Ligas Feministas was the sponsorship of women's conferences and meetings. Topics discussed at these conferences and meetings included birth control, the Catholic Church, Liga organizational matters, women's emancipation, and suffrage. At a large conference held in October 1922, three key Ligas Feministas members, Elvia Carrillo, Rosa Torres, and Eusebia Pérez Vda. de MacKiney, were honored by being elected to represent the Ligas at the Liga Central meetings.[80]

The center of feminist activity in Yucatán was the Liga "Rita Cetina Gutiérrez," located in Mérida. Elvia Carrillo served as its president. Founded January 19, 1919, and named after the state's leading poet and teacher, the Liga Feminista "Rita Cetina Gutiérrez" was an active club that engaged in a wide range of activities. Liga members endorsed candidates at both local and national levels, even though women were not allowed to vote in the national elections;[81] made frequent trips from Mérida to the countryside to attend meetings and to generate interest in the formation of new Ligas Feministas; and actively supported a variety of educational programs.[82] In early February 1922, for instance, the Liga Feminista "Rita Cetina Gutiérrez" inaugurated a school, and Liga members participated in the governor's reading program. As the Liga president, Elvia Carrillo offered a prize of fifty pesos for any woman who could teach a group of twenty or more to read and to write within three months.[83]

In addition to endorsing political candidates, sponsoring women's conferences, and supporting educational endeavors, the Liga "Rita Cetina Gutiérrez" published a monthly magazine, *Feminismo: Organo de la Liga Feminista "Rita Cetina Gutiérrez" (Feminism: Voice of the "Rita Cetina Gutiérrez" Feminist League)*. Elvia Carrillo served as the magazine's director. *Feminismo* had a strong feminist-Socialist tone, featured a variety of poetry, contained notices of future women's meetings, and printed articles written by both Mexican and foreign women. Photographs of some of the Liga's most prominent women, including Elvia Carrillo and Rosa Torres, and of such notables as Alma Reed, also appeared in *Feminismo*.[84]

Regarding the Ligas Feministas and suffrage, the governor, reflecting the revolutionaries' traditional distrust of women's loyalties, declared: "I shall foment all Feminist Leagues with the object . . . of granting identically the same rights to women as to men, *but only to organized women with ideals parallel to those of the South East Socialist Party.*"[85] Nevertheless, under Governor Carrillo Puerto, all women were granted suffrage and all were permitted to run for both municipal and state offices.

The first woman in Mexican history to occupy a position by popular election was Socialist Rosa Torres, who was elected president of the Mérida City Council in 1922. In the 1923 election, in which only PSS members ran, Elvia Carrillo, Raquel Dzib (a local schoolteacher), and Beatrice Peniche de Ponce (a teacher and librarian) won seats in the State Assembly, becoming the state's first female legislators.[86]

The Divorce Law

The Yucatán Divorce Law of 1923, making divorce not only permissible by mutual consent but also quick and inexpensive, was part of the restructuring of women's societal roles that the Socialist government hoped to make acceptable to Yucatecos. The law was based on Carrillo's belief that "marriage is a voluntary union based on love entered into for the purpose of founding a home" and is therefore to be dissolved "when either contracting party desires it." Carrillo believed that marriage, instead of enslaving women, should be "a union of equals based on mutual love and respect, not on possession."[87]

Whatever Carrillo's stated reasons for instituting the Divorce Law, he was accused of promoting divorce to free himself to marry his fiancée, North American writer Alma Reed. These accusations seem to be unfounded because the blueprints for the Divorce Law were drawn before Carrillo made plans to remarry.[88] His first marriage, in February 1898, was to María Isabel Palma Puerto of Motul. (It is interesting to note that this was the second marriage between the Palma Puerto and the Carrillo Puerto families. Enriqueta, the eldest Carrillo child, had married Pedro Palma, Isabel's brother.)[89] While the marriage between Felipe and Isabel was hardly ideal, it was satisfactory and the couple had four children. Because of the different interests that each developed through the years, Carrillo and his wife grew apart.[90] As was common in Yucatán at the time, Carrillo acquired a mistress.[91] Then, in February 1923, while separated from his wife, who had been living in Cuba for three years, Carrillo met Alma Reed. Reed was a twenty-seven-year-old *New York Times* reporter from San Francisco who was traveling with a group of American archeologists and writing about Mayan ruins. Carrillo did not divorce his wife until November, and the plans for Yucatán's Divorce Law were made prior to this. Thus, while Alma Reed may have approved of the law, she was not responsible for its inception.[92]

The new Divorce Law was used infrequently by Yucatecan couples. But Americans, who were permitted to obtain a divorce after thirty days' residence, quickly took advantage of it.[93] North American Counsul O. Gaylord Marsh considered the law immoral and recommended that the United States denounce it. Marsh believed that the Divorce Law was an effort by Mexican Socialists, with connections in Russia, to demoralize American civilization. Yucatán, in his opinion, was merely serving as a base for Bolshevik operations in the Western Hemisphere.[94] As late as December 1924, there were complaints about the number of United States citizens obtaining divorces under the law; subsequently, the law was amended so that foreigners were required to reside at least six months within the state before they could be granted a divorce.[95]

The Birth Control Program

Yucatán's state-supported birth control program was unique for its time. While women in the United States and other industrialized countries were being jailed for discussing the subject publicly, women in Yucatán were encouraged to participate in the state-supported birth control program.[96] Governor Carrillo explained his reasons for supporting the birth control program: "Parents are the ones to determine when and how many children they shall have, not ignorant blind chance."[97]

As with many other social reform efforts, Yucatán's birth control program was organized under the jurisdiction of the Liga Central, with local support provided by the Ligas Feministas. The Yucatán program received assistance from the American Birth Control League. In August 1923, Mrs. Anne Kennedy and Mrs. George H. Rublee visited Yucatán to help establish the first government-supported birth control clinics in the Western Hemisphere.[98]

An important phase of the government's birth control project was the distribution of birth control pamphlets to those about to be married. The pamphlet most commonly distributed was a short translation of *Family Planning*, by North American birth control advocate Margaret Sanger. Its Spanish title was *La regulación de la natalidad, o la brújula del hogar* (*Family Planning: Birth Control Issues*). The pamphlet's introduction cited Margaret Sanger as "one of the most important women of the epoch." The text provided the reader with a detailed and specific account of how to prevent conception, and the final section included a statement supporting the birth control program, signed by more than one hundred prominent Yucatecos. The pamphlet confronted such stereotypic notions as "large families are happy" by countering that large families were sometimes forced financially to place their children into domestic service.[99] Basically, the point of the state leaflet was that women should have control over their bodies.

Another widely disseminated birth control pamphlet was written by Esperanza Velázquez Bringas in 1922. In it, Velázquez defended Margaret Sanger's work and discussed birth control clinics in Holland and New Zealand. Supporting the concept of limited family size, Velázquez stated that birth control would "liberate women and benefit all humanity."[100] In an article in El Popular, Velázquez asked her readers if it were not "more immoral to allow children in a working family to grow up with inadequate nourishment, sick, and [as] poor citizens" than to limit family size.[101]

The birth control program caused an even greater reaction than did the Divorce Law. Yucatecos were horrified by Sanger's graphic descriptions and worried that children might be exposed to ideas expressed in her pamphlet. The controversy received daily coverage in local newspapers. For example, in March 1922, the staff of the Socialist newspaper El Popular launched a counterattack on critics of the birth control program, and later that month the signatures of more than two hundred teachers appeared in support of the birth control program.[102]

The controversy over the distribution of birth control information reached its peak when members of the Catholic Knights of Columbus and their wives demonstrated against the dissemination of the pamphlets. The demonstration ended in a scuffle between Catholics and Socialists. Nevertheless, with the governor's support, the Ligas Feministas continued to distribute birth control information. The controversy flared again in late 1923 when Rosa Torres distributed pamphlets to representatives of the press during the Mexican Press Association's convention in Mérida.[103]

The governor's ambitious birth control program was not particularly successful, not only because of strong political and religious opposition but because it was impractical to try to reach illiterate women with pamphlets and the targeted women had little knowledge of basic hygiene practices. As a case in point, where would Yucatecas who could afford it purchase syringes, douche bags, and suppositories when most of them did not even have access to purified water?

The Leadership of Elvia Carrillo Puerto

Elvia Carrillo Puerto explained her basic feminist objectives in an interview printed in El Popular in the summer of 1922: "I want all my sisters to enjoy the same freedoms as men but in a dignified and honorable way." Calling her the "soul and life" of the feminist movement, the article praised Elvia Carrillo's success in allying the Yucatán feminist movement with that in the nation's capital. Carrillo made frequent trips to Mexico City to strengthen these contacts and, to this same end, brought several feminists to Yucatán.[104]

Elvia Carrillo's closest political contacts in Mexico City were with Socialists Esperanza Velázquez Bringas and Elena Torres. Velázquez, a linguist, lawyer, and writer for the newspaper *El Heraldo de México* and for the magazine *Zig Zag*, was born in Veracruz and educated at the University of the Southeast in Yucatán. Torres, who had moved from Yucatán to Mexico City, was a professor, a writer, and an authority on rural education. Both women visited Yucatán in 1922. Velázquez arrived in late January for a three-month stay and worked with Elvia Carrillo, with the Ligas, and with local educators. During her stay in Yucatán, Velázquez also contributed to *Tierra* and *El Popular*. After participating in the League of Rationalist Teachers Conference in Campeche, Velázquez returned to Mexico City in April. Later, Velázquez became the first woman to head the Department of Libraries in Mexico City.[105] Elena Torres visited Yucatán in early July and, with Elvia, observed state projects and attended numerous Liga functions. In an interview with *El Popular*, Torres noted that of all the states in Mexico, Yucatán was the most advanced. "The women," Torres affirmed, "are not only better prepared to interpret the idea of suffrage in its true sense, but they are already organized into leagues and parties."[106]

Despite their many successes, Elvia Carrillo Puerto and her collaborators did not have the support of all women in Yucatán. *La Lucha*, an anti-Socialist newspaper, maintained a constant barrage of criticism. At one point, *La Lucha* called Elvia Carrillo's efforts on behalf of women "ridiculous." To disassociate themselves from the work and ideology of the Ligas Feministas, Catholic women formed the Asociación Yucateca Protectora de la Mujer (Yucatán Women's Protective Association). Imitating the Liga in its efforts to appeal to women, Asociación members established an orphanage and planned a women's school that stressed domestic arts.[107]

The Asociación Yucateca Protectora de la Mujer used *La Lucha* as a vehicle to express its viewpoint. In an argument voiced frequently, members of the Asociación called feminism "the hysterical product of spinsters" who have not succeeded "in captivating some man's heart." They denounced feminism and socialism as a "disgrace"; free love and birth control were condemned outright. Conservative author Pilar de Fontanar articulated the Asociación's views in a column in *La Lucha* called "The Lies of Feminism," in which she called feminism and its supporters "crude" and anti-male.[108]

However, criticism did not deter Elvia Carrillo Puerto. Even after her brother's assassination in January 1924, Elvia Carrillo continued to expand her field of feminist activity. In 1925, she established residence in the state of San Luis Potosí in order to be eligible to run for the office of deputy. This would be the first time since Hermila Galindo's 1917 campaign for deputy in Mexico City that a woman had run for a state office. Carrillo

Puerto's candidacy was possible in San Luis Potosí because literate women had been allowed to vote in municipal elections since 1924 and in state elections since 1925.[109]

In his reports from San Luis Potosí, the United States consul compared the status of feminism in San Luis Potosí in 1925 to the status of women in the United States immediately after the Civil War. The consul described San Luis Potosí as having only a weak feminist movement because of the dominating influence of the church. However, the consul did note that the role of women was in transition: more women were working, and the Instituto Científico y Literario (Scientific and Literary Institute) of the University of San Luis Potosí had begun to admit women, although they comprised less than 5 percent of the student population.[110]

In her bid for election, Elvia Carrillo sought support at both the state and the national level. From the state Minister of the Interior, Adalberto Tejeda, she received assurances that because the Constitution of 1917 did not specifically bar women from voting or running for office, her candidacy was legal. Carrillo also received support from the governor of San Luis Potosí, Aurelio Manrique, and from his chief of operations, General Saturnino Cedillo.[111]

Carrillo felt it essential to have a woman as her *suplente* (substitute), even though local politicians urged her to select a male *suplente* because they thought it would be impossible to find another woman who was not "reactionary and Catholic." Carrillo reminded them, "What about your mothers, your wives, your sisters, and your daughters? Fine liberals you must be, if not a single one of . . . you have been able to convert your women folk to your point of view."[112] Finally, after a desperate house-to-house search for a woman willing to run with her for public office, Carrillo chose Hermila Zamarrón, a stenographer employed in a local internal revenue office.

Her ticket established, Carrillo faced yet another challenge. Up to that point, her candidacy had been unopposed. After July 1925, however, the governorship of the state changed hands and Governor Abel Cano assumed power. Unlike his predecessor, Cano did not support women's rights. In the last days of Carrillo's campaign, Cano endorsed an opposition candidate, Florencio Galván. Attempting to put an end to his opponent, Cesareo Vásquez, Galván's *suplente*, fired eight shots at Elvia Carrillo, all of which missed their intended target.[113]

Despite the efforts of the opposition, Carrillo won handily in San Luis Potosí. Then, after having her credentials approved by local authorities, Carrillo traveled to Mexico City for her election certification by the Preparatory Junta of the Chamber of Deputies. In accordance with Article 60 of the 1917 Constitution, the Preparatory Junta, selected by a permanent committee of each chamber, met in August to verify election returns from the previous month. Deputies whose credentials were in order were then recommended for seating when the regular session began in September. Despite her overwhelming victory at the polls and the approval of her election by state authorities in San Luis Potosí, Carrillo was unable to secure verification of her credentials by the Preparatory Junta; consequently, she was denied her seat for the 1925 session.[114] Without legal recourse, Carrillo had to drop the matter temporarily. The following year she sent a long letter to the Chamber of Deputies, with thousands of women's signatures, demanding that the constitution be altered to include women's suffrage.[115]

Following her election reversal, Elvia Carrillo continued her feminist activities in Mexico City. In 1927, she founded the Liga Orientadora Socialista Femenina (Feminine Socialist Guiding League), composed of employees from the Department of Agriculture. In 1932, Carrillo helped organize the Liga Orientadora de Acción Femenina (Feminine Action Guiding League), and she traveled to Europe on government business at the request of President Abelardo Rodríguez. One of her last public posts was the presidency of the Liga Orientada de Mujer (Women's Guiding League). In 1938, Carrillo retired from public life.[116]

During her last years, Elvia Carrillo suffered poor health and lived in poverty. Consequently, she granted few interviews.[117] However, in December 1952, as members of the Congress discussed and prepared to vote on women's suffrage, Carrillo agreed to a rare interview with the chief of information of the magazine *Atisbos*. After briefly outlining her lifework, Carrillo commented, "My life is wrapped in mist and adorned with ironies." She proudly acknowledged that she had been recognized by the Mexican government on two occasions: when she received an award presented by President Cárdenas in 1939 and when she was a recipient of the prestigious Legion of Honor presented by President Ruiz Cortines in 1952.[118] However, these were the only acknowledgments given Carrillo by the Mexican government.

The Collaborators of Elvia Carrillo Puerto

In Yucatán, Elvia Carrillo Puerto organized the Ligas Feministas to coordinate women's activities and to support the PSS and her brother's administration. Carrillo's key Yucatán collaborators were Eusabia Pérez Vda. de MacKiney, Aurora Abán Puga, Nelly Aznar Gutiérrez, Susana Betancourt, Raquel Dzib Cicero, Rosa Torres, and Beatrice Peniche. Besides accompanying Carrillo on field trips and speaking engagements, each held posts in feminist organizations. Eusabia Pérez served as chairperson pro tempore for the Liga Feminista "Rita Cetina Gutiérrez" in Elvia Carrillo's absence and was one of three representatives to the powerful Liga Central; Aurora

Abán held the important post of president of the Liga Feminista; Nelly Aznar directed the magazine *Rebeldía*, which defended the rights of women; and Susana Betancourt, a vital participant in the 1916 feminist congresses, served as treasurer for the Liga "Rita Cetina Gutiérrez."[119]

Elvia Carrillo's closest collaborators were Raquel Dzib Cicero, Rosa Torres, and Beatrice Peniche. Dzib, a schoolteacher, served with Carrillo and with Peniche in the twenty-eighth legislature, where she staunchly supported the rights of women and the rights of the poor. Born in 1882 into a working-class family, Dzib had been a student of Rita Cetina Gutiérrez at the Instituto Literario de Niñas. She later taught at the Instituto and at other schools in Mérida. During the administration of Governor Alvarado, Dzib participated in both the pedagogical and feminist congresses. She died in March 1949 after fifty years of championing popular education.[120]

The relationship between Elvia and Rosa Torres was especially close. Constant companions, they participated together in worker and feminist congresses. Torres, a graduate of the Escuela Normal de Mérida, a schoolteacher, and an outspoken Socialist, related some of her revolutionary experiences in her short autobiography, *Mi actuación en el h. ayuntamiento de Mérida, Yucatán, México en el año de 1923* (*My Position and Record on the City Council of Mérida, Yucatán, México, in 1923*). In a 1954 interview published in *Excelsior*, when asked why she participated in the Revolution, Torres replied that "the campesino's slavery in Yucatán always made an impression upon me." After President Madero's assassination, Torres joined the Constitutionalists. She summarized her life's basic tenet very simply: "My object has been to always be useful." Torres was the first woman elected to the Mérida City Council, where she served as president and on many Socialist and feminist committees.[121]

In 1976, Beatrice Peniche was the only woman of the Elvia Carrillo Puerto collaborators still living. In an interview in her home in Mérida, Peniche reaffirmed her commitment to socialism and to feminism. Peniche's participation in feminism began early in her youth, when Raquel Dzib Cicero was her teacher. Peniche served as a schoolteacher, a librarian, a poet, and an active participant in both the Pedagogical Congress and the feminist congresses. She continued her activities under Governor Carrillo as a state representative and as a member of many feminist committees.[122]

The End of Reforms

Politics and armed rebellion shifted Yucatán's destiny to shoulders other than those of Felipe Carrillo Puerto. On December 3, 1923, after General Guadalupe Sánchez of Veracruz allied with Adolfo de la Huerta against President Obregón's "appointment" of Plutarco Calles as his presidential successor, Governor Carrillo pledged to support President Obregón and to fight the rebels. Governor Carrillo's Ligas were armed, but federal troops in Mérida revolted and tipped the balance of military power against Carrillo, who was then forced to flee. His path led from his home town of Motul to the east coast, where he and twelve supporters boarded a small escape vessel, but the vessel was forced back to shore by a storm known locally as a "norther." On December 23, 1923, while attempting to locate another boat, Carrillo was captured by the rebels and jailed in Mérida. On January 2, 1924, tried for thirty-six continuous hours for crimes allegedly committed by his PSS supporters, Governor Felipe Carrillo Puerto, his three brothers, and nine companions were found guilty and condemned to death. In the early morning hours of January 3, 1924, the thirteen men were driven to a Mérida cemetery and executed by a firing squad.[123]

Governor Felipe Carrillo's death marked an end to Yucatán's leadership in the women's rights movement in Mexico. Writer Ernest Gruening lamented, "Thus perished the most enlightened, the most courageous, the most lovable man in Mexico. Her [Mexico's] tragic history of blood and tears has offered no nobler, no sweeter figure as a sacrifice to human freedom."[124]

The next period in Yucatán's history was one of turmoil. The rebellious de la Huerta forces attempted to destroy former Governor Carrillo's government, the PSS, and the Ligas, which were declared illegal. Finally, President Obregón's supporters toppled de la Huerta's supporters and regained control of the government. The Socialists then tried to reinstate themselves. But confusion reigned because President Obregón sent his own representatives to Yucatán, where the local legislators had already selected Miguel Cantón as governor. The new Obregón-appointed legislators then selected a replacement for Governor Cantón. Ironically, in a move to maintain his power, Cantón, who had been a supporter of feminist programs, declared that the actions of the Obregón-appointed legislators were illegal because the Obregón legislature contained women, who were denied the right to vote and to hold office by the national constitution.[125] Ultimately, the Obregón faction gained control.

President Obregón immediately took steps to reduce the power of the Ligas Feministas. Members of Ligas were dismissed from public posts, and Elvia Carrillo, now with a price of 10,000 pesos on her head, complained that all that remained of the Liga Central was its name. In a letter to President Obregón, Elvia Carrillo reported that women in municipal and state government had been forced out of their positions and that members of the Carrillo family had been hounded out of their government posts. Elvia Carrillo later maintained that socialism in Yucatán was buried with her brothers, and that socialism today "is little more than a deceitful and coarse farce."[126]

Assessing the magnitude of Governor Felipe Carrillo Puerto's lasting influence on the Mexican women's movement is difficult because his Yucatán projects were halted abruptly by his execution and the subsequent transfer of power to conservatives. Further, the depth of his influence is difficult to measure because most of Felipe Carrillo's social programs were instituted from the administrative level rather than the grass-roots level. Carrillo's birth control program, divorce law, and rationalist system of education often met uncompromising resistance from members of the Catholic Church, the *hacendados*, and, ironically, the very people Carrillo strove to convert to socialism.

However, in post-Carrillo Yucatán, there remained considerable residual influence from the Yucatán feminist programs. The Ligas Feministas continued to function long after Governor Carrillo's execution in 1924, but in a politically hostile atmosphere. For example, even as late as 1930, the Liga Revolutionaria Feminista "Aurora Abán" (named after a prominent Yucatán feminist) published a pamphlet affirming its complete accord with the ideas of Felipe Carrillo Puerto.[127] Further, many of the feminists active in the era of strong support from governors Salvador Alvarado and Felipe Carrillo continued their efforts without government support.

Ultimately, the antifeminist successor administrations in Yucatán, coupled with the cancellation of such reform laws as state suffrage, served to diffuse the momentum of the Yucatán feminist movement. Although Elvia Carrillo Puerto never lost her enthusiasm for improving women's conditions, she was forced to leave Yucatán. After running for political office in San Luis Potosí, Carrillo moved to Mexico City, where feminists in the 1920s and 1930s were organizing on a massive scale. It was at this time that the center of the Mexican feminist movement shifted from Yucatán to Mexico City, and Yucatán was never again the lodestar of the women's movement in Mexico.

Porfirio Díaz, president of Mexico for three decades preceding the revolution. Photograph by Brown Brothers.

Ricardo Flores Magón, "Fugitive Wanted" photograph, 1906. Reprinted by permission of the Bancroft Library, University of California, Berkeley.

Margarita Magón de Flores, mother of the Flores Magón brothers. Reprinted from *Revista de la Universidad de Mexico*, XXVIII, no. 3 (November 1973), p. 17.

Teresa Urrea, La Santa de Cabora. Reprinted by permission of the Arizona Historical Society/Tucson.

Lifestyle of the wealthy during
the Porfiriato (note the
European influence on attire).
Reprinted from John Kenneth
Turner, *Barbarous Mexico*.

Lifestyle of the poor during the Porfiriato. Reprinted from John Kenneth Turner, *Barbarous Mexico*.

Illiteracy was widespread, and the poor hired scribes to transact business and to write letters. Reprinted by permission of the Huntington Library, San Marino, California.

Yaqui Indian women and children being shipped to Yucatán to serve as slaves. Reprinted by permission of the Huntington Library, San Marino, California.

Juana B. Gutiérrez de Mendoza, revolutionary leader, activist, writer, and teacher, shown with two Indian boys she adopted. Reprinted from Juana B. Gutiérrez de Mendoza, ¡Por la Tierra y por la raza!

Dolores Jiménez y Muro, revolutionary leader, activist, poet, and teacher. Reprinted from Gustavo Casasola, *Historia gráfica de la revolución mexicana, 1900-1960*, vol. II, p. 837.

Women demonstrate in support of striking miners at Cananea, 1906. Reprinted by permission of the Bancroft Library, University of California, Berkeley.

Francisco I. Madero,
president of Mexico,
1911-1913, and wife
Sara (on step behind
Madero) in Ciudad
Juárez, 1911. Reprinted
by permission of the
Library of Congress.

Madero (center) with
members of the Hijas
de Cuauhtémoc.
Reprinted from
Casasola, vol. I,
p. 405.

Carmen Serdán, revolutionary
leader in Puebla. Reprinted from
*Revista de la Universidad de
Mexico*, XXVIII, no. 3 (November
1973), p. 16.

Serdán home in Puebla,
today a regional museum.
Balcony to the left of
doorway (surrounded by
bullet holes) is where
Carmen Serdán urged
townspeople to join the
revolution. Photograph by
the author.

María Arias Bernal (at right) with General Obregón at Madero's gravesite. Reprinted from Casasola, vol. II, p. 837.

Women revolutionaries, 1911. Reprinted by permission of the Library of Congress.

Soldadera (possibly
Valentina Ramírez).
Reprinted from Casasola,
vol. I, p. 263.

Soldadera on train with the
federal troops, ca. 1911.
Reprinted from Casasola,
vol. I, p. 720.

Soldadera in action.
Reprinted from Casasola,
vol. III, p. 1788.

Soldadera and
compañeros. Reprinted
by permission of the
El Paso Public Library.

Soldaderas and
compañeros. Reprinted
by permission of the
El Paso Public Library.

Soldadera
saying
good-bye
to her
"Juan."
Source
unknown.

Zapatistas (note women marching in foreground). Photograph by International Vargas.

Madre Conchita (front center, dressed in black), José de León Toral (bottom left), and others implicated in the assassination of Obregón. Reprinted from Casasola, vol. III, p. 1874.

Felipe Carrillo Puerto,
governor of Yucatán,
1922-1924. Photograph
by Ernest Gruening.

Elvia Carrillo Puerto,
sister of Governor
Carrillo Puerto, organizer
of Ligas Feministas,
Socialist, and feminist
leader. Personal photo.

Lázaro Cárdenas, president of Mexico, 1934-1940 (at right in dark suit). Photograph by Steinheimer.

Women in Alameda Park in Mexico City demonstrating against sex education in 1930s. Reprinted from Casasola, vol. III, p. 2138.

Amalia Caballero de Castillo
Ledón, feminist and diplomat.
Source unknown.

Margarita Robles de Mendoza
picketing in front of Congress
for women's suffrage.
Reprinted from Casasola, vol.
III, p. 2195.

Mexican women standing in line to vote in their first presidential election, 1958. Source unknown.

Cover photo:

Soldadera. Reprinted from
Gustavo Casasola, *Historia
gráfica de la revolución
mexicana, 1900-1960*, vol. I,
p. 263.

▪ 4 ▪

Implementing the
Goals of the Revolution:
The Second Phase, 1920-1934

The period from 1920 to 1934 brought significant changes to every facet of Mexican society, and to Mexico's political leadership in particular. Although the widespread violence of the preceding ten years decreased dramatically, revolts and political assassinations continued on a lesser scale. Emiliano Zapata's movement was all but destroyed by his assassination in April 1919. Pancho Villa was assassinated in July 1923, after having retired to private life in 1920.

Mexican politics of the 1920s was dominated by a trio from Sonora known as the "Sonoran Triangle"; these leaders were Adolfo de la Huerta, Alvaro Obregón, and Plutarco Calles. De la Huerta served as interim president of Mexico for six months in 1920 and led the 1923 revolt against President Obregón's imposition of Calles as his presidential successor; Alvaro Obregón, a farmer who rose quickly to political prominence during the Revolution, was elected president of Mexico in 1920; Calles, a former schoolteacher, served as president of Mexico during the stormy 1924-1928 period, years characterized by intense church-state conflict. After president-elect Obregón's assassination in 1928, three succeeding presidents completed his six-year term (1928-1934)—Emilio Portes Gil, Pascual Ortiz Rubio, and Abelardo Rodríguez.

The 1920s were not a propitious time for women's rights. Despite women's widespread participation in the Revolution, the federal government demonstrated a marked indifference to their plight. A principal reason for this indifference was that Mexican presidents during this tumultuous political period considered women to be too much under the influence and

control of the church. Consequently, the succession of presidents, preoccupied with both national and international crises, chose neither to give
women's issues a high priority nor to include women's needs in their programs for meeting the goals of the Revolution. President de la Huerta was
absorbed in a maelstrom of political controversy, and his six-month administration was too short to address adequately any of Mexico's pressing problems. President Obregón held an old-fashioned gentleman's view of women
that did not include them as political equals, so women's issues did not
receive a high priority. President Calles, arrogant and aggressive, was a
successful politician from a male-dominated world, where women's opinions counted for little. Unfortunately for the women's movement, the three
successors to Calles's presidency devoted no more attention to women's
issues than did their predecessors. Of the three, Portes Gil was probably
most aware of women's needs, but he was unwilling to work politically to
improve the status of women.

The lack of presidential support during the 1920s resulted in a major
political setback for women in general and for women within the labor
movement in particular. Without high-level government support for
women's issues, male union officers, believing that women were too reluctant to risk antagonizing management and too indifferent to general union
goals, began to recruit more and more men to fill factory positions. Accordingly, access to skilled factory jobs through apprenticeship and technical
education (both controlled largely by male union officials) was rarely made
available to women. Thus, the unions, in collusion with high officials in
the federal government, limited the number of opportunities for women in
the work force.[1]

In addition to the setbacks in the labor movement, Mexican women fared
poorly in the political arena of the 1920s. Because so many women had
sympathized with the conservative de la Huerta Rebellion, openly supported
the Catholic Church in the Cristero Rebellion (an open rebellion by the
church against the state during the years 1926-1929), been implicated in the
assassination of President-elect Obregón, and refused to support the government's Socialist education program, male revolutionary leaders were generally suspicious of women's political allegiance. An additional political
liability for women was the extreme ideological differences exhibited at
women's conferences, such as the 1925 Congress of "Mujeres de la Raza"
described on pages 107-108. The few women who assumed important government and university positions during the 1920s were indeed exceptions
to the rule.

Principal legal changes affecting women during the period 1920 to 1934
resulted from the following legislation: passage of the 1923 Homestead
Decree, passage of women's suffrage legislation in four Mexican states,
revision of the Mexican Civil Code of 1928, and passage of the federal

Labor Law of 1931. The 1923 Homestead Decree granted widows who were Mexican citizens and heads of families the same rights as men in holding ownership of those portions of national or uncultivated land not reserved by the government. (Title to such unclaimed land was to be granted to the claimant after two years of cultivation or stock-raising.)[2] Of the four states that granted women suffrage (Yucatán, San Luis Potosí, Chiapas, and Tabasco), three had Socialist governors and one had a progressive governor (San Luis Potosí). The Civil Code of 1928 addressed concubinage and legal recognition of children of such unions. President Calles recommended the measure, explaining that concubinage was so common that it was necessary to recognize its existence legally for the sake of the children.[3] Adoption of the federal Labor Law in 1931 did result partly from demands by women's organizations. The law prohibited women and minors from overtime work, night work, and work in unhealthy and dangerous environments. Under this law, pregnant women could be required to work a maximum of only eight hours, and were to have one day off per week, rest periods at work, and time off before and after childbirth. Further, because the labor sections of the Constitution had not been enforced, the 1931 law provided again for a minimum wage and for equal wages for men and women.[4]

By the end of the 1920s, members of the newly formed Partido Nacional Revolucionario (National Revolutionary Party [PNR]), Mexico's official political party, began to recognize the potential in women's political participation and attempted to incorporate women into the party. The 1929 PNR platform included two planks in support of women: the full right of women's participation in political life and the full incorporation of the *campesina* into the economic life of the country, thereby "liberating her from hard labor." To these ends, the PNR sought to produce publicity "to influence public opinion so that woman will begin to be a partner and cease to be a slave."[5]

EDUCATION AND HEALTH PROGRAMS

During the 1920s, leaders of the "Sonoran Triangle" sought to overcome a series of obstacles to implement the goals of the Revolution. The major obstacles were foreign commercial domination, influence of the Catholic Church, and inadequate education and health services for the masses. To these ends, "Sonoran Triangle" leaders negotiated more favorable agreements with foreign governments having major holdings in Mexico; invoked federal enforcement of the anti-clerical provisions of Mexico's Constitution (thereby triggering the Cristero Rebellion, the assassination of President-elect Obregón, and the controversy over church-state jurisdiction in education);

and initiated bold new programs for mass education and health care. Education and health care programs of the 1920s impacted particularly the status of Mexican women because implementation of the programs was dependent upon teachers and nurses, nearly all of whom were women.

Major growth in public education resulted in the creation of the Ministry of Education in 1921, during the presidency of Alvaro Obregón. This ministry was directed by dynamic José Vasconcelos, former rector of the National University, who aspired to use education as an instrument of social reform and thus to elevate the general welfare of the Mexican people. Introducing education into rural areas was a prime goal of this reform, and because women constituted over half of all rural teachers, they were key participants in the rural education program.[6]

Vasconcelos utilized innovative methods to bring education to the countryside, including the establishment of educational "missions." A Congress of Missioners met in Mexico City in September 1922 to discuss implementing educational "missions" as a means of bringing education to remote rural areas, where education was virtually non-existent. "Missionary" teachers studied specific educational needs of remote areas, developed educational programs tailored to meet those needs, and then recruited local teachers to implement the programs. These local rural teachers, who constituted the vanguard of the administration's rural education program, received their training at mobile "Cultural Missions" operated by the federal government. Professor Elena Torres, who had organized the rationalist educational program in Yucatán, and who had directed a free breakfast program for 12,000 children in the capital, became chief of the Bureau of Cultural Missions. The first educational missionary personnel left Mexico City in 1923 to begin work in the state of Hidalgo. The mission's main purpose was to provide Socialist-oriented cultural and professional training for primary-school teachers. In 1926, under Torres's direction, six missions served more than 2,000 rural teachers. In the next decade, the number of missions grew to eighteen, serving more than 4,000 teachers.[7]

Special classes for women, new kindergartens, rural schools in remote areas, and education centers for teachers were introduced rapidly by the Obregón administration. New schools offered women training in clerical skills, home economics, and domestic-related industries. By 1924, Mexico City had five trade schools for young women (but only three for young men, as men were more likely to learn trades outside of school). One of the four schools of commerce in Mexico City was exclusively for women, and held both day and night classes. By 1925, more women than ever were enrolled in university courses in preparation for professional careers.[8]

Development of a preschool program in the Department of Education was directed by Rosaura Zapata (1876-1963) from La Paz. After obtaining a degree in primary education in Mexico and then studying extensively abroad, Zapata returned to Mexico to establish the first kindergartens and a private child welfare organization called the Pestalozzi-Froebel Society. The society's goals were to establish a kindergarten and a parent-teacher association, to provide legal protection for women, and to provide for the scientific study of children.[9]

Rosaura Zapata's work was so highly regarded that she was awarded many honors. In 1954 she became the first recipient of the prestigious Medalla Altamirano, awarded by the Mexican Senate. The aims of the Pestalozzi-Froebel Society coincided with many of those of the Children's Aid Society. Headed by Mexico's First Lady, María Tapia de Obregón, the Children's Aid Society was founded to help needy children by providing a variety of services ranging from housing assistance to classroom instruction.

The federal campaign against illiteracy was directed by Eulalia Guzmán. Guzmán, a former student of feminist Dolores Correa Zapata, was an educator whose extensive field experience ranged from educating Yaquis in Sonora to the founding of schools for poor children in Mexico City. In 1930, after studying three years in Berlin, Guzmán returned to Mexico to become inspector of primary schools. For the national government's literacy drive, Guzmán recruited six thousand men and women and two thousand student volunteers, all to teach reading.[10]

A determined effort was made by the Obregón administration to institute mass health care programs because this area had been neglected badly during the first phase of the Revolution (1910-1920). In 1920, Francisco Bulnes, historian and former advisor to Porfirio Díaz, commented grimly upon health conditions in the capital:

> According to the civil register of Mexico City, 70 percent of the births were of natural (illegitimate) children. Violation of the women of the humble classes was an established and respectable custom . . . ; sixty percent of the population suffered with chronic alcoholism. In 1919 the medical service of the Department of Education declared that the majority of the children attending school were afflicted with hereditary syphilis.[11]

Health programs begun under Obregón were expanded under President Calles. Included in Calles's massive effort were a vaccination program; increased health inspections; passage of stricter sanitary and housing codes; opening of additional prenatal and children's clinics; increased research in tropical diseases; and dissemination of information on health care delivered via public lectures, radio messages, films, and pamphlets. Mobile health brigades were formed to travel to remote parts of the republic to promote sound health practices. There were even limited efforts to distribute birth control information. One of the earliest birth control efforts occurred in 1925, when a clinic was opened in the capital, where thousands of copies of Margaret Sanger's pamphlet on family planning were distributed. In 1926, Dr. Bernardo J. Gastélum, director of the Department of Health during the Calles administration, addressed the widespread problem of prostitution and social diseases at the first Pan American Conference of Public Health Officers:

> In Mexico . . . 60 per cent of the inhabitants suffer from syphilis; in the capital more than 50 per cent. Of the prostitutes, who number around twenty thousand, eighteen thousand have it; in the population between fifteen and twenty-five years of age, 35 per cent are afflicted with it.[12]

Because prostitution was so widespread, the Department of Health abandoned the practice of licensing prostitutes. Instead, efforts were concentrated on providing them with health care. Clinics were established in various parts of Mexico City, where prostitutes reported every six days for examination and for free treatment. Medical staffs were instructed to treat these women with the same respect accorded any other patient. When ill, prostitutes were sent to a hospital. During convalescence, literate prostitutes were taught a trade; if illiterate, they were taught to read and to write.[13] Particular concern over prostitution continued throughout the period, and in June 1934, a Congress on Prostitution was held in the capital. Delegates to the congress, representing the views of both Communists and political moderates, agreed that the government should end its policy of merely regulating brothels and close them instead. However, there was strong disagreement over the cause of prostitution and how to curtail it. Communists believed that poverty and ignorance were the causes and that funds for social and educational reforms should be augmented; moderates believed that the causes were alcoholism and vice and that the focus should be upon censorship and moderation of behavior.[14]

Alcohol abuse was a topic on which women of all political persuasions agreed, and they campaigned vigorously for its prohibition. Because prohibition was supported by both the federal and state governments, especially those under Socialist administrations, prohibition laws were passed in several Mexican states.[15]

In the early 1920s, women focused particular attention on women's and children's issues. In 1922, the Sociedad Protectora de la Niñez Escolar (School Children's Protective Society) expanded its membership further under the leadership of feminist María Gómez Vda. de Bacmaister. In 1923, the Asociación de Mujeres Cristianas (Young Women's Christian Association [YWCA]) was founded by María Elena Ramírez. Operating under the auspices of its international division, the YWCA concentrated on women's issues. In 1924, in Mexico City, the YWCA opened a baby clinic and a center to help lower-class women.

In 1928, medical students organized the Rosalia Slaughter Medical Society, which was affiliated with the Pan American Round Table. The Medical

Society's purpose was to improve the education of women medical students.[16] In 1929, interest in women's health was stimulated further by the founding of the Association of Mexican Women Doctors, which encouraged women to attend medical school, and by the founding of the National Association of Children's Welfare, which was organized by Carmen García de Portes Gil, wife of President Portes Gil.[17]

Several prominent professional women provided leadership in children's welfare and health care. Amalia Caballero de Castillo Ledón, born in northeastern Mexico in 1902, was a feminist, writer, professor, and well-known playwright. She served as a member of the board of directors of the National Association of Children's Welfare and as a leader in the Pan American Women's League. Women's and children's health care received special attention from three top women physicians: Matilde Rodríguez Cabo, Esther Chapa, and Antonia Ursúa. Dr. Rodríguez Cabo and Dr. Esther Chapa began their friendship and collaborative reform efforts while medical students in Mexico City. They focused their efforts on such topics as prison reform, prostitution, and welfare for women and children. Dr. Ursúa devoted her attention mostly to improving health conditions for women, especially poor women.

WOMEN'S ORGANIZATIONS AND THE INTERNATIONAL WOMEN'S NETWORK

The number of women's organizations increased dramatically between 1920 and 1934. Masses of Mexican women, convinced of the value of national and international unity, organized for political and economic purposes. Mexican women of this period founded three important organizations: 1) the Consejo Feminista Mexicana (Mexican Feminist Council); 2) the Liga Feminista Mexicana (Mexican Feminist League); and 3) the Unión de Mujeres Americanas (Union of American Women [UMA]).

In 1920, the Consejo Feminista Mexicana was begun by women activists, including Elena Torres and María del Refugio García. The organization's ambitious goal, the economic, social, and political emancipation of women, was discussed at length in the journal *La Mujer*, edited by Julia Nava de Ruisánchez. The Consejo was particularly successful in attracting large numbers of working women.

The Liga Feminista Mexicana, a women's suffrage organization, was organized in 1923. Liga officers included a distinguished group of educators and feminists, including Eulalia Guzmán, Julia Nava de Ruisánchez (charter member of the Hijas de Cuauhtémoc and Regeneración y Concordia), and Luz Vera Córdova (educator, writer, and organizer).

The UMA, begun in 1934 by Margarita Robles de Mendoza, was oriented toward improving relations between women in the Americas. Suffrage for women of the Americas was its main goal.[18]

In April 1922, a delegation of Mexican women, led by Elena Torres and composed of Eulalia Guzmán, Julia Nava de Ruisánchez, and Luz Vera Córdova, traveled to Baltimore, Maryland to attend the Pan American Conference of Women. The Liga Feminista "Rita Cetina Gutiérrez" from Yucatán also sent a delegation, headed by Elvia Carrillo Puerto.[19] This Baltimore meeting of 2,000 delegates was the largest of any meeting of women of the Americas. Delegates formed the Pan American League for the Advancement of Women, and Mexican delegate Elena Torres was elected vice-president for the area comprising the United States, Mexico, and Canada.

The goals of the newly formed Pan American League for the Advancement of Women focused upon issues raised by progressive women in Mexico. These goals were:

> . . . to promote the general education of women and to secure for them higher standards of education; to secure the rights of married women to control their own property and earnings; to secure equal guardianship; to encourage organizations, discussion, and public speaking among women and freedom of opportunity for women to cultivate and use their talents; to educate public opinion in favor of granting the vote to women; to secure their political rights; and finally to promote friendliness and understanding among all Pan American countries. . . .

In late May 1923, the Mexican branch of the Pan American League for the Advancement of Women hosted the First Feminist Congress of the Pan American Women's League (Primer Congreso Feminista de la Liga Pan Americana de la Mujer) in Mexico City; more than one hundred women were in attendance. Most of the congress delegates were professional women, including Mexico's first woman medical doctor, Matilda P. Montoya; Julia Nava de Ruisánchez; Luz Vera Córdova; and Margarita Robles de Mendoza. Elena Torres, who had issued invitations to the congress and had led the Mexican delegation to the Baltimore meeting the year before, served as president of the congress.

From the beginning, the Yucatán delegates, led by Elvia Carrillo Puerto and Susana Betancourt, attempted to dominate the meetings. However, the more radical ideas of the Yucatecas on sex education, sexual relations without marriage, and birth control were tempered by those of the moderate delegates.[20] A wide range of topics was discussed, including birth control, economics, labor problems, social problems, and civil rights. The resolutions that passed suggest that the delegates were reluctant to endorse fully the radical ideas of the Yucatán feminists, especially those on free love and birth control. The birth control issue was defeated mainly because Mexico had suffered a dramatic population decline through the loss of lives during the Revolution and through the large numbers of Mexicans who migrated to the United States to escape the ravages of the Revolution.

Delegates recommended that the inequities in the Law of Family Relations be removed so that "a single sexual standard for men and women apply," that pre-natal and post-natal clinics with women administrators be established to combat Mexico's high infant mortality rate, and that more coeducational and industrial schools be founded. Delegates also requested greater protection for domestic workers employed by foreign companies, establishment of more kindergartens and juvenile courts, installation of eating facilities in factories, and access to women officials at borders and ports. Unlike delegates at the Feminist Congress in Yucatán, delegates to the First Feminist Congress of the Pan American Women's League viewed women's rights to political and civil equality as an essential need. Two key spokespersons, Luz Vera Córdova and Margarita Robles de Mendoza, both educators and writers, led the demand that women be granted national suffrage.[21]

Luz Vera Córdova had worked in educational "missions" in Puebla and later worked in educational "missions" in her home state of Veracruz. In 1934, she became the first woman to receive a Doctor of Philosophy degree from the National University. A devoted feminist, Vera participated in both the 1923 and the 1925 women's congresses in Mexico City.

Margarita Robles de Mendoza was from the upper class and had a distinguished career as a language professor, feminist writer, and one of the founders of the Unión de Mujeres Americanas (UMA). (With a membership of 200,000, the UMA launched a vigorous campaign for women's suffrage.) Robles provided leadership in many feminist organizations: in 1929, she represented Mexico on the Inter-American Commission on Women in Washington; in 1935, she served as director of the Acción Femenina (Feminine Action) section of the Partido Nacional Revolucionario (PNR), Mexico's main political party; and in 1931, her feminist study *La evolución de la mujer en México* (*The Evolution of the Mexican Woman*) was published.[22]

Throughout the 1920s and 1930s, Mexican women's interest in international organizations was strengthened even further. The international peace movement attracted large numbers of Mexican women, and as contact with women from other countries increased, Mexican women showed even greater determination to continue their fight for equal rights.[23]

In November 1920, the Women's Society was founded in the capital. The society's purpose was to promote closer ties between women in American nations. Officers included activist Esperanza Velázquez Bringas.[24] That same year, Mexican women joined other Latin American women in affiliating with the International Council of Women (ICW). The ICW, originally organized in 1888, was dedicated to promoting peace and to achieving general improvement in the status of women worldwide. The ICW had held its first meeting in 1910-1911 in Buenos Aires, and by the mid-1920s it had many Latin American members. By 1930, the ICW had adopted Spanish as a semi-official language.[25]

In 1925, university women founded the Asociación de Universitarias Mexicanas (Association of Mexican University Women) to promote cultural and scientific exchanges between Mexican women and women abroad.[26] In 1928, the Pan American Round Table of Mexico City, which espoused ideas similar to the 1920 Women's Society, was founded. Its goals were to promote interest in social life, to foster interest in customs of the American nations, and to engender goodwill among those nations.

Women on the political Left were especially active between 1920 and 1934. Several of these women formed a study group, "Leona Vicario," named after the Independence heroine, to investigate problems confronting the Mexican family and the status of the woman as mother and wife. Its organizers included Dr. Esther Chapa, Dr. Matilde Rodríguez Cabo, Professor Esperanza Balmaceda de Joseph, and Consuelo Uranga. Elvia Carrillo Puerto collaborated with María "Cuca" García to unionize women government employees. García realized quickly, when first President Obregón and later President Calles reneged on their political support of women's rights, that if women were ever to be an effective political force, they would have to organize themselves.[27] Juana B. Gutiérrez de Mendoza's interest in indigenous races and rural education was reflected in the numerous organizations she founded in the 1920s. After working in rural schools in 1922, Gutiérrez collaborated with *campesinos* in the state of Morelos to establish an experimental agrarian colony called "Santiago Orozco."[28] The colony failed when Gutiérrez tried to curb the church's power, and the *campesinos* abandoned the community shortly after its founding. After the *campesinos* left, the Spanish *hacendados*, whom Gutiérrez despised, were able to reclaim the land.

After the failure of the agrarian colony, Gutiérrez continued to study anthropology in Zacatecas, where she also worked as an inspector of rural federal schools. In 1923 she founded the Consejo de los Caxcanes (Council of Caxcanes) in Juchipila, Zacatecas, to promote and to preserve indigenous culture. Later Gutiérrez worked in a cooperative in Morelia, Michoacán.[29]

WOMEN'S CONFERENCES

During the 1920s, there was phenomenal growth in the number of Mexican women who participated in a variety of domestic and international women's conferences. The first Mexican women's meeting to be held in the second decade of the twentieth century was a Workers' Conference organized by Elvia Carrillo Puerto, attorney Florinda Lazos León, and journalist María Efraína Rocha. The conference delegates demanded that *campesinas* and *obreras* be granted greater political rights, land, and farm tools.

A highly controversial meeting of the Congress of "Mujeres de la Raza" was held in early July 1925 in Mexico City. Even though congressional delegates were mainly from the middle and upper classes, the congress painfully exposed the vast ideological differences separating these women. The congress was sponsored jointly by the Liga de Mujeres Ibéricas e Hispanoamericanas (League of Iberian and Hispanic-American Women) and the Unión Cooperativa "Mujeres de la Raza" (Cooperative Union of "Mujeres de la Raza"). Sofía Villa de Buentello, a moderate who was one of the founders of the Unión Cooperativa "Mujeres de la Raza" and the author of *La mujer y la ley* (*Women and the Law*), presided over the meeting of more than two hundred Spanish-speaking women from Mexico, Latin America, and Spain. In an interview in *Excelsior* in December 1924, Villa had expressed her high aspirations for the congress.[30] However, the congress began with disputes over registration and voting procedures, and ended on a bitter note. Serious differences between conservatives, trying to maintain the status quo, and Communists and Socialists (led by Elvia Carrillo Puerto and Cuca García), trying to radically change the existing order, were a major cause of the disruptions. This political rift was exemplified by the schism that manifested itself during the session on moral problems. Villa recommended that public billboards carry inscriptions reading "Swearing and begging prohibited," to which García objected immediately: "How can one prevent begging when there is no work, when salaries are so meager, and you have the poor in complete helplessness? Work is the social salvation," García concluded. On the following day, García stressed the importance of education for indigenous peoples and launched a vigorous protest against domination by political conservatives.[31]

During the next few days, the controversy polarized the congressional delegates into two distinct factions. As arguing increased, several delegates left the meeting in disgust. Frustrated, a visibly shaken Villa reminded the audience: "This is an international congress, not a Socialist or worker congress; the foreign delegates have abandoned us and now there is no congress." Rising, Elvia Carrillo Puerto responded, "If it is to be said that this congress, to be international, is for people of class, why have you invited us, the workers?" Carrillo continued her protest, "The heart, the very fiber of the country, protests against the parasites that suck [the lifeblood] from it." In the confusion, Villa finally obtained a promise for order, and García proposed that members refrain from passing any measures in the passion of the moment. With order restored, delegates began to filter back into the meeting.[32]

Delegates to the Congress of "Mujeres de la Raza" did not confine their discussion to areas of traditional concern for women, but broadened it to include international problems as well. Elvia Carrillo Puerto gave a presentation on the successful activities of the Ligas Feministas (Feminists Leagues) in Yucatán, which the conservatives protested immediately. The following week, amid vigorous protests, the political radicals succeeded in passing a proposal that reactionaries be purged from the Mexican government, especially from the Ministry of Education.[33]

Believing the delegates had strayed from purposeful action, Villa tried to adjourn the congress. She met with a wall of protest, mostly from leftists, who accused congress planners of selecting themes that confined discussions to the subject of women in their role as wife and mother. When Villa insisted that the congress adjourn, conservatives joined with Communists and Socialists to elect a new board of directors and voted to continue the meeting. The board's newly elected president sent a message to President Calles stating that the congress would continue with truly revolutionary women and that this would signal another triumph for the Revolution. Villa's scheduling of a concert, so that delegates could not hear subsequent speakers, grated on already uneven tempers. The congress continued until July 15, even though only ninety-eight delegates (roughly one-half) were present on the last meeting day to participate in discussions on the need for education of indigenous people and for political equality for women and children.[34]

On the last day of the congress, a scathing editorial entitled "A Defeat of Feminism" appeared in the Mexico City daily *El Universal*. Referring to the disintegration and poor organization of the congress, the unsigned editorial reminded women that if this were an example of their participation in public life, their participation was a fraud, and that the Congress of "Mujeres de la Raza" was nothing more than a caricature of the national congress, superficial and scandalous, and conducted by women trying to behave like men. The author concluded by calling the congress a defeat for the feminist cause.[35]

In the 1930s, for the first time in Mexican history, women from the upper, middle, and lower classes came together for a series of congresses that marked a growing concern over the conditions of working-class women. The National Congress of Women Workers and Peasants (Congreso Nacional de Mujeres Obreras y Campesinas) held its first congress in October 1931; its second congress in November 1933; and its third congress in September of the following year. On the positive side, these congresses represented a high point of progress and organization for working women; on the negative side, they exposed the sharp ideological divisions within women's ranks. Many of the issues addressed in these three congresses, such as the government's failure to address women's needs, would provide part of the rationale for the 1935 platform of the Frente Unico Pro Derechos de la Mujer (Sole Front for Women's Rights [FUPDM]), Mexico's largest women's rights organization.

On October 1, 1931, the first National Congress of Women Workers and Peasants convened in Mexico City. Organized by members of the Partido Feminista Revolucionario (Feminist Revolutionary Party) of the PNR and the Bloque Nacional de Mujeres Revolucionarias (National Bloc of Revolutionary Women), the congress attracted some six hundred delegates from all parts of Mexico. President Ortiz Rubio and other government officials attended briefly, reflecting the government's keen interest in the meetings. Themes of the congress were cooperation between *obreras* and *campesinas*, organization of women at the national level, founding of a women's bank, definition of women's civil and political condition, and establishment of an organization to protect children.[36]

On the afternoon of October 2, Cuca García addressed the *campesinas'* struggle:

> Thousands of women work the land like *peones* for a small salary,
> or work the miserable parcel of their husband, father, or brother,
> because they are almost completely limited in their right to the land.
> The Agrarian Law states that they can obtain land [*ejidos*] only as the
> female head of the family, [or] as adult *campesinas* who have suitable
> needs. The young *campesinas* don't have a right to the land; that is,
> the agrarian legislation condemns them to always live at the poor
> economic level of their father, their husband, [or] their brother, and,
> as we have already said, economic independence is the base of political
> independence for women.[37]

The following day, María Ríos Cárdenas, an organizer of the National Congress of Women Workers and Peasants and the founder and publisher of the feminist journal *Mujer*, presented a plan for a nationwide women's organization headquartered in Mexico City, with branches in every state. Ríos recommended that all feminist organizations be merged into a single confederation and establish formal relations with the government, with labor unions, and with peasant groups. This plan immediately factionalized the delegates. One faction, led by Florinda Lazos León, a lawyer from Chiapas, supported the idea that an organization for women only be formed; and the other faction, led by Cuca García, recommended working within already existing mixed-gender peasant and labor unions. Lazos's faction maintained that whenever women worked with men, women's needs were subordinated. García, joined by Communists Consuelo Uranga (a teacher and an activist since her student days) and Concepción (Concha) Michel (a well-known singer), maintained that the congress should have broader aims than feminism, and that feminism diverted attention away from the basic struggle to liberate the masses. However, the majority of delegates agreed with Lazos, and her proposal for a nationwide organization of women's groups was adopted.[38]

The Communists at the 1931 congress created an uproar, not unlike the one created by the Yucatán delegates at the First Feminist Congress of the Pan American Women's League in 1923. Nevertheless, the delegates succeeded in passing proposals for establishing social services and education programs for *campesinas*, establishing minimum wages, ensuring paid maternity leaves for female employees, seeking electoral reforms, and amending Article 34 of the 1917 constitution to permit women the right to vote and to run for office.[39] Probably the most controversial measure passed by the congress was the anti-Catholic recommendation that the government limit the number of priests and that it not employ members of the Catholic Knights of Columbus. This recommendation aroused considerable protest, and Mexico City newspapers soundly criticized the delegates.[40]

Generally, this first National Congress of Women Workers and Peasants ran smoothly, with a few notable exceptions. On October 4, the Communist delegates walked out of a session in protest; and, at the closing session, fourteen Communists (including Concha Michel) were arrested for denouncing officials of the Ortiz Rubio administration. However, once at police headquarters, the women were released.[41]

Despite the unwillingness of Communists and Socialists to form a unified feminist organization, the political moderates, led by María Ríos Cárdenas, proceeded with their plans to unify women's groups under a single organizational umbrella. To this end, delegates from the National Congress of Women Workers and Peasants formed both an executive committee and a permanent commission to plan for the second congress.[42]

The Second National Congress of Women Workers and Peasants, also held in Mexico City, lasted from November 25 to 30, 1933. There were even more delegates present than at the first congress, and because of worsening economic conditions there was increased tension between political leftists and political moderates. Delegates addressed such issues as minimum wages for women, the creation of special departments for women in government agencies, establishment of a bank for women's cooperatives, and education for workers. Conflict erupted when Communist Consuelo Uranga spoke critically of government manipulation, which so offended many delegates, the majority of whom were long-time government employees, that they walked out and refused to return to the congress.

On November 28, Juana Gutiérrez de Mendoza, a veteran of the Revolution, spoke on the need for *campesinas* to have the same opportunities as *campesinos* to acquire land under the agrarian reform program. Ana María Hernández reported on efforts to organize working-class women. The most tense episode of the second congress occurred when police entered the meeting, ordered all Communists to leave, and apprehended two Communist delegates. Communist Party member Uranga ignored the order to leave and continued to stress her point that the only path to emancipation was through social revolution. Several delegates objected to having the police disrupt their meeting. However, order was restored quickly and the business of the congress proceeded.[43] Nevertheless, the congress board of directors, angered by the disruption, protested to the police and demanded immediate release of the women delegates and a guaranty by the police that in the future no delegates would be barred from attending the meetings. Uranga and Lazos continued an unresolved argument over whether women should organize only with other women's groups or work with existing organizations that included men.[44]

Despite the disruptions and arguments, delegates succeeded in passing proposals for minimum wages, unification of women's organizations, repeal of certain taxes, free schools, committees to organize agrarian communities, and a denouncement of persons who monopolize public posts. Before closure of the second congress, the delegates issued an international statement that supported solidarity with China but took a stand against payment of foreign debt, obligatory military service, the Seventh Pan American Conference, American intervention in Cuba, Japanese aggression in China, and war as a means of settling political disputes.[45]

The Third National Congress of Women Workers and Peasants met in September 1934 in Guadalajara with 260 delegates. The delegates approved proposals that supported the legal protection of women as workers, wives, and mothers; coeducation; unification of women's organizations; "defanaticization" (elimination of religious fanaticism) of the Mexican people; Socialist education; and women's suffrage. Also, delegates to the third congress urged that the military budget be reduced to provide more funds for social and educational reforms. The only tense moment occurred when a number of delegates accused the delegates from the Partido Feminista Revolucionario of the PNR of being allied with Catholic bourgeois elements. These accusations led to some disorder and the police were called, but the presiding officer, María Ríos Cárdenas, was able to adjourn the congress without a major incident.[46]

THE SUFFRAGE QUESTION

In spite of the ideological divisions so evident at the three National Congresses of Women Workers and Peasants, it was clear that all feminists supported suffrage. However, the Mexican government continued to avoid the issue. Neither Obregón nor Calles considered the granting of suffrage to women to be a political necessity; furthermore, Calles was especially opposed to suffrage because groups such as the League of Catholic Women, organized in 1924, vehemently resisted his anti-clerical policies.

During the period 1920 to 1934, only four Mexican states amended their laws to include women's suffrage. States that allowed women to vote were

Yucatán, under Felipe Carrillo Puerto's governorship (1922); San Luis Potosí, under governor Rafael Nieto (1923); Chiapas (1925); and Tabasco, under Socialist Tomás Garrido Canabal (1931 to 1934).[47] In an atmosphere reminiscent of that in Yucatán in the early 1920s, Tabascan women were organized into leagues and cooperatives, and participated actively in civic affairs. Quick divorces were permitted, and education was rationalist, compulsory, coeducational, and free.[48]

None of the other Mexican states followed the examples of Yucatán, San Luis Potosí, Chiapas, and Tabasco. Indeed, before the end of the 1920s, both Yucatán and San Luis Potosí had revoked their suffrage laws. In addition to the loss of suffrage in these two states, the women's movement suffered other liabilities: the activities of the League of Catholic Women increased the government's suspicion that women served as a political tool of the Catholic Church; women's participation in the Cristero Rebellion of 1926, in which Catholics took up arms against the government, continued to be used as a counter-suffrage argument; and women's involvement in the assassination of President-elect Obregón (1928) kept women suspect in the eyes of revolutionary politicians.[49]

While Mexican men distrusted women's political loyalties and their ability to organize politically, there was another fundamental factor that made them reluctant to grant women suffrage. In this regard, a Mexican colonel wrote:

> . . . [W]e Latins consider that if our women are brought into the
> rough political melee of public life they would immediately lose their
> womanly charm and femininity; besides we are endowed with a radical
> sentimental temperament which tends to forbid them [women] from
> mixing in our public affairs.

The colonel indicated that although he did not personally accept this viewpoint, and that those who did were either blind or stupid, these opinions were quite common. He admitted that sooner or later "we shall have to share with them [women] equal rights willingly, as they are bound to win that equality by the people's vote."[50] In 1926, the colonel had no way of knowing that suffrage would not be granted Mexican women for another twenty-seven years.

Of the three interim presidents (Portes Gil, Ortiz Rubio, and Rodríguez), Portes Gil was the only one who dealt directly with women's issues. During his presidency (December 1928 to February 1930), Portes Gil's attitude toward women's suffrage was mid-point between the negative reactions of Obregón and Calles and the positive reaction of Cárdenas. Portes Gil's wife Carmen, at twenty-four, was Mexico's youngest first lady and one of the most active. Besides founding the National Association of Children's Welfare, Carmen Portes Gil worked to educate poor children and helped to organize a national campaign against alcoholism. President Portes Gil was acquainted with the most important feminists of the time and held long discussions with them on the suffrage question. Nonetheless, when he expelled Italian Communist Tina Modotti because of her attacks against the government and refused to support women's suffrage, the reason he gave was the traditional one, namely, the church controlled women, making them enemies of the Revolution.[51]

In an interview with feminist Margarita Robles de Mendoza during his presidency, Portes Gil stated that although the Constitution proposed to limit the vote to men, women could and should participate in politics. However, he contended that women would have to be educated first and prepare themselves to hold public positions. When the president was shown a long list of professional women, he responded by stating that he was pleased to know that so many women were ready to work for the social advancement of the country.[52] Portes Gil's remarks, which received considerable publicity, encouraged further agitation among feminists.

THE WOMEN'S MOVEMENT, THE BRIGADAS FEMENINAS, AND THE CATHOLIC CHURCH

During the 1920s, the stormy relationship between the Catholic Church and the Mexican government grew increasingly violent. The church (and a large segment of the army) supported both the de la Huerta Rebellion against the federal government in 1923 and the revolt of generals Serrano and Gómez against the federal government in 1927. In 1926, the church openly defied the federal government by taking up arms in the Cristero Rebellion; and in 1928 the assassination of President-elect Obregón by Catholics kept the church and state conflict at fever pitch. Trouble flared again over government attempts to institutionalize Socialist education. These battles between church and state had a negative effect on the political future of Mexican women because male government officials were further convinced that women generally would not vote independently but would follow church direction and thereby negate the hard-won goals of the Revolution.

President Obregón, in attempting to diminish church influence, had placed the church in the defensive posture of developing its own organizations aimed specifically at the proselytization and politicization of youths, workers, journalists, and women. In 1919, during a church-sponsored social week held in Puebla, priests openly urged the people to confront the rising tide of socialism. Several speakers equated socialism with free love and feminism, both of which the church had condemned.[53]

In 1920, Catholic Social Action leaders created an umbrella organization, called the Confederation of Catholic Associations of Mexico, to coordinate association activities. At the same time, a Mexican Social Secretariat was formed. This Secretariat was responsible for organizing and holding association conferences; organizing labor unions; forming women's organizations; and publishing *La Paz Social* (*Social Peace*), a monthly devoted to social questions. In 1920, the Secretariat founded the Unión de Damas Católicas de México (Catholic Ladies' Union of Mexico), whose goal was to proselytize and to recruit women through publication of *La Dama Católica* (*The Catholic Lady*). The editors of *La Dama Católica*, asserting that women's place was in the home, assured their readers that while they were not "feminists in the exaggerated sense of the word," feminine influences (except in politics) could aid greatly in solving many of Mexico's social problems.[54]

The backbone of Social Action was the Confederación Nacional Católica de Trabajar (National Catholic Labor Confederation), formed in 1922. Social Action members called for the preservation of the family by keeping women out of the labor force and in the home. In 1925, the seventy-five-year-old Archbishop of Mexico, José Mora y del Río, issued a pastoral letter censuring adoption of "a North American custom" of women working outside the home. Father Medina, S.J., in his monthly review for *La Paz Social*, echoed Archbishop del Río's sentiments that women working outside the home would lead to its ruin. In the April issue, Father Medina was even more explicit: "The woman, from the moment that she becomes a worker, ceases to be a woman."[55] Although the clergy held to its hard-line position against women working, the church's negative position on women's political participation changed quickly because it needed political support in its battles with the Mexican government.

By the mid-1920s, the conflict between the church and state had heated to the boiling point. During the previous eight years, the anti-clerical provisions of the constitution had rarely been enforced. Then, in mid-June 1926, President Calles began stricter enforcement by prohibiting foreign priests from working in Mexico, closing religious schools, monasteries, and convents, and ordering all Mexican priests to register with civil authorities. By July 31, church officials had reacted by declaring a strike, suspending all religious services, and calling an economic boycott on the purchase of goods and services "to paralyze in every way possible the social and economic life of the country."[56]

During the summer and fall of 1926, there were scattered incidents of violence between church and government supporters, with women visible on both sides of the conflict. In Mexico City, police fired into a crowd of women in the Church of San Rafael after the women refused to leave the building. Anti-government riots in Guadalajara and Torreón involved large numbers of women participants. Conversely, there were many women who demonstrated in favor of the government's anti-church policies. For example, on August 1, 1926, masses of women marched in a pro-government parade sponsored by the labor union Confederación Regional Obrera Mexicana (Regional Confederation of Mexican Workers [CROM]).[57]

During the winter of 1926, thousands of Cristeros (Catholic guerrillas) were in armed rebellion against the government. The centers of Cristero resistance were mainly rural, and were located mostly in western and southern Mexico. The Cristero rebels were primarily poor farmers who did not understand the complexities of the church-state conflict, and who reacted to what they considered to be government wickedness.[58] These rebels blew up trains, burned government schools, and attacked "Socialist" teachers. The fact that a large percentage of rural schoolteachers were women did not deter the Cristeros. In a tragic incident, not unlike those that occurred elsewhere in Mexico, a young woman in a small Zacatecan village ran out of her classroom when she heard men approaching on horseback. After being lassoed, she was dragged feet first over miles of rocky ground until there was almost nothing left to bury. Federal troops retaliated by taking hostages, raiding villages suspected of sheltering rebels, and mercilessly looting the countryside.[59]

In many areas, women served at the very heart of the Cristero movement. Although most were not directly involved in combat, women served as spies; organizers; and suppliers and carriers of arms, ammunition, food, and medicines. The famous Brigadas Femeninas (Feminine Brigades), founded in June 1917 by Luis Flores González, played a critical role in the Cristero operation. General Jesús Degollado Guizár, commander of the Cristero army, stated: "They [the Feminine Brigades] had become the principal means by which the Guardia Nacional was supplied with arms and ammunition." In January 1928, the Brigadas established headquarters in Mexico City and planned to take jurisdiction over the entire republic. By the end of 1928, the Brigadas had increased in number from six in the states of Jalisco and Colima to more than twenty throughout the republic. These Brigadas maintained six branches of activity—finance, war, provisions, welfare, information, and health care—and had over 10,000 members, the majority of whom were single women of working-class background.[60]

A principal activity of the Brigadas Femeninas was the provisioning of supplies to men on the battlefields. Thousands of women carried munitions and supplies from the cities to the Cristero camps. Brigada members hid munitions in baskets that appeared to be filled with maize, or in containers filled with milk; they also carried arms hidden in specially made vests called *chalecos*. Often under cover of night, groups of six to ten women, disguised as *campesinas*, trudged between cities and camps; by day, the women hid in fields or in deserted ranch houses.[61]

In the latter part of 1928, the Liga Nacional Defensora de la Libertad Religiosa (National League of Defense of Religious Liberty), which had been responsible for organizing many Catholic lay groups, clashed with the Brigadas Femeninas over jurisdictional matters. The Brigadas demanded autonomy, and the Liga Nacional refused to grant it. The main center of Brigada resistance to Liga authority was located in the Federal District. Repeated efforts to prevent a schism were unsuccessful, and the Liga finally branded the Brigadas as illegitimate. The conflict, which was never really resolved, damaged the overall Cristero effort and ended many of the Brigada's activities, especially the flow of ammunition, which, in turn, seriously impeded the Brigada's effectiveness.

In the tense atmosphere created by the Cristero Rebellion, women's political loyalty was even more strongly suspect. Mexican government officials, preoccupied with domestic and international crises, continued to be unreceptive to demands for women's political equality, especially when they suspected that women's primary allegiance was to the church. Women were accused frequently of being implicated in plots to kill government officials, but such accusations were generally unsubstantiated.

Women in religious orders suffered severely. Every convent in the republic was dispersed by President Calles's ruling of 1926. An indirect consequence of the church-state conflict was the seizure, deportation, shooting, and sometimes raping of nuns. Thousands of nuns were expelled from their positions in schools and hospitals; but because they constituted a large part of the teaching and nursing staffs, it was often necessary to then rehire them as lay teachers and lay nurses.[62]

Nuns, and lay women sympathetic to the church, turned their homes into meeting places, harbored fugitives, and served as messengers for anti-government insurgents. After the assassination attempt against Obregón in Chapultepec Park in November 1927, women hid the would-be assassins until the government finally captured and executed four of them. Madre María Concepción Acevedo de la Llata, known simply as Madre Conchita, the abbess of a Capuchin convent, used her Chopo Street home in Mexico City for anti-government political purposes. One room served as a chapel, where the devoted could attend mass; but other rooms of the house served as a center of anti-government conspiracy. One of the plans discussed at the Chopo Street residence was the assassination of either Obregón or Calles. A hypodermic needle containing poison was the planned instrument of death. The assassination plan called for a girl with a needle hidden in a bouquet to dance with one of the men, and then to inject the poison. Although this particular plan was eventually abandoned, the anti-government plotting continued.[63]

Probably the most sensational incident regarding Catholic women's involvement in anti-government activity occurred in 1928 when a twenty-six-year-old artist and mystic named José de León Toral shot and killed President-elect Obregón at a banquet in a restaurant in Mexico City. Toral greatly admired Madre Conchita, and through her inspiration had decided to give his life for the cause. After Obregón's assassination, Madre Conchita and twenty nuns were arrested. The church denounced the assassination and disclaimed any responsibility. Archbishop de la Mora of San Luis Potosí stated that Madre Conchita was mentally abnormal, and the Unión de Damas Católicas de México refused to defend her.[64] At their much-publicized trial in November 1928, Toral was condemned to death and Madre Conchita received a twenty-year sentence. (The law forbade the execution of women.) Madre Conchita was sent to prison at Islas Marías, where she served as governess to the director's children and later married a fellow prisoner.[65]

Fanatical Catholics were determined to prevent Toral's execution. A telegram from Toral's lawyers asking for clemency from President Portes Gil was followed by a letter from the representatives of the League of Defense of Religious Liberty; the letter threatened that members of the Portes Gil family would be killed unless the president pardoned Toral. Portes Gil denied the pardon, and on the morning of February 10, 1929, the presidential train was dynamited in the state of Guanajuato. The presidential party was uninjured, but one person was killed and two pullman cars and a locomotive were destroyed. The execution of Toral was carried out on schedule by a firing squad. However, Catholics made a final point when attendance at Toral's funeral was so great that police and firemen could hardly preserve order.[66]

Although the church-state controversy was alleviated temporarily by an agreement concluded in June 1929, the residue of bitterness remained on both sides.[67] For example, legislators in several Mexican states continued to hound the church by limiting the number of priests and by severely restricting the few that remained. Churches were closed in almost half the states of Mexico in the early 1930s. The most extreme case of anti-clerical legislation occurred in Tabasco, where Governor Tómas Garrido Canabal ordered priests to marry and churches to be destroyed. Catholics in Tabasco were even forbidden to celebrate holy days of obligation and were ordered to eat meat on Fridays.

Education was a major point of contention between church and state. At the Unión de Damas Católicas national convention, Catholic women called for a repeal of the constitutional ban on religious primary education and insisted upon the right of parents to determine the kind of schooling their children received.[68] Narcisco Bassols, minister of education from 1931 to 1934, further stoked the fires of controversy when he placed Catholic schools under federal control and ordered instructors to teach socialism. But it was the institutionalization of "sex education," which included physiology and hygiene courses, that caused the greatest distress. Many Catholic parents refused to allow their children to attend classes, and they openly challenged the government educational program. Lay teachers were often attacked and harassed. While there was not as much widespread violence as in the 1920s, teachers did occasionally lose their lives.[69] The agitation over education was so great that Minister Bassols had to resign in May 1934.[70] Riots and protests continued until President Cárdenas reached an agreement with the church in the late 1930s.

WOMEN JOURNALISTS

Throughout the 1920s, women continued to assume leadership positions in the field of journalism. In 1920, lawyer María Sandoval and professor Julia Nava de Ruisánchez edited a new magazine called *Mujeres*. *Mujeres* was not successful, and only a few issues were published before 1923, at which time it was revived as a publication of the National Congress of Women Workers and Peasants. In 1922 and 1923 in Yucatán, Elvia Carrillo Puerto and Rosa Torres edited a short-lived radical publication called *Rebeldía*. In 1926, *Mujer*, one of the most staunchly feminist magazines since Hermila Galindo's *La Mujer Moderna*, was begun by María Ríos Cárdenas, a professor in the Normal School in Mexico City and organizer of the National Congresses of Women Workers and Peasants. *Mujer*'s subtitle— "For the moral and intellectual elevation of women"—characterized its contents. Published by and for women, *Mujer* featured articles about the women's movement in Mexico and abroad, as well as articles on divorce, free union, and other areas of interest to progressive women.[71] Possibly because of the forthright manner in which controversial subjects were presented, *Mujer* did not attract a wide reading audience and was discontinued in 1929.[72] Guadalupe Ramírez, daughter of noted statesman and journalist Ignacio Ramírez, founded *Luz* in 1929 with five other women. *Luz* was known for its progressive ideas.[73]

During the 1920s, two significant trends for women journalists were the growing interest that many publications displayed in women's activities and the increasing number of women contributors who published in other than "women's" magazines. Two general magazines, *La Revista de Revistas: El Seminario Nacional* and *El Universal Ilustrado*, provided extensive coverage of women's activities. Besides focusing upon female personalities of the day, these publications included articles on women's conferences and on women's organizational campaigns.

Increasingly, then, more and more women contributors began to venture outside the bailiwick of "women's" magazines. Juana Gutiérrez collaborated with the staff of the capital's daily newspaper *El Heraldo de México* (which was directed by her old PLM friend, engineer Camilo Arriaga) to produce a series of social articles covering a wide range of topics—from women's schools to the reconstruction of Mexico. Socialist Esperanza Velázquez Bringas, who served as director of all libraries in Mexico for the federal Ministry of Education, published widely throughout this period; and Catalina D. Eznell, a playwright and drama critic, served as an editor for the important Mexico City daily newspaper *Excelsior*.[74]

Leftist women wrote prolifically throughout the 1920s and 1930s. Feminists Artemisa Sáenz Royo ("Xóchitl") and Cuca García wrote for the Communist newspaper *El Machete*.[75] In addition to her other projects, Juana Gutiérrez de Mendoza continued to write. In May 1920, she published a twelve-page pamphlet, *Comentarios de actualidad* (*The Current State of Affairs*), under the pseudonym "Juan Bernal." The pamphlet was not a feminist tract but a diatribe against Carranza and Obregón. After criticizing "legalists," Gutiérrez concluded that the Mexican Revolution had degenerated into "a legalistic fossil." Her despair over the direction of the Revolution was also evident in her private papers. In January 1922, she noted that the struggle during the period 1910 to 1920 was not really revolutionary. Demanding "effective suffrage and no re-election is not revolutionary, but conservative," because these do not alter the societal structure.[76] In 1924, Gutiérrez wrote *Por la Tierra y Por la Raza* (*For the Land and For the People*), in which she outlined the history of indigenous peoples in Mexico and discussed their most pressing problems.

In the late 1920s, Gutiérrez collaborated on the newspaper *América India: Por la Unión Indoamericana* (*Indian America: For Indo-American Union*), the product of a group attempting to create an Indo-American Union to promote the welfare of the indigenous community. The group's goals included protection against Yankee imperialism. In an article in *América India*, Gutiérrez explained the group's purpose as being "to conserve and improve the indigenous race, freeing it from all foreign influence."[77] In 1933, she edited *Radiográficas Revolucionarias* (*Revolutionary X-Rays*), a monthly that addressed a variety of subjects, including women's issues. Gutiérrez's *El Cauce* (*The Source*) focused on women's issues and appeared for the first time on May 31, 1934; published from the capital, *El Cauce*'s format was similar to *Vésper* (which was reissued in 1932).

In an interview in January 1928, Emilia Enríquez de Rivera, founder and director of *El Hogar* (*The Home*), revealed the difficulties she encountered in establishing a new publication. For *El Hogar*, Enríquez confided that, for the first issues, she had to write every line, solicit announcements, and distribute copies. She explained, "My magazine has been my children and my total life." Enríquez attributed her literary success to her willingness to steer clear of controversial political questions. Because Enríquez's magazine focused on women in the home, it was one of the few magazines not suspended during the Revolution.[78]

Women's journalism flourished in the early 1930s, and many new newspapers and magazines were published by women's organizations. *La Voz de la Mujer* (*The Voice of Women*), published by the Bloque Nacional de Mujeres Revolucionarias, under the direction of lawyer Florinda Lazos León, gave extensive coverage to women. The June 22, 1932 issue of *La Voz de la Mujer* contained an open letter to former President Calles and to President Pascual Ortiz Rubio demanding that women be incorporated into the political structure. Later, the Bloque published a small periodical on women called *Flama* (Flame), directed by Dr. Esther Chapa and writer Adelina Zendejas.[79]

SUMMARY

The period from 1920 to 1934 drew to a close with few solid political gains for women. Women had helped to win the Revolution and to institutionalize the government's educational and health programs, but they were excluded from receiving their promised share of revolutionary benefits. Paradoxically, the Mexican government used women to disseminate Socialist education designed to reduce the influence of the church, yet it refused to give women political rights because of their ties to the church. Women's lack of organization and their sharp divisions over ideology further damaged their credibility as a political force.

Women in the period 1920 to 1934 did organize on a wider scale than ever before, and a few educated women did assume prominent positions in government and in the universities. However, it was not until after 1934 that the key ingredients for women to win equal political rights were present—a supportive president and a sufficiently large number of women organized in support of suffrage.

▪ 5 ▪

An Era of High Hopes:
The Third Phase, 1934-1940

The final period of the Revolution, 1934 to 1940, can be characterized as an era of high hopes for supporters of the women's movement in Mexico. This era was dominated by the policies and personality of President Lázaro Cárdenas, who strove to fulfill the goals of the Revolution by transforming Mexico into a Socialist state. Cárdenas's strategy for achieving those goals was to implement a Six-Year Plan that addressed specifically the needs of groups that had been largely ignored and excluded by previous administrations (such as the *campesinos*, Indians, *obreros*, and women); to attack the shortcomings in the nation's education programs by overcoming the resistance of the Catholic Church to Socialist programs; and to eliminate the domination of the Mexican economy by foreign interests.

To implement his Six-Year Plan, Cárdenas often aimed directly at changing the mores of the Mexican people. In an attempt to halt those habits which he believed corrupted society, Cárdenas banned gambling, conducted an anti-alcohol campaign, prohibited the manufacture and sale of dice and cards, closed red-light districts in Mexico City, and fought graft in government. Cárdenas's Six-Year Plan was the principal vehicle he employed in his effort to attain the goals of the Revolution and, concomitantly, to elevate the general status of the Mexican people. The plan's principal thrusts included agrarian reform, labor reorganization, and the expansion of secular, Socialist education.

The Cárdenas administration redistributed more land (both private and public) than had any previous administration; oversaw labor's reorganization into the powerful Confederación de Trabajadores de México (Confederation of Mexican Workers [CTM]); and brought about dramatic educational growth, including construction of thousands of new schools. Under Cárdenas, the number of rural schools, rural schoolteachers (mostly women), and rural pupils doubled in less than a decade.[1] The president was less successful in his efforts to curb the church's political power; however, after years of struggle with the church over control of education, a *modus vivendi* finally was reached during Cárdenas's last years in office. With regard to foreign economic influence and foreign affairs, Cárdenas faced two major crises during his tenure: the Spanish Civil War in 1936 (Mexico supported the Spanish Republic) and the foreign oil expropriations in 1939 (Mexico nationalized the foreign oil firms).

Cárdenas came from a background not unlike that of many other leaders of the Revolution. This extraordinary figure was born in 1895, in the state of Michoacán, into a poor family. Cárdenas worked first in a tax collector's office and then became the town jailer. When the Revolution began, he joined General Calles's forces, was steadily promoted, and ultimately attained the rank of brigadier general. Prior to his presidency, Cárdenas had served as governor of Michoacán, as head of the Partido Nacional Revolucionario (National Revolutionary Party [PNR]), and as Minister of War. In June 1933, when Cárdenas was nominated as the PNR's presidential candidate, he aroused only minimal interest because he was still considered a Calles man. However, once elected to office, Cárdenas made it clear that his only political masters were the Six-Year Plan and the Constitution of 1917.[2]

As stated earlier, the Cárdenas era was one of enormous hope for Mexican women. President Cárdenas was supportive of women, and women during this period were well organized. Unlike many revolutionary leaders, Cárdenas viewed the incorporation of women into the political structure as an essential goal of the Revolution. As governor of Michoacán, in 1928 he had encouraged women to organize in order to combat alcoholism and to counter religious fanaticism. As part of his agrarian reform program, he had even encouraged women to guard the fields with guns while their husbands worked.[3] During his presidency, in affirmation of his support for women's suffrage, Cárdenas stated, "A sound basis for social revolution will not be achieved until the Constitution is reformed to grant equal rights." North American authors Nathaniel and Sylvia Weyl were so impressed that they called Cárdenas an "uncompromising feminist."[4] The philosophical basis for Cárdenas's views, however, was not feminism but socialism. Further, unlike many Mexican politicians during the Revolution, Cárdenas was consistent in both his public and private life—he did not publicly support women's rights and then forbid his wife to pursue her own interests. Betty Kirk, a North American reporter, confirmed this when she interviewed First Lady Amalia Solórzano de Cárdenas in October 1940 and found her to be a modern and progressive woman.[5]

During the Cárdenas presidency, both church and state viewed women as a largely untapped, latent political force; and each undertook vigorous campaigns to compete for women's political loyalties. In 1934, the church began publication of the monthly *El Boletín Católico* (*The Catholic Bulletin*), aimed at the organization of Catholic women "in defense of the family" and, more specifically, at preventing women's acceptance of the government's new socialistic education. In every diocese in Mexico, Catholic women formed committees to promote traditional values and to fight against encroachment by the state. For example, clubhouses equipped with sewing machines and hand irons were established by Catholic women to attract lower-class women and thus to build greater community support for church programs.[6]

In the tug of war between church and state, Cárdenas offered women both political participation and suffrage in exchange for their support of his candidacy in the 1934 election. Edelmira Rojas Vda. de Escudero organized the Partido Feminista Revolucionario to work with the PNR in promoting Cárdenas by sponsoring women delegates to the party and establishing political committees for women throughout the republic. Through such efforts, Ligas Feministas were organized and young girls were incorporated into juvenile brigades.[7] Women in the PNR addressed a variety of family-related problems, including health care, alcoholism, drugs, illiteracy, prostitution, and recruitment by exploitative employers.[8] They also formed vigilante groups to monitor consumer prices on items of prime necessity and publicly denounced price infractions.[9]

In return for women's assistance, Cárdenas agreed to support a nation-wide drive for suffrage.[10] In his presidential message to Congress on September 1, 1935, he pledged to create a women's sector of the party, stating that "working women have the right to participate in electoral struggles." Shortly after his speech to Congress, the president approved the incorporation of the Partido Feminista Revolucionario into the PNR, under the title Acción Femenina (Feminine Action). Acción Femenina had the following goals: incorporation of women into the civic and political life of the nation; acquisition of equal rights for women to develop their faculties to the extent of their capabilities; establishment of campaigns against alcoholism, illiteracy, and religious fanaticism; and attainment of equal rights for women in the civil, social, economic, and political arenas of Mexico.

Margarita Robles de Mendoza was appointed director of the Acción Femenina section by PNR top official and former president Emilio Portes Gil, despite protests from leftist women such as Elvia Carrillo Puerto and Juana Gutiérrez de Mendoza. Carrillo Puerto, Gutiérrez, and others believed that Robles de Mendoza had no understanding of working-class women and *campesinas* and thus was incapable of representing them. They asked that her salary be awarded to a more representative woman. President Cárdenas, responsive to the charges against Robles de Mendoza, removed her as Mexico's representative to the Inter-American Commission on Women and then appointed writer and feminist Amalia Caballero Castillo de Ledón to serve in her stead.[11]

Several members in the Cárdenas cabinet were strongly supportive of women's rights. The Ministry of Agriculture (directed by Tómas Garrido Canabal), the Ministry of Communications (directed by Francisco Múgica), and the Ministry of Public Education established women's associations, and women served on the staffs of these ministries. Moreover, in 1935, Cárdenas appointed Palma Guillén, psychology professor and head of the Office of Secondary Education, as Mexico's Minister to Colombia, making Mexico the first Latin American country to appoint a woman diplomat.[12]

Because of increased networking, Mexican women during the 1930s were well integrated into the international feminist movement. During this period, Mexican women founded several new women's organizations that attracted followers from all social classes and further united Mexican women. Among these organizations were: the Ejército de Defensa de la Mujer (Women's Defense Army), organized in 1934 to protect and to defend Mexican women; the Ateneo Mexicano de Mujeres (Mexican Women's Cultural Club), founded in 1936 by Amalia Caballero de Castillo Ledón; and the Liga de Acción Femenina (League of Feminine Action), led by Elvia Carrillo Puerto.[13]

Many of the new organizations had a strong international orientation, such as the Club Internacional de Mujeres (International Women's Club), founded in June 1933 by Amalia Caballero de Castillo Ledón and a group of women from other countries such as Switzerland, Russia, Holland, and the United States; and the Unión Femenina Ibero-Americana (Ibero-American Feminine Union), founded by Palma Guillén in February 1936 to promote social, cultural, and civic advances for women in the Americas, Portugal, and Spain.[14] Mexican women in the 1930s also participated in several international conferences held in the United States, Mexico, Europe, and Latin America.

Mexican women of the 1934-1940 period demonstrated a continuing interest in developing better health and welfare programs for women and children. In February 1937, the First National Congress of Industrial Hygiene was held in Mexico City, with 576 delegates attending. The congress adopted hundreds of resolutions dedicated to the improvement of working conditions for women and children. Considering the socialistic goals of the president, it is not surprising that the importance of women's and children's welfare was recognized nationally in 1937 by the creation of a Children's Welfare Bureau, a designated department of the federal government. In 1938, the combination of a supportive president and an organized feminine constituency resulted in the establishment of both the

Association of Women Physicians, founded by Dr. Matilde Rodríguez
Cabo, and a League of Mental Hygiene. The commitment by the Cárdenas
administration to improve the lot of women and children was reinforced
again in July 1939 when the National Committee for Mother and Child was
established in Mexico City.[15]

THE ALL-OUT DRIVE FOR THE VOTE

In her 1938 book *El derecho al voto para la mujer* (*Woman's Right To
Vote*), Dr. Esther Chapa noted with dismay that the law excluding women
from voting placed them automatically "in the same category as vagabonds,
inmates of insane asylums, owners of houses of prostitution, ex-convicts,
gamblers, fugitives from justice, and other public charges to whom the vote
is also denied."[16] After years of struggle and disappointment, Mexican
women leaders decided to concentrate their major efforts upon achieving
suffrage. In July 1930, delegates to the Seventh Congress for the Women's
International League for Peace and Freedom proclaimed suffrage a primary
goal.[17] In 1931, the PNR, recognizing women's enormous political potential, called the first officially sponsored PNR meeting that specifically
addressed women's rights, problems, and needs. It was at this meeting that
Cuca García accused former President Calles and President Ortiz Rubio,
both present, of murdering *campesinos*. García was immediately arrested
and imprisoned. However, within a few hours, as word of the event spread,
thousands of women converged on the jail and the police, fearing a riot,
were forced to release García.[18]

In January 1932, feminists Florinda Lazos León, Elvia Carrillo Puerto,
Edelmira Rojas Vda. de Escudero, and María Ríos Cárdenas resolved to
go directly to Congress to demand women's suffrage. Amid the congressmen's laughter, Elvia Carrillo protested, "We [women] need to live.
Women ought to go to the Congress, because the nation is not made up of
men only. . . . "[19] However, despite the pressure of repeated requests for
suffrage, the congressmen refused to comply.

In 1935, women founded the most powerful Mexican women's organization of the 1930s. Cuca García, in an attempt to provide greater organizational and ideological coherence to the women's movement, organized the
Frente Unico Pro Derechos de la Mujer (The Sole Front for Women's
Rights [FUPDM]) and served as its first secretary general. García was
described as "a short, round little woman of forty with a serene face, an
inexhaustible wealth of physical energy and the utter simplicity of all those
who have dedicated their lives to a cause that is beyond all thought of self."
Increasingly, García came to be associated with Mexico's radical Left, led
by Minister of Communications Francisco Múgica and Senator Ernesto Soto

Reyes. Former President Emilio Portes Gil identified García with the Communist women (led by Dr. Matilde Rodríguez Cabo) who were directing a campaign to discredit him as president of the National Executive Committee of the party in order to advance Múgica to the presidency in the upcoming 1940 election.[20]

The women working in close collaboration with Cuca García in the FUPDM were mostly Socialists and Communists, and they included Consuelo Uranga, Dr. Esther Chapa, Soledad Orozco Avila (who participated in the Red Battalions during the Revolution), and Frida Kahlo (painter and wife of muralist Diego Rivera). The FUPDM's goal was to expand women's awareness beyond the demand for suffrage, and thus to develop a basis for collective solidarity from which women could advance their general status. In an attempt to incorporate women from all social classes and ethnic backgrounds, the FUPDM presented a comprehensive program with the following objectives: 1) the unrestricted right of women to vote and to be elected to office; 2) modification of the Civil Code of 1928 to allow for equalization of legal rights between the sexes; 3) modification of the federal Labor Law of 1931 to allow for women's maternity needs; 4) amendment of the Agrarian Code to allow those women who fulfilled the same qualifications as men to be eligible for land distribution; 5) protection of women government employees; 6) integration of indigenous women into Mexico's social and political life; 7) establishment of employment centers for unemployed women; 8) creation of special programs for treatment of children's problems and for protection of infants; and 9) establishment of a broad program of cultural education for women. In addition to women's issues, the FUPDM's platform included public praise for democratic countries, and public condemnation for both imperialism and fascism. The success of the FUPDM was reflected both in the composition of its constituency and in the size of its membership. By 1939, the FUPDM had consolidated hundreds of women's groups and was composed of eight hundred organizations whose membership totaled more than fifty thousand women.[21]

In the spring of 1936, the PNR granted women the right to vote in party primaries and to hold full membership in the labor union section, *campesino* section, and women's section (Acción Femenina). It was reported that 2,550 women participated in these primaries in the Federal District (the district in which women's political activity was greatest). Almost simultaneously, Mexican states began to grant women suffrage. Guanajuato allowed limited suffrage in 1934; Puebla followed in 1936; and suffrage was granted shortly thereafter in the states of Veracruz, Durango, Tamaulipas, and Hidalgo.[22]

Nevertheless, the tempestuous nature of Mexican politics in 1936 caused women's issues to be temporarily subordinated to other political affairs as Cárdenas became preoccupied with both internal political dissension and foreign affairs. Internally, the nation was polarized politically by radicals and conservatives, who were fighting pitched battles in the streets, especially over church-state jurisdiction; Mexican labor was in the throes of a major reorganization; and PNR "in-fighting" had escalated greatly. Externally, Mexicans were paying close attention to the developing civil war in Spain, and foreigners were continuing their efforts to exploit Mexico commercially.

One of the president's immediate political concerns was the struggle within the PNR's upper echelon. The political battle raged between conservative Portes Gil (who, before becoming president, had served as Calles's Attorney General and later had served as head of the PNR Executive Committee) and the radicals led by General Múgica. The Múgica faction viewed Portes Gil as a conservative Calles hold-over, and they demanded his resignation. Many leftist women, including Cuca García, Dr. Esther Chapa, Professor Esperanza Balmaceda de Josefe, and Dr. Matilde Rodríguez Cabo, joined the radicals in their attempt to oust Portes Gil from power. In August 1936, the leftists finally succeeded. Feminists were overjoyed by his overthrow because they thought it would speed the passage of suffrage. General Múgica, who had presidential ambitions, had openly courted the women's support. Múgica's attempt to portray himself as a suffrage advocate was ironic because he had been absent in 1917 when his own committee voted on suffrage at the Constitutional Congress and had provided little support for women afterward.[23] However, Múgica's exreme leftist politics made him unacceptable to Cárdenas as a presidential candidate, and Múgica withdrew his candidacy.

Church-state disputes also absorbed a great deal of the president's attention. However, unlike the 1920s, which were filled with widespread violence, the 1930s were characterized by serious but scattered clashes between church and state supporters, mainly over control of education. In October 1934, Congress adopted the Cárdenas Six-Year Plan, with socialized education as one of its basic goals. In an attempt to extricate the church from education, the Plan extended federal control over primary, secondary, and normal schools.

New definitions outlining the rights and duties of both student and teacher arose from the Plan. For example, the definitions stated that children deserved good schools and good teachers, as well as the companionship of members of the opposite sex. The boys "have a right to be educated with the girls, and the girls with the boys, because . . . man does not live in a world exclusively masculine, or . . . woman in one exclusively feminine." With Socialist education, teachers (mainly women) assumed an even more crucial societal role. Cárdenas stated, "The revolutionary teacher must be a social leader, an advisor, an orientor" who "must not only teach how to read and write, but . . . also show the proletariat the manner of living together better, of creating a more human and just existence." The government's official position was that the school was "the determining factor in the new economic and social order" and the child was to be "an agent of social transformation."[24]

Despite Cárdenas's optimism and good intentions, many parents were deeply resentful over the institutionalization of a Socialist education program. In September 1934, at least thirty thousand Catholic women in Mexico City protested the closing of churches and the establishment of Socialist education.[25] There was even an attempt to launch another Cristero Rebellion, and physical attacks were renewed on teachers and schools. Between 1935 and 1939, almost three hundred rural schoolteachers were murdered.[26] To allow them to defend themselves, Cárdenas directed that all rural teachers be armed. In addition, the government leveled a fifty-peso fine on parents who refused to send their children to state-required classes. Although considerable violence was perpetrated by both sides, church-state tension had eased greatly by 1940.

The Spanish Civil War, in which Mexico supported the Republic, absorbed a great deal of the president's time and diverted attention from the Mexican women's movement. In addition, the Spanish Civil War was detrimental to the women's suffrage issue in Mexico because it raised serious questions about women's political loyalties. When Spanish women voted for the first time in municipal elections in April 1933, and for the first time nationally in November of the same year, the Spanish Socialist party suffered serious setbacks. The Spanish Catholic Church, bitterly resisting the anti-clerical reforms of the Spanish Republic, openly exerted its influence on women voters and successfully controlled their votes. By 1936, political parties in Spain had become severely polarized, permitting General Franco to launch an attack against the Republic. The disastrous Spanish Civil War that followed caused many Mexican legislators to reconsider giving Mexican women the right to vote, fearing that the same fate might befall Mexico.

In 1936, despite the president's absorption in many pressing national and international issues, it appeared that Mexican women would soon be granted suffrage. The National Council of Women's Suffrage decided, at its January 1936 meeting, to launch a renewed all-out drive for the vote. This meeting was attended by Mexico's most illustrious feminist leaders: Margarita Robles de Mendoza, Juana Gutiérrez de Mendoza (representing the Amigas del Pueblo), Elvia Carrillo Puerto, and Cuca García, among others. Women from the FUPDM planned to take the suffrage issue directly to the president and to Congress.[27]

The year 1937 began with particularly positive signs for the women's movement. In January, political asylum was arranged for Leon Trotsky and his wife, both known to favor equal rights for women; and in February, Cárdenas gave an interview to Joseph Freeman of *New Masses*, in which he indicated his continuing support of the women's movement. Cárdenas stated, "We intend to give to the women of Mexico all the opportunities to participate in social life in equality of circumstances with men."[28]

In the PNR primary elections of April 1937, women participated in large numbers nationally for the first time. FUPDM Secretary General Cuca García and Soledad Orozco Avila were selected as candidates for the Chamber of Deputies in Uruapán, Michoacán and in Guanajuato, even though the National Election Law still restricted eligibility to males. As had been the case with Hermila Galindo and Elvia Carrillo Puerto, García and Orozco sought election on the basis that the Mexican Constitution did not specifically exclude women from citizenship. The women's plan was to run for office in the regular June election and then, if elected, to appeal to the Mexican Supreme Court to overrule Article 37 because it conflicted with Articles 34 and 35, which conferred citizenship upon all Mexicans. Although opposed by four PNR-supported candidates, García won her election in Uruapán. Orozco, a journalist and widow with six children, also won her race. The challenge to male exclusivity in the Chamber of Deputies posed by these two women forced a decision upon the PNR National Executive Committee, which ruled that a constitutional amendment would be needed before women could vote or stand as candidates in national elections. Accordingly, the Electoral Committee of the Chamber of Deputies awarded the contested seats to the women's male opponents.[29]

In response to the election reverses of García and Orozco, women demanded that President Cárdenas clarify his position on women's rights. Frustrated by delays, in August 1937 the women undertook their most extreme action; they staged a hunger strike outside the president's home in Mexico City. The strike continued for two weeks until Cárdenas, unwilling to allow the protesters to become political martyrs, promised in a speech before the Mexican Feminine Confederation in Veracruz to introduce a bill in the next congressional session that would establish equal political and civil rights for women.[30]

Subsequent to the president's pledge, an outpouring of mail from both within and outside Mexico urging suffrage for women flooded the government palace in Mexico City. Elvia Carrillo Puerto, Margarita Robles de Mendoza, Cuca García, Matilde Rodríguez Cabo, and even Hermila Galindo, who had been in retirement since Carranza's death, sent messages encouraging the passage of suffrage legislation.[31] Telegrams poured in from all over the world. Women in the United States expressed a special interest in the fate of their Mexican sisters. North American Anna Kelton Wiley, representing the National Women's Party, visited Mexico in May 1937 to meet with members of the FUPDM. García gave her a message for women in the United States, asserting that the Mexican government had "taken advantage of services, [and] sent us [women] back home" but "we are not discouraged by the indifference of our Government in denying us our rights." García related how she had been nominated for Congress with a ten-thousand-vote margin but had not been allowed to take her seat, expressing outrage over the decision of the PNR Board because it "does not represent the will of the people." Defiantly, García vowed to run again and to continue the fight for women's equality.[32]

On November 23, 1937, Cárdenas sent to the Senate his proposed amendment of Article 34 providing suffrage for women. He stated that women had participated in the revolutionary struggle and deserved recognition and that if it were true that many women were ignorant and unprepared to participate politically, the same was true for men. Also, if women remained outside the political structure, they could be susceptible to church influence. When the Senate committee recommended changes to the amendment, the president, pressured by the powerful labor union Confederación de Trabajadores de México (CTM) and by numerous feminist organizations, returned the amendment to Congress. On December 18, 1937, the committee recommended passage of the original amendment, and on December 21 the Senate approved the measure by unanimous vote. Two days later, the amendment went to the Chamber of Deputies, where it was referred to the Committee on Constitutional Questions. This committee then adjourned without acting on it. Even though passage of the amendment was postponed, women remained optimistic, sensing imminent victory. With no intention of letting the opportunity slip away, they accelerated their lobbying activities.[33]

The president's attention, however, was soon absorbed by his pending proposals for PNR reorganization and by international crises. By the end of 1937, Cárdenas's PNR reorganization plans were complete: the party name was changed to the Partido Revolucionario Mexicano (Mexican Revolutionary Party [PRM]); a popular sector of the PRM was formed that provided for individual membership (in which women members had the same rights as men); and a special women's section was established, with representation on the PRM National Executive Committee.[34]

In the spring of 1938, international conflict was barely avoided when Mexico expropriated foreign oil companies. Expropriation resulted partly from a dispute begun in 1936 between labor and management within the petroleum industry. When Mexican oil workers struck for higher wages and better working conditions, the oil companies refused to negotiate seriously with union representatives. As the strike in the oil industry began to affect other sections of the economy, Cárdenas ordered the dispute settled by an arbitration board. The board ordered an increase in wages and improved conditions. The oil companies refused to accept the decision and appealed to the Mexican Supreme Court, which then upheld the decision of the arbitration board. When the companies refused to obey the Supreme Court decision in its entirety, Cárdenas nationalized the holdings of seventeen foreign oil companies.

In this time of international crisis, the entire Mexican nation, including the church, united behind the president. Feminist Leagues helped rally women to the aid of the republic. In the capital, the president's wife, Amalia Solórzano de Cárdenas, headed a collection drive to help defray the expenses of expropriation. Thousands of women from all social classes contributed everything from candelabras to turkeys to gold wedding bands. The first lady remarked, "I feel happy to see how the Mexican woman responds when she is called upon in the name of her country." Ironically, although Mexican political leaders praised the generosity of the Mexican woman and her strong sense of nationalism, they still refused to give her the vote.[35]

In June 1938, Cárdenas called a special congressional session for early July. On July 6, the proposed amendment to Article 34 came up again for consideration by the Chamber of Deputies. Because no one was willing to openly defy the president, the amendment was unanimously approved the same day and then referred to the state legislatures for ratification.[36]

During the period between Congress's adjournment in July and its opening session in September 1938, women continued their all-out drive for the vote. On September 1, in his annual address to Congress, Cárdenas called for quick ratification of the measure:

I hope . . . that the counting of the ratifications of the reform of
Constitutional Article 34 which concedes full political rights to women,
[will] be accomplished as soon as possible, [by] urging the legislatures
of the states to send in their votes, for this reform corrects the injustice
with which up to now Mexican women have been treated.[37]

By the end of 1938, a majority of Mexican states had ratified Cárdenas's amendment to Constitutional Article 34. In May 1939, however, with the congressional session near adjournment, no congressional action had been taken on the amendment, even though all twenty-eight states had ratified it.[38] It appeared that Mexican women were defeated in their quest for suffrage.

The issue of women's suffrage was preempted once again, this time by the struggle within the PRM to select a presidential candidate for the 1940 election. This selection was viewed as a crucial political decision because conservatism had made a strong resurgence, especially in areas of western Mexico where Cristeros had been active. Also, a conservative organization called the "Anti-Communist Center" had attracted wide support. The center issued a call for *hispanidad* (cultural, historical, religious, and linguistic unity of the Spanish world) and for maintenance of the institutions of the family and the church within a corporate state under a hierarchical, authoritarian government. *Hispanidad* adherents were mostly Catholics frustrated by the actions of a revolutionary government which they felt did not respect their religious convictions.

Mexico's extreme political divisions were foremost in Cárdenas's mind when he selected his successor. Fearful that General Múgica's candidacy would further disrupt the delicate political balance, Cárdenas turned reluctantly to moderate General Manuel Avila Camacho, his National Defense Minister. Camacho assured the public that although he and his wife were faithful Roman Catholics, he would continue to support women's interests.[39]

The conservatives, who were consolidated behind the Partido de Acción Nacional (National Action Party [PAN]) and its candidate, General Juan Andreu Almazán, posed the most serious threat to Camacho. Almazán campaigned against Communist influence, atheists, the "godless public schools," and the immigration of Spanish refugees. Capitalists, the clergy, the wealthy, the Cristeros, the fascists, unorganized labor, and *campesinos* who had not converted to socialism provided Almazán's principal support. In 1939, to garner women's support, the pro-Almazán coalition organized the Partido Femenino Idealista (Feminine Idealist Party), which maintained women's groups in all parts of the country and threatened to control most of the women's votes if suffrage were granted before the upcoming election.[40]

With time running out for Congress to adopt the amendment to Article 34, feminists went directly to the National Council of the PRM, as well as to individual members of Congress, to demand the vote. What happened next is still unclear, but Congress adjourned in July 1939 without having altered the National Election Law.[41] In a valiant last effort, Cárdenas pressed for action on the pending suffrage amendment in the September 1, 1939 opening session of Congress:

> From the very beginning of my term I have been urging that the
> grave injustice be rectified that cheats Mexican women of substantial
> rights while, on the other hand, it imposes upon them all the obliga-
> tions of citizenship. Suffrage in Mexico should be made complete by
> giving women the right to vote. Otherwise, the electoral function
> remains incomplete. . . . Although the idea commonly prevails that
> women's suffrage, if enacted, will be accompanied by problems of a
> reactionary nature, this should not prevent the enactment of the meas-
> ure, for it is one of our basic duties to organize and guide along chan-
> nels that are favorable to the nation, the fundamental functions of the
> sovereign prerogatives of the people.[42]

The moderate political stance of President-elect Avila Camacho and the lack of congressional action caused women's hopes to fade. Realizing that only drastic action would have any effect upon the decision-making process, the Acción Femenina Section of the PRM, its affiliated organizations, and other feminist groups sent Cárdenas a telegram on March 24, 1940 urging him to call a special session of Congress as soon as the regular session ended, and to designate the pending suffrage amendment as the sole subject for consideration.[43]

No further action was taken on the women's suffrage amendment, however, because Cárdenas refused to call a special session of Congress. Another opportunity for victory for women's suffrage slipped away, and then Mexico had to turn its full attention to the problems of World War II, which erupted the following month.

WOMEN JOURNALISTS

The 1930s was a period of intense activity for Mexican women journalists, with many women's groups starting their own publications. For example, the Frente Unico Pro Derechos de la Mujer (FUPDM) published the magazine *Mujer Nueva* (*New Woman*), directed by María Efraína Rocha; the Feminine Coordinating Committee for the Defense of the Homeland published *Unidad* (*Unity*), under the direction of María Efraína Rocha and Adriana Lombardo, and later *Rumbos Nuevos* (*New Directions*); and the Democratic Union of Mexican Women, with the National Union of Mexican Women, published *Mujeres*.[44]

In addition to feminist periodicals, women wrote for major newspapers (*Excelsior*, *El Nacional*, and *El Universal*) and for dozens of general-interest magazines. *Revista de Revistas: El Semanario Nacional* covered feminist activities, women in sports, and general news items, although by 1936 gossip about Hollywood stars began to predominate. *El Universal Ilustrado* also covered women's topics, but again interest in Hollywood prevailed by the end of the 1930s. Throughout the 1930s (and until 1943), Emilia Enríquez de Rivera published *El Hogar*, focusing on women in the home. Soledad Orozco Avila collaborated with her husband on the publication *El Bajio*, assuming control after his death, and in 1933 moved to the capital, where she often contributed to the newspaper *El Nacional*.[45]

Juana Gutiérrez de Mendoza continued to write extensively, with most of her work reflecting her interest in indigenous culture and rural education. In 1936, she served as director of a women's school called the Industrial Femenina "Josefa Ortíz de Domínguez" in Morelia. Although Gutiérrez always maintained a keen interest in women's rights and education, her involvement in the late 1930s lacked the intensity of her earlier efforts, perhaps because of her advancing age, her disenchantment with feminist leadership, or both. She eventually broke away from feminists, including Communist colleagues such as Cuca García and Adelina Zendejas, because of their "dogmatism."[46]

Gutiérrez spent most of her time writing for magazines and newspapers and authoring pamphlets. Her publication *Alma mexicana: Por la Tierra y*

Por la Raza (*Mexican Heart: For the Land and for the People*) appeared in 1935. The magazine was published for only a short while in Mexico City and then reappeared in Morelia in 1941. Gutiérrez's despair, prompted by thirty-five years of incessant struggle, surfaced in the November 1, 1935 issue, when she lamented:

> My sixty years have not served me for anything. I can't use them to make a blindfold for my eyes or a shroud for my conscience. It is a problem that has only this solution: to bear however possible these sixty years with all their impediments and to continue the task with the sad understanding that it is futile.

Gutiérrez explained that she had the right to shrug her shoulders or to go to a corner in any part of the world to rest, but she had not found that corner. Gutiérrez refused to retreat in silence, which she considered "the most repugnant of complicities." Instead, she chose to remain active and to publish *Alma Mexicana* to symbolize the "soul" of an inextinguishable race.

In the November 15, 1935 issue, Gutiérrez discussed the disagreements and the hostility raging at the time between moderate and leftist feminists. In a candid article entitled "Las mujeres sin patria" ("Women without a Country"), she expressed her disenchantment with some of the feminist leadership, which she considered bourgeoise and "un-Mexican." Gutiérrez directed her criticism at upper-class feminist Margarita Robles de Mendoza, whom she believed had failed to identify with the egalitarian goals of the Revolution. To illustrate her point, she recalled the time that Robles, introducing a musical trio from Michoacán, made no attempt to pronounce the musicians' names because she found it too difficult. Gutiérrez objected to Robles's lack of national pride in indigenous culture, noting that Robles knew how to pronounce the names of foreign enemies of Mexico. What Mexico needed, Gutiérrez maintained, was not "women without a country" but Mexican women who understood what a homeland and home represent.[47]

Gutiérrez continued to write on a wide range of topics for various publications, such as *El Heraldo de México*, directed by former PLM leader Camilo Arriaga.[48] She also wrote several short pamphlets, including *El cuatatapa*, a children's story, and *Los tres problemas nacionales* (*The Three National Problems*), in which she focused on the constitution, national unity, and economic reintegration, both published in 1933.[49] In 1935, Gutiérrez published the following: *Preliminarias de combate* (*Combat Preliminaries*), sponsored by the Amigas del Pueblo, which was dedicated in part to the Bloque Nacional de Mujeres Revolucionarias;[50] *Camisas de colores* (*Colored Shirts*), also sponsored by the Amigas del Pueblo; *Antorcha nueva* (*New Torch*), a long poem about struggle that paid homage to teachers and to her granddaughters; *La campana de la escuela* (*The School Bell*), written for the families of students in the Benito Juárez

School (where Gutiérrez worked), urged parents to take an active interest in the education of their children; and *La republica femenina* (*The Feminine Republic*), an important pamphlet in which Gutiérrez described her attitudes about women's role in society. (In this pamphlet Gutiérrez stated her belief that the parallel to class antagonism was the biological antagonism between the sexes; accordingly, she advised women not to imitate men but to develop their own interests.)

Gutiérrez also reactivated the Amigas del Pueblo, in May 1936, and helped to found another women's group, La Republica Femenina (The Feminine Republic), whose members included Concha Michel, Laura Mendoza, and Aurora Martínez. La Republica Femenina called for the formation of a separate feminist republic and for organization of *campesinas* into communities with day-care centers, cooperatives, *ejidos* (communal lands), and banks. These communities were to be located in south-central Mexico. In 1940, Gutiérrez co-authored *Llamada la atención a la conciencia nacional* (*Call to National Attention*), a short pamphlet that criticized the church, called attention to women's welfare issues, and demanded that women have the vote and at least 50 percent of all employment opportunities. These demands were signed by co-authors Concha Michel, Dr. Antonia Ursúa, Elena Torres, and several others.[51]

In 1941, Gutiérrez prepared a proposal and plans for a girls school in Morelia. The project was never realized, however, because Gutiérrez died the following year.[52]

WOMEN REVOLUTIONARY LEADERS

The revitalization of the women's movement in the 1930s was due in large part to a supportive president and the formation of numerous politically active women's organizations. Many women leaders who had been inactive reemerged during this important period. Carmen Parra Vda. de Alaniz, a revolutionary leader from Casas Grandes, Chihuahua, who had been imprisoned during the Revolution, served as a representative for the Frente Unico Pro Derechos de la Mujer (FUPDM) in Chihuahua and was active in anti-Fascist groups. Puebla's Guadalupe Narváez, who had worked with Carmen Serdán and the Constitutionalists, helped found the FUPDM and served as an officer. Julia Nava de Ruisánchez, a prominent professor, feminist writer, and editor, originally from Nuevo León, who since shortly after the turn of the century had participated in such revolutionary feminist organizations as the Hijas de Cuauhtémoc and Regeneración y Concordia, continued her feminist activities and served as president of the Ateneo Mexicano de Mujeres in the 1950s. Soledad Orozco Avila, a teacher and writer from Jalisco who had been part of the Casa del Obrero Mundial and had worked for the government for years, ran for office in Guanajuato at the same time as did Cuca García and remained active in the PRM.[53]

In addition to the reemergence of these women leaders of the 1920s, some women who had been relatively unknown in the 1920s assumed prominent leadership positions in the 1930s. Dr. Matilde Rodríguez Cabo, Dr. Esther Chapa, Margarita Robles de Mendoza, Amalia Caballero de Castillo Ledón, Palma Guillén, Eulalia Guzmán, and Leonor Llach were professional women who played a seminal role in the 1930s' women's rights movement.

Dr. Matilde Rodríguez Cabo and Dr. Esther Chapa continued to collaborate politically on projects aimed at improving the welfare of both women and children. Rodríguez Cabo wrote numerous articles as well as the book *La mujer y la revolución (Women and the Revolution)* (1937), in which she outlined the contributions of many women to the Revolution and made a strong case for women's suffrage. Chapa wrote for numerous scientific journals and for newspapers, such as *El Nacional*, and was the first woman named to be head of the Microbiology Department in the Faculty of Medicine at the Universidad Nacional Autónoma de México (UNAM) in Mexico City. An active member of the Communist Party, Chapa made several trips to the People's Republic of China before her death from cancer in December 1970.[54]

Margarita Robles de Mendoza continued her feminist activities, serving as the first president of the Unión de Mujeres Americanas (UMA), director of the Acción Femenina sector of the PRM, and delegate to a peace conference in Buenos Aires sponsored by the Inter-American Commission of the Pan American Union. Amalia Caballero de Castillo Ledón had a distinguished writing and diplomatic career. She was a founder of the Ateneo Mexicano de Mujeres and the Club Internacional de Mujeres, and served in several government posts, including Undersecretary for Cultural Affairs in the Ministry of Education (1959). In addition, during the 1940s and 1950s, Caballero de Castillo Ledón represented Mexico in several international women's conferences and was elected vice-president and then president of the Inter-American Commission of Women. She also represented Mexico on the United Nations Commission on the Status of Women and was appointed to serve as Minister to Sweden and later as Minister to Switzerland.[55] Palma Guillén, a prominent educator, had an equally distinguished diplomatic career. In 1935, Cárdenas appointed her Minister to Colombia, the first woman to hold such a post. Then she served as Minister to Denmark, and as Consul in Milan, Italy, and later as Ambassador to the League of Nations. In addition to her diplomatic service, Guillén continued to write and to publish.

Writer Leonor Llach was a founder of the Ateneo Mexicano de Mujeres and of the Organización Nacional Femenina of the PRM. Llach held a variety of government positions in the Department of Public Education, Department of Health, and Department of the Library. Although Eulalia Guzmán lived abroad during most of the 1920s, and for a good part of the 1930s, when she returned to Mexico she participated actively in women's organizations and became head of the Department of Archeology at the National Museum of Anthropology.[56]

Much of the women's leadership in the 1930s came from members of the Communist party. Dr. Esther Chapa, Dr. Matilde Rodríguez Cabo, Consuelo Uranga, Concha Michel, Esperanza Balmaceda, and Adelina Zendejas, all Communists, helped to focus attention on human rights and women's issues. In her student days, Consuelo Uranga, originally from Chihuahua, had represented Mexico at the Feminist Congress against the War in 1914, and had been imprisoned for her radical ideas. Concha Michel, an active and versatile personality, was a writer and singer from Jalisco. In 1935, she helped organize the Bloque Nacional de Mujeres Revolucionarias and, along with two hundred women and three hundred children, participated in the takeover of a hacienda. Michel also founded an industrial school near the pyramids of San Juan Teotihuacán. Professor Esperanza Balmaceda continued her revolutionary feminist activities in the FUPDM and as the second president of the Unión de Mujeres Americanas. Although Adelina Zendejas, born in Toluca in 1915, was a young woman in the 1930s, she participated actively in the women's movement. Today, she continues to write for newspapers and magazines, often under the pseudonyms "Victoria Miranda," "Yolia," and "Mara Blanco."[57]

Some of the women who had been active leaders earlier in the Revolution either retired during this period or continued their political activities in a limited way. Carmen Serdán, who had been at the center of the Madero movement in Puebla, was granted a small government pension upon retirement, but it was not adequate to support her and she was forced to work in the library of the National Teachers School. Serdán died in 1948 in Mexico City, and her remains are located in the Serdán tomb in her hometown of Puebla.[58] Sara Pérez de Madero left Mexico after her husband's assassination and lived in New York until 1916, at which time she returned to Mexico, where she died in 1951 at the age of seventy-nine.[59] Elisa Acuña y Rossetti, after collaborating with the PLM and the Zapatistas, limited the scale of her political activities following Zapata's assassination in 1919 and ended up working at the National Library. Acuña died in 1946 and is buried in Mexico City.[60] Elvia Carrillo Puerto remained active throughout the 1920s and 1930s; she died in Mexico City in 1965, destitute and largely forgotten.[61]

There was a very special, small group of women leaders still living during this period who had participated actively in all phases of the three decades of revolutionary struggle. Cuca García and Juana Gutiérrez de

Mendoza were among the few survivors who lived to carry the spirit of the Revolution into the 1930s. It is a sad commentary that both died unrewarded for their efforts. García died in the 1970s, possibly of malnutrition; Gutiérrez, poor and forgotten, died on July 13, 1942.[62]

SUMMARY

In the period from 1934 to 1940, it appeared that women would be granted suffrage and assume their rightful place in Mexican society. They came closer than ever before to acquiring basic political equality, but because of their traditional link with the church, male revolutionaries did not trust women sufficiently to grant them suffrage. In addition to the church-state controversy, internal political dissension (political intrigue and presidential succession struggles) and external political influences (the Spanish Civil War and the expropriation of foreign oil companies) stole the political focus away from women's demands for equality. Further, it appears that male chauvenism continued to play a significant role in the refusal of Mexican men to recognize women as their political equals.[63] During this period of such high hopes, Mexican women came tantalizingly close to obtaining their goal, only to have that hard-fought victory slip away at the last minute because of pressures resulting from unforeseen political and international events.

▪ 6 ▪

Conclusion

The thirty-year period of the Mexican Revolution, 1910 to 1940, was a time of profound change for Mexican women. Changes in women's status resulted from the expansion of women's educational opportunities; the advances in industrialization that provided new jobs for women; the impact of socialism and communism upon Mexican politics; and the interaction of Mexican women with European and U.S. feminists, which greatly encouraged Mexican women in their struggle to attain equality.

During the Revolution, Mexican women undertook new social, economic, and military responsibilities; they traveled throughout the republic as never before; and they organized themselves on a broad scale for political purposes. Women participated in the actual warfare of the Revolution as *soldaderas*; they were instrumental in the formation of revolutionary plans, goals, and objectives; and they were actively involved in virtually all other phases of the efforts to implement revolutionary goals.

Despite their myriad contributions, women were neither recognized adequately nor granted the political equality promised them. While a few revolutionary women were awarded small pensions, and some were even commissioned with rank, many of them lived out their lives in poverty and died unknown. Tragically, there was truth in the observation of North American writer Ernest Gruening that "the Revolution has done little, purposefully, toward the emancipation of women."

For Mexican women, a major break in the laws, customs, and traditions that discriminated against them took place during the Porfiriato (1876-1910). The most dramatic opportunities for advancement for women in this pre-revolutionary period occurred in education; consequently, many middle-class women attended schools and universities, and then entered the labor market as teachers, nurses, and government employees. During the Porfiriato, the situation was dismal for lower-class women, who worked for a pittance as domestics or as factory hands, and many had to turn to prostitution to survive. Politically, women founded women's labor organizations and organized anti-Díaz political groups. Women began to write extensively, and were published in books, magazines, and periodicals. No longer confining their subjects to music and religion, women wrote revolutionary pieces that were critical of the Díaz regime and that questioned women's submissive role in society.

It must be remembered that Mexican women of all social classes traditionally suffered severe legal discrimination. Women's lives were strictly circumscribed by laws prohibiting them from entering professions and locking them almost exclusively into marriage and family roles. In addition to the gender-discriminatory nature of Mexican law, the Catholic Church reinforced institutionalized sexism by encouraging women to confine their interests to the family, the home, and the church.

Despite Mexican law and tradition, from the onset of the Revolution (1910-1920) many women welcomed the new social, economic, and political challenges that forced them from traditional roles. Because they traveled extensively for the first time, acquired training previously unavailable to them, assumed positions which in the past had been closed to them, and had opportunities to join women's groups for socioeconomic and political ends, revolutionary women set into play an irresistible momentum that culminated eventually in the attainment of suffrage for all Mexican women.

Women did gain limited legal rights during the early revolutionary period (1910-1920). Divorce was permitted for the first time, and the 1917 Constitution guaranteed some rights for working women. However, political equality remained elusively outside women's grasp, primarily because of the lack of a large broad-based women's movement and women's traditionally close relationship with the church. (Revolutionaries were convinced that church influence had to be destroyed if the Revolution were to succeed.)

Some of the immediate effects of the revolutionary fighting—rape, pillage, death, and disintegration of the family—were particularly devastating to women. Women's traditional existence as wife and mother was disrupted by separation, death, and the establishment of new liaisons. Unprotected women were often pressed into service, kidnapped, and abused. Under such adverse circumstances, women were compelled further to organize in order to correct injustices and to demand equal rights.

Between 1915 and 1924, the most intense struggle for women's rights in Mexico centered in the state of Yucatán. Site of the first two feminist congresses, Yucatán was the scene of the most active social, political, and economic participation by women in Mexico. Yucatán's leadership in the women's movement resulted from the support of its two Socialist governors, the progressive ideas and activism of its women leaders, and the considerable wealth it derived from henequen production. Yucatán was one of the first Mexican states to provide education for women. Socialist Governor Salvador Alvarado expanded women's educational opportunities and greatly improved working conditions for women, in an attempt to incorporate them into his structure for a new society.

Alvarado's reform programs were expanded by his successor, Socialist Governor Felipe Carrillo Puerto. Under Governor Carrillo Puerto, women were granted suffrage, were permitted to run for elective office, and were given access to birth control information. Elvia Carrillo Puerto, the governor's younger sister, organized women into Ligas Feministas, which sponsored women's meetings, conducted night schools, and launched statewide campaigns against illiteracy, superstition, alcoholism, poor hygiene, and improper child care.

The execution of Governor Carrillo Puerto in 1924 abruptly halted nine years of Yucatecan social reform. The conservative administration that succeeded Carrillo Puerto dissolved the Ligas Feministas, removed women from their positions in municipal and state government, cancelled women's suffrage, and halted government social programs. As a consequence, by 1924 the momentum of the Mexican women's movement shifted from Yucatán to Mexico City, where feminists in the 1920s and 1930s organized on a massive scale in an effort to gain equality.

Mexican women continued to achieve only limited success in their struggle for equality in the period from 1920 to 1934. After helping to win the Revolution and to carry out many revolutionary reforms, especially in the fields of education and health, women received few immediate benefits. There were several reasons why women's needs were ignored: the ruling "Sonoran Triangle" did not view women's rights as an integral part of the goals of the Revolution; national and international crises preempted attention to the cause for women's rights; and women's continued support of the church embittered and threatened revolutionary leaders, who felt they must protect the gains of the Revolution against this conservative "fifth column" within Mexico.

Arguments favoring women's rights were weakened politically by women's open sympathy for the de la Huerta Revolt against the central government in 1923; their support of the Cristero Rebellion in 1926; the role of women conspirators in planning and carrying out the assassination of President-elect Obregón in 1928; and the resistance of many women to the government's program of Socialist education. Moreover, women's conferences such as the 1925 Congress of "Mujeres de la Raza" revealed serious weaknesses in their organizational, political, and ideological unity. These weaknesses damaged women's image as a political force.

Nevertheless, during the period from 1920 to 1934, women organized on a broader scale than ever before and sponsored several successful women's conferences. A few highly educated women even assumed prominent positions in government and in the universities. By the mid-1930s, the PNR, recognizing women's political potential, acted to incorporate women into the party. However, the key ingredients for acquisition of political equality for Mexican women, such as a supportive president and a strongly organized women's movement, were absent prior to 1934.

During the six-year presidency of Lázaro Cárdenas (1934-1940), women worked concertedly and enthusiastically to achieve suffrage. They faced fewer political obstacles than in the past because both the church and the state, each struggling to protect its own interests, sought women's allegiance. Many women rallied to President Cárdenas because he offered them suffrage and wide participation in government. Under Cárdenas, women's groups were organized and incorporated into the official party. In 1936, the party granted women the right to vote in party primaries, and a few states enacted women's suffrage. In 1938, a national suffrage amendment passed both houses of Congress and was ratified by all twenty-eight states. However, Congress adjourned without completing the ratification process, and the suffrage amendment never became law.

Women's major political stumbling block for political equality in the 1930s continued to be their allegiance to the Catholic Church. Women's overwhelming support of the conservative candidate in the 1940 presidential election confirmed the lingering suspicions held by many radicals about women's political loyalty to the revolutionary government. In addition, Mexico's internal problems (conflict with the church, political intrigue, and bitter controversy over presidential succession) and external problems (the Spanish Civil War and foreign oil expropriations) directed the political focus away from the women's struggle for equality.

* * *

Despite their extraordinary revolutionary efforts and the extensive support they marshalled in their quest for equality, women remained disenfranchised long after the Revolution. Although women had learned to organize politically and had acquired considerable experience in working together to achieve common goals, they were unable to maintain the political focus on women's suffrage during the 1940s because when World War II swept the globe, the women's cause was subjugated politically to the war.

In the post-World War II period, Mexican women finally won their battle for political equality. On December 31, 1946, they received the right to vote in municipal elections. Seven years later, on December 31, 1953, after the church and state had arrived at a *modus vivendi* and the Partido Revolucionario Institucional (PRI) was firmly in control of Mexican politics, women were granted national suffrage. But it was not until 1958 that Mexican women voted in their first presidential election.

Since 1958, several women have served in Mexico's Congress. More Mexican women continue to enter the universities, to join the work force, to have access to birth control information, and to participate in international women's organizations. Mexico now offers opportunities for women in virtually all fields, including medicine, engineering, law, and business. Moreover, interest in women's studies programs has increased, and currently such courses are offered at the Universidad Nacional Autónoma de México and at the Colegio de México.

In 1974, Mexico adopted the equivalent of the proposed U.S. Equal Rights Amendment, giving equality to both sexes. That same year the Civil Code was revised to give women equal rights and obligations in marriage and divorce. In 1975, Mexico assumed an international leadership role in women's rights by hosting the United Nations Año Internacional de la Mujer (International Women's Year) meeting in Mexico City.

In spite of significant gains in the 1980s, serious socioeconomic inequalities persist and are waiting to be addressed by a new set of leaders from the ranks of modern Mexican women. The emergence of these modern Mexican women has resulted directly from the experiences, dedication, and sacrifices of their predecessors in the Mexican Revolution. These heroic predecessors have left a rich cultural heritage that challenges both Mexicanas and Chicanas to persevere in the quest for legal, economic, and social equality.

List of Feminist Organizations, 1870-1936

Date Organized	Name of Organization	Emphasis
1870	La Siempreviva (Yucatán)	Women's rights
1904	Admiradoras de Juárez	Social change and women's rights
	Sociedad Protectora de la Mujer	Social change and women's rights
1907	Hijas de Anáhuac	Social change and women's rights
1909	Amigas del Pueblo	Social change and women's rights
1910	Hijas de Cuauhtémoc	Social change and women's rights
	Liga Femenina Anti-reelectionista "Josefa Ortiz de Domínguez"	General social change
1911	Regeneración y Concordia	Social change and women's rights
1913	Club Lealtad	Social change and women's rights
1919	Consejo Nacional de Mujeres Mexicanas	Social change and women's rights
1920	Consejo Feminista Mexicano	Women's rights
	International Council of Women (ICW)	Social change and women's rights

Date Organized	Name of Organization	Emphasis
1922	Ligas Feministas (Yucatán)	Social change and women's rights
	Mexican branch of the Pan American League for the Advancement of Women	Women's rights
1923	Liga Feminista Mexicana	Women's rights
	Unión Cooperativa "Mujeres de la Raza"	International networking and women's rights
1933	Club Internacional de Mujeres	International networking and women's rights
1934	Unión de Mujeres Americanas (UMA)	International networking and women's rights
1935	Frente Unico Pro Derechos de la Mujer (FUPDM)	Social change and women's rights
1936	Unión Femenina Ibero-Americana	International networking and women's rights
	Liga de Acción Femenina	Women's rights

List of Women's Congresses Held in Mexico, 1916-1934

Date	Congress
1916	First Feminist Congress (Mérida)
	Second Feminist Congress (Mérida)
1923	First Feminist Congress of the Pan American Women's League (Mexico City)
1925	Congress of "Mujeres de la Raza" (Mexico City)
1931	First National Congress of Women Workers and Peasants (Mexico City)
1933	Second National Congress of Women Workers and Peasants (Mexico City)
1934	Third National Congress of Women Workers and Peasants (Guadalajara)

Notes

CHAPTER I

1. Moisés González Navarro, *El porfiriato: La vida social*. Vol. IV of Daniel Cosío Villegas, ed., *Historia moderna de México*, 9 vols. (México: Editorial Hermes, 1957), p. 370.

2. José E. Iturriaga, *La estructura social y cultural de México* (México: Fondo de Cultura Económica, 1951), p. 16.

3. John Kenneth Turner, *Barbarous Mexico* (Austin: University of Texas Press, 1969), pp. 42, 49-52, 65, 92.

4. Silvia Hilda Celorio Guevara, "Delincuencia femenina" (Thesis, Universidad Nacional Autónoma de México, 1964), p. 166; González Navarro, *El porfiriato: La vida social*, pp. 413-14.

5. Luis Lara y Pardo, *La prostitución en México* (México: Librería de la Vda. de Ch. Bouret, 1908), pp. 18-20, 22, 26-27, 29, 108. Dr. Lara y Pardo reported that only 5 percent of the prostitutes were literate.

6. Hermila Galindo, *Estudio de la Srita. Hermila Galindo con motivo de los temas que han de absolverse en el Segundo Congreso Feminista de Yucatán* (Mérida: Imprenta del Gobierno Constitucionalista, 1916), p. 14.

7. Ernest Gruening, *Mexico and Its Heritage* (New York: The Century Co., 1928), p. 625.

8. Génaro García, *Apuntes sobre la condición de la mujer* (México: Compañía Limitada de Tipógraficos, 1891), pp. 7, 42-46.

9. Ibid., pp. 71, 78-79.

10. Wilfrid Hardy Callcott, *Liberalism in Mexico, 1857-1929* (Palo Alto: Stanford University Press, 1931), pp. 80-81.

11. Ibid., p. 81.

12. Frederick C. Turner, *The Dynamic of Mexican Nationalism* (Chapel Hill: University of North Carolina Press, 1968), p. 91.

13. María del Carmen Ochoa Flores, "Desarrollo social de la mujer mexicana" (Thesis, Universidad Nacional Autónoma de México, 1968), p. 35; Callcott, *Liberalism in Mexico*, p. 120; "Acceso a la educación en todos los niveles," in *Derechos de la mujer mexicana* (México: XLVII Legislatura del Congreso de la Unión, 1969), p. 69.

149

14. "Acceso a la educación," p. 70, stated that the opening date for the Escuela Comercial was 1901, but Ana María Flores, "La mujer en la sociedad," in *México: Cincuenta años de revolución*, 4 vols., Vol. II: *La vida social*, ed. by José Iturriaga, Humberto Romero, and Génaro Vázquez Colmenares (México: Fondo de Cultura Económica, 1961), p. 331, stated that the opening date was 1903.

15. "Acceso a la educación," pp. 67-70; "Feminismo," *Enciclopedia de México*, 1970, IV, p. 168.

16. Callcott, *Liberalism in Mexico*, p. 146.

17. Iturriaga, *La estructura social*, p. 14. In the 1890s, a relatively small number of women were government employees; by 1910, 1,785 women were working for the government.

18. "Acceso a la educación," p. 70. For a more detailed account of the life of Margarita Chorné, see "Acceso," p. 115. For a further account of Matilda P. Montoya, see p. 116; María Elvira Bermúdez, "La familia," *México: Cincuenta años de revolución*, 4 vols., Vol. II: *La vida social*, eds., José Iturriaga, Humberto Romero, and Génaro Vázquez Colmenares (México: Fondo de Cultura Económica, 1961), p. 87. *New York Times*, September 26, 1920, p. 14, incorrectly identified Matilda P. Montoya as Teresa Montoya. María Sandoval struggled long to obtain her education. After receiving her degree, Sandoval became so well known that she was invited by President McKinley to come to the United States, become a U.S. citizen, and practice law; but she declined because she preferred a career in her own country.

19. Yolanda Tanabe Velasco, "La mujer y la profesión de contador público en México" (Thesis, Universidad Nacional Autónoma de México, 1962), p. 15; Ana María Flores, "La mujer en la sociedad," p. 331.

20. González Navarro, *El porfiriato: La vida social*, pp. 497-99.

21. "La instrucción nocturna para obreras," *La convención radical obrera*, a. 12, No. 531 (January 16, 1898), p. 1.

22. Ignacio Gamboa, *La mujer moderna* (Hoctún, Yucatán: Imprenta "Gamboa Guzmán," 1906), pp. 92, 121. For examples of other anti-feminist writings, see: P. S. Moebius, *La inferioridad mental de la mujer* (México: Maucci Hermanos, n.d.), and Roberto Nova, *La indigencia espiritual del sexo femenino* (Valencia: F. Sempere y Compañía, Editores, 1908). Nova maintained that women's inferiority stemmed from the limited capacity of their small skulls.

23. For examples of student theses about women, written during the period 1902-1904 at the Instituto Normal del Estado de Pueblo, see the collection at the University of Texas in Austin.

24. Rodney D. Anderson, *Outcasts in Their Own Land: Mexican Industrial Workers, 1906-1911* (DeKalb: Northern Illinois University Press, 1976), p. 41.

25. Dawn Keremitsis, *The Cotton Textile Industry in Porfiriato, Mexico 1870-1910* (New York: Garland Pub., 1987), p. 195.

26. Dawn Keremitsis, *La industria textil mexicana en el siglo XIX* (México: SepSetentas, 1973), p. 65.

27. Ibid, p. 209. Keremitsis noted that in the twentieth century, no more than 18 percent of the textile workers have been women, and that it has been estimated that since the 1950s no more than 5 percent of the textile workers have been women. Keremitsis explained this trend as resulting from the availability of male workers at low wages. Therefore, there has been no need to hire women to reduce labor costs. See ibid., pp. 200-201, and Keremitsis, *The Cotton Textile Industry*, p. 196.

28. Adelina Zendejas, "El movimiento femenil mexicano," *El Día* (June 16, 1975), p. 16. Zendejas concluded that the organization of women textile workers was a precursor of the women rights movement in Mexico.

29. Keremitsis, *The Cotton Textile Industry*, p. 188; Turner, *Barbarous Mexico*, p. 168.

30. Keremitsis, *The Cotton Textile Industry*, pp. 189-90, quoting Veracruz (state), Gobernador, *Memoria del estado, 1900-1902*.

31. Ramon Eduardo Ruiz, *Labor and the Ambivalent Revolutionaries: Mexico, 1911-1923* (Baltimore: The Johns Hopkins University Press, 1976), p. 7, quoting Julio Sesto, *El México de Porfirio Díaz* (Valencia: F. Sempere y Compañía, Editores, 1910), pp. 131, 134, 253.

32. Ana María Hernández, *La mujer mexicana en la industria textil* (México: Tipografía Mod., 1940), p. 25.

33. Keremitsis, *The Cotton Textile Industry*, pp. 190-91; Anderson, *Outcasts*, p. 77.

34. Victor Alba, *Historia de la mujer* (México: Editorial Patria, S.A., 1953), p. 83; Anderson, *Outcasts*, pp. 67-69. Zendejas, "El movimiento," p. 16, listed 1872 as the date of the first Permanent Congress. The date should be 1876. Vivian M. Vallens, "Working Women in Mexico during the Porfiriato, 1880-1910" (Unpublished M.A. thesis, California State University, Long Beach, 1975), p. 69, and John M. Hart, *Anarchism and the Mexican Working Class, 1860-1931* (Austin: University of Texas Press, 1978), p. 55, stated that Huerta focused her organizational activities in the Orizaba region during the 1880s and 1890s.

35. Alvarado Morales Jurado, "La mujer campesina mexicana" (Thesis, Universidad Nacional Autónoma de México, 1954), p. 69; Hernández, *La mujer mexicana*, pp. 35-38. (Hernández was a federal work inspector.) In 1912, after founding the Hijas, María del Carmen Frías and her sister Catalina continued with the Casa del Obrero Mundial in Mexico City. María del Carmen died forgotten in 1935. For more biographical information on the sisters, see Hernández, pp. 40-41.

36. González Navarro, *El porfiriato: La vida social*, pp. 294-97, 310-12. Wages for women varied from 12 to 50 centavos daily.

37. Ibid., p. 310.

38. Ibid., p. 348.

39. Ibid, p. 415. María Antonieta Rascón, "La mujer y la lucha social," *Imagen y realidad de la mujer*, ed. by Elena Urrutia (México: SepSetentas, 1975), stated that the Admiradoras de Juárez was founded in 1906.

40. "Feminismo," p. 172.

41. Mario Gill, "Teresa Urrea, La Santa de Cabora," *Historia Mexicana*, VI, No. 4 (April-June, 1957), pp. 628-30; Frank Bishop Putnam, "Teresa Urrea, The Santa of Cabora," *Southern California Quarterly*, XLV, No. 3 (September 1963), pp. 246-50.

42. Putnam, "Teresa Urrea," pp. 250-55; Gill, "Teresa Urrea," pp. 632-34.

43. Putnam, "Teresa Urrea," pp. 253-54.

44. Ibid., pp. 255-57; Gill, "Teresa Urrea," p. 643.

45. Putnam, "Teresa Urrea," pp. 258-59, 261-64; Gill, "Teresa Urrea," p. 644.

46. James D. Cockcroft, *Intellectual Precursors of the Mexican Revolution, 1900-1913* (Austin: University of Texas Press, 1968), pp. 4-5; Myra Ellen Jenkins, "Ricardo Flores Magon and the Mexican Liberal Party" (Unpublished Ph.D. dissertation, University of New Mexico, 1953), pp. v-vi.

47. Juan Gómez-Quiñones, *Sembradores: Ricardo Flores Magón y El Partido Liberal Mexicano: A Eulogy and Critique*, "La Mujer," Monograph No. 5 (Los Angeles: UCLA Chicano Studies Center, 1973), p. 108.

48. Ricardo Flores Magón, *Semilla libertaria*, 3 vols., Vol. II (México: Ediciones del Grupo Cultural "Ricardo Flores Magón," 1923), pp. 136-37, quoting *Regeneración*, February 12, 1916. In the same article, Ricardo Flores Magón praised Salvador Alvarado for sponsoring the First Feminist Congress. The importance of women in the liberal movement is illustrated further by the extensive correspondence Ricardo maintained with both U.S. and Mexican women radicals while he was imprisoned in Leavenworth, Kansas from 1918 to 1922. For details see ibid., p. 154.

49. Cockcroft, *Intellectual Precursors*, pp. 239-45, has a copy of the PLM reform program.

50. Ibid., p. 86; María de los Angeles Mendieta Alatorre, "Las mexicanas en la revolución," *Novedades* (Suplemento, "México en la cultura"), November 6, 1966, p. 1; Gómez-Quiñones, *Sembradores*, pp. 13-14.

51. María de los Angeles Mendieta Alatorre, *La mujer en la revolución mexicana* (México: Talleres Gráficos de la Nación, 1961), pp. 38, 41, 77, 89; Ethel Duffy Turner, *Ricardo Flores Magón y el partido liberal mexicano*, trans. Eduardo Limón G. (Morelia: Editorial "Erandi" del Gobierno del Estado, 1960), p. 310. Dolores Arriaga later married Liberal Party member Santiago R. de la Vega.

52. Aurora Martínez Garza Vda. de Hernández, ed., *Antorchas de la revolución* (México: Gráficos Galeza, 1964), pp. 33-35.

53. Turner, *Barbarous Mexico*, p. 279; Turner, *Ricardo Flores Magón*, pp. 174, 310, 359; Antonio Barbosa Heldt, *La mujer en las luchas por México* (México: Editora y Distribuidora, S.A., 1972), pp. 80-81.

54. Other women leaders who joined the liberal cause included Veracruz journalists Emilia Minn and Josefa Arjona de Pinelo. For information on Minn, see Matilde Rodríguez Cabo, *La mujer y la revolución* (México: n.p., 1937), pp. 20-22. For information on Arjona de Pinelo, see Mendieta Alatorre, *La mujer*, pp. 39-40. Veracruzana Donaciana Salas often served the liberal cause as a messenger between Veracruz and Mexico City. For information on Salas, see Heldt, *La mujer*, p. 64. In Chihuahua, Silvina Rembao de Trejo published articles for the liberals, founded a revolutionary center that was active from 1907 to 1913, and became known as "La Matrona de la Revolución en Chihuahua." For information on Rembao de Trejo, see Martínez, ed., *Antorchas*, p. 6.

55. "La mujer en la vida sindical y el artículo 123," *Derechos de la mujer mexicana* (México: XLVII Legislatura del Congreso de la Unión, 1969), p. 62; "Feminismo," pp. 170-72; Turner, *Ricardo Flores Magón*, p. 43. Rossetti was sometimes spelled Rosete.

56. Mendieta Alatorre, *La mujer*, p. 34.

57. Ibid.; Enrique Flores Magón, "Profa Elisa Acuña y Rosete," *El Nacional*, November 27, 1946, pp. 3, 7; Cockcroft, *Intellectual Precursors*, pp. 109-110.

58. Mendieta Alatorre, *La mujer*, p. 33; Susana Mendoza, Juana's great-niece, interview, Cuernavaca, August 12, 1976. It is difficult to determine the first publication date of *Vésper*. Juana B. Gutiérrez de Mendoza, "Memoirs" (unpublished), listed April 5, 1901; Juan Gerónimo Beltrán, "Una precursora," *El Popular*, July 15, 1942, p. 5, stated that the first publication date was 1900; Cockcroft, *Intellectual Precursors*, p. 102, noted that the date was June 15, 1901. Cockcroft incorrectly stated that Elisa Acuña and Rossetti helped to found *Vésper*; Acuña joined Gutiérrez to work on *Vésper* after 1903.

59. Cockcroft, *Intellectual Precursors*, p. 114. Laura Mendoza, "Datos biográficos de doña Juana Gutiérrez de Mendoza," in *Antorchas*, ed. by Martínez Garza, pp. 17-19, presents a thorough overview of Gutiérrez's life. Laura was Gutiérrez's oldest daughter.

60. Gutiérrez de Mendoza, "Memoirs"; Inés Hernández Tovar, "Sara Estela Ramírez: The Early Twentieth Century Texas-Mexican Poet" (Unpublished Ph.D. dissertation, University of Houston, 1984), p. 25.

61. Cockcroft, *Intellectual Precursors*, pp. 118-19. Hernández Tovar, "Sara Estela Ramírez," pp. 138-43, contains a copy of the March 9, 1904 letter from Ramírez to Ricardo Flores Magón.

62. Susana Mendoza, interview, Cuernavaca, August 13, 1976; Turner, *Ricardo Flores Magón*, pp. 65-66.

63. Ibid., August 12, 1976.

64. Turner, *Ricardo Flores Magón*, p. 66. Gutiérrez published her criticisms of the Liberal Party Constitution in *Vésper* on Sunday, May 6, 1906. Santiago R. de la Vega, "Las mujeres en la revolución," *El Universal*, February 1, 1950, pp. 4, 9.

65. Rodríguez Cabo, *La mujer*, pp. 16-18; Biographical Collection at the Biblioteca Nacional under "Jiménez." Some sources stated that Dolores Jiménez y Muro was born in San Luis Potosí, but most sources indicated Aguascalientes.

66. González Navarro, *El porfiriato: La vida social*, pp. 298, 322.

67. Anderson, *Outcasts*, p. 156, disputed the depth of the PLM's involvement in the Río Blanco strike, which he contends was not politically motivated.

68. Ruiz, *Labor*, p. 7. Owners of the Cananea mines paid between 3 and 8 pesos per day; and owners of the Río Blanco textile mills paid men 1.25 pesos and women 50 to 80 centavos per day.

69. Turner, *Barbarous Mexico*, pp. 168-69.

70. Ruiz, *Labor*, pp. 23-25; Hart, *Anarchism*, pp. 95-96.

71. Moisés González Navarro, "La huelga de Río Blanco," *Historia Mexicana*, VI, No. 4 (April-June 1957), p. 520, stated that Garcín was the owner of the company store and that he was a Spaniard. Heriberto Peña Samaniego, *Río Blanco* (México: Centro de Estudios Históricos del Movimiento Obrero Mexicano, 1975), p. 72; Carlo de Fornaro, *Diaz Czar of Mexico* (New York: The International Publishing Co., 1909), p. 53; and Anderson, *Outcasts*, pp. 155-59, stated that Garcín was a Frenchman. Hernández, *La mujer mexicana*, pp. 31-32; Hart, *Anarchism*, pp. 96-97.

72. Fornaro, *Diaz Czar*, pp. 54-55; Peña Samaniego, *Río Blanco*, pp. 71-78; Ochoa Flores, "Desarrollo social," p. 39; Anderson, *Outcasts*, pp. 163-64.
73. González Navarro, "La huelga," p. 523; Hart, *Anarchism*, p. 98. Anderson, *Outcasts*, pp. 167-69, argued that the figures for the dead were exaggerated and that an accurate count of workers killed was between fifty and seventy. It was, however, widely believed at the time that hundreds of workers had been massacred.
74. Hart, *Anarchism*, p. 98.
75. F. Ibarra de Anda, *El periodismo en México*, Vol. II: *Las mexicanas en el periodismo*, 2nd ed. (México: Editorial "Juventa," 1937), pp. 23, 31, 45-46; Jane Herrick, "Periodicals for Women in Mexico during the Nineteenth Century," *The Americas*, XIV, No. 3 (October 1957), pp. 136-41.
76. Herrick, "Periodicals," pp. 141-44.
77. For more information on Dolores Correa Zapata, see Leonor Llach, "Tres escritoras mexicanas," *El Libro y El Pueblo*, XII, No. 4 (April 1934), pp. 166-68.
78. Ibarra de Anda, *Las mexicanas*, p. 114; Herrick, "Periodicals," p. 143.
79. Adelina Zendejas, "La mujer mexicana en el periodismo," *El Gallo Ilustrado* (June 22, 1975), p. 3; Luz Elena Galván, *La educación superior de la mujer en México: 1876-1940*, No. 109 (México: Cuadernos de la Casa Chata, 1985), p. 20.
80. Maria del Carmen Millán, *Diccionario de escritores mexicanos* (México: U.N.A.M.-Centro de Estudios Literarios, 1967), p. 52; Sidonia Carmen Rosenbaum, *Modern Women Poets of Spanish America* (New York: Hispanic Institute, 1945), p. 42. Using pseudonyms, Dolores Jiménez contributed to the following anti-Díaz newspapers: *El Malcriado*, *La Voz de Juárez*, *Juan Panadero*, *El Diario del Hogar*, and *La Libertad*.
81. *Mexican Herald*, July 3, 1911, p. 3.
82. See Ibarra de Anda, *Las mexicanas*, p. 63, for biographical information on Guadalupe Gutiérrez de Joseph.
83. Zendejas, "La mujer mexicana," p. 3.
84. Ibarra de Anda, *Las mexicanas*, pp. 92-93; *Mujeres mexicanas notables* (México: Talleres de la Cámara de Diputados, 1975), p. 220-22.
85. Rodríguez Cabo, *La mujer*, pp. 20-22; Zendejas, "La mujer mexicana," p. 3.
86. *Vésper*, July 1903, pp. 2-3. As did Dolores Jiménez, María Enriqueta, and many other women revolutionaries, Juana Gutiérrez used pseudonyms in her work. "Juan Bernal" was her favorite pseudonym. Susana Mendoza, interview, Cuernavaca, August 12, 1976.

CHAPTER 2

1. *New York Times*, May 10, 1911, p. 2.
2. Frederick C. Turner, *The Dynamic of Mexican Nationalism* (Chapel Hill: The University of North Carolina Press, 1968), p. 188. Women were especially successful in smuggling operations along the United States–Mexican border. At the El Paso–Ciudad Juárez border crossing, for example, men traveling on streetcars were searched regularly, but women were searched only randomly, permitting many opportunities for smuggling. Frederick C. Turner, "Los efectos de la participación femenina en la revolución de 1910," *Historia Mexicana*, Vol. 64, No. 4 (April-June, 1967), p. 608.
3. Turner, *The Dynamic*, p. 185.
4. Mrs. E. Alex Tweedie, *Mexico As I Saw It* (London: Thomas Nelson and Sons, 1911), p. 211.
5. Edith O'Shaughnessy, *A Diplomat's Wife in Mexico* (New York: Arno Press, 1970), p. 187.
6. Turner, *The Dynamic*, p. 120. Because of diseases, epidemics, food shortages, and deaths, Mexico's population growth leveled off for the first time in years. *The Mexican Herald*, February 2, 1914, p. 1, reported that women complained because they had little communication with their husbands and were left without funds. The War Department took the position that it would take care of the wives of officers on active duty.
7. Many attacks against women were reported in newspaper and journal accounts. *The Mexican Herald*, September 5, 1912, p. 1, reported that rebels in Cananea carried away a number of women; ibid., January 20, 1913, p. 1, stated that five men and five women were kidnapped by Zapatistas. Turner, *The Dynamic*, p. 123, discussed the large consignments

of women and young girls transported through Veracruz to Quintana Roo and Campeche. O'Shaughnessy, *A Diplomat's Wife*, pp. 58, 67.

8. O'Shaughnessy, *A Diplomat's Wife*, pp. 124-25.

9. Ibid., p. 89, from a letter to O'Shaughnessy's mother dated December 14, 1913, underlining in original.

10. Rip-Rip [Rafael Martínez], "Las mujeres en la revolución," *El Gráfico*, September 8, 1930, p. 2; Teodoro Hernández, "Hay que hacer justicia a las mujeres revolucionarias de principios del siglo," *El Nacional*, November 30, 1958, p. 8. Aurora Martínez Garza Vda. de Hernández, ed., *Antorchas de la revolución* (México: Gráficos Galeza, 1964), pp. 16-17, contains a list of women who signed the proposal to bring their protest to the national level.

11. C. J. Velarde, *Under the Mexican Flag, the Mexican Struggle Outlined* (Los Angeles: Southland Pub. House, 1926), pp. 307-308, contains a copy of the manifesto of the Cuauhtémoc League. Blas Urrea [Luis Cabrera], *Obras políticas del Lic. Blas Urrea . . .* (México: Imprenta Nacional, S.A., 1921), p. 327; Adelina Zendejas, "Precursoras y lideres del voto femenino en México," *Mujeres*, No. 65 (July 5, 1961), p. 42. Ruisánchez was sometimes written as Ruiz Sánchez.

12. Fausto Fernández Ponte, "Mary Petre, correo de Madero," *Excelsior*, December 7, 1966, pp. 1, 13, 14.

13. María de los Angeles Mendieta Alatorre, *Carmen Serdán* (México: Editorial Bohemia Poblana, 1971), p. 152; María de los Angeles Mendieta Alatorre, *La mujer en la revolución mexicana* (México: Talleres Gráficos de la Nación, 1961), p. 56.

14. Mendieta Alatorre, *La mujer*, pp. 51-57; Artemisa Sáenz Royo ["Xóchitl"], *Historia político-social-cultural del movimiento femenino en México, 1914-50* (México: M. León Sánchez, 1954), pp. 37-39.

15. Mendieta Alatorre, *Carmen Serdán*, p. 115, has a photograph of Carmen on the day of her release from prison. There is a complete deposition by Carmen Serdán of the events of November 18, 1910, pp. 128-45. *La Semana Ilustrada*, Año II, No. 86, June 23, 1911, also contains a photograph taken with the Madero women in Puebla. Mendieta Alatorre, *La mujer*, p. 50; Aurora Fernández y Fernández, *Mujeres que honran a la patria* (México: n.p., 1958), p. 216.

16. *Diario del Hogar*, June 19, 1911, p. 1. Del Valle's baby daughter was born in prison.

17. Fernández y Fernández, *Mujeres*, p. 216.

18. *Cronica ilustrada revolución mexicana*, XLI (1967-68), related by María Narváez, p. 13. Rosa and Guadalupe helped with Carmen's mission to Zapata. To pay for the trip, Rosa was forced to pawn the few pet birds owned by the family.

19. Mendieta Alatorre, *Carmen Serdán*, p. 154, has a photograph of Carmen Serdán and the others with Carranza.

20. Ibid., p. 165, has a photograph of the group.

21. Ibid., p. 155; *Derechos de la mujer mexicana* (México: XLVII Legislatura del Congreso de la Unión, 1969), p. 114.

22. *Derechos de la mujer*, p. 114. *New York Times*, May 10, 1911, p. 2, reported that Sara shared Francisco's prison cell in Monterrey and in San Luis Potosí, cooking his food because she feared that he would be poisoned.

23. *New York Times*, May 11, 1911, p. 2.

24. Edith O'Shaughnessy, *Diplomatic Days* (New York: Harper and Bros., 1917), pp. 75, 335.

25. Ernest Gruening, *Mexico and Its Heritage* (New York: The Century Co., 1928), pp. 570-73. Sara Pérez de Madero's only success with Ambassador Wilson was that he agreed to send a telegram from Madero's mother to President Taft.

26. Matilde Rodríguez Cabo, *La mujer y la revolución* (México: n.p., 1937), p. 18; Lucina Villarreal G., *Heroinas de la independencia; Adelitas de la revolución; Legionarias del ejército nacional* (México: n.p., 1940), p. 12.

27. Rodríguez Cabo, *La mujer*, p. 20.

28. Villarreal G., *Heroinas*, p. 13; Mendieta Alatorre, *La mujer*, pp. 76-77.

29. María Antonieta Rascón, "La mujer y la lucha social," in *Imagen y realidad de la mujer*, ed. by Elena Urrutia, Sepsetentas, No. 172 (México: Secretaría de Educación Pública, 1975), pp. 155-56; María Efraína Rocha, *Semblanzas biográficas de algunas luchadoras mexicanas contemporáneas* (México: Ediciones del Comité Coordinador Femenino, 1947), pp. 6-7. Alaniz was also spelled with an *s*.

30. Turner, *The Dynamic*, pp. 197-98; Ward M. Morton, *Woman Suffrage in Mexico* (Gainesville: The University of Florida Press, 1962), p. 2.

31. *Mexican Herald*, August 5, 1912, p. 6.

32. O'Shaughnessy, *Diplomatic Days*, p. 27. Mexican women were encouraged by the worldwide struggle for equality. The activities of women in Great Britain and in the United States received extensive coverage in Mexican magazines and newspapers.

33. Ibid., p. 260. This information was taken from a letter O'Shaughnessy wrote to her mother on April 24, 1912.

34. Rodríguez Cabo, *La mujer*, p. 17. Bacmaister was often spelled Bakmaister or Baicmaster.

35. James D. Cockcroft, *Intellectual Precursors of the Mexican Revolution, 1900-1913* (Austin: University of Texas Press, 1968), pp. 189-99, quoting Teodoro Hernández, "Precursores de la revolución: José Edilberto Pineal," *El Popular*, July 12, 1943. The six states were Tlaxcala, Guerrero, Michoacán, Campeche, Puebla, and México.

36. *New York Times*, May 8, 1911, p. 2. Díaz left Mexico permanently on May 31, 1911.

37. Ibid., June 1, 1911, p. 2. Juana B. Gutiérrez de Mendoza, "Memoirs" (unpublished), stated that the founders of the Amigas del Pueblo were Juana Gutiérrez de Mendoza, Manuela Peláez, Rosa G. Vda. de Maciel, and Laura Mendoza. *Mexican Herald*, June 25, 1911, p. 1. Yolando Tanabe Velasco, "La mujer y la profesión de contador público en México" (Thesis, Universidad Nacional Autónoma de México, 1962), p. 12, contains a long list of women who were instrumental in the fight for women's rights.

38. *Revista de Revistas*, Año II, No. 89, October 8, 1911, p. 3.

39. Rocha, *Semblanzas biográficas*, p. 16.

40. Wilfrid Callcott, *Liberalism in Mexico, 1857-1929* (Palo Alto: Stanford University Press, 1931), p. 219.

41. Mendieta Alatorre, *La mujer*, p. 41. Mendieta Alatorre incorrectly states that María Elvira Bermúdez was a member of the Club Lealtad. Bermúdez was not born until 1916. María Elvira Bermúdez, interview, Mexico City, July 25, 1976.

42. *Mujeres mexicanas notables* (México: Talleres de la Cámara de Diputados, 1975), pp. 138-41.

43. Francisco Ramírez Plancarte, *La ciudad de México durante la revolución constitutionalista* (México: Ediciones Botas, 1941), pp. 65-66. Rosa Seldi, "María Arias," Biographical Collection of the Biblioteca Nacional, states that María Arias was actually horrified by her title "María Pistolas" because she was so gentle that she "could not kill an ant."

44. Seldi, "María Arias"; *Derechos de la mujer*, p. 15; Rodríguez Cabo, *La mujer*, pp. 22-23; biographical sketch written by Eulalia Guzmán in the Biographical Collection of the Biblioteca Nacional.

45. Ricardo Flores Magón, *Semilla libertaria*, 3 vols., Vol. II (México: Ediciones del Grupo Cultural "Ricardo Flores Magón," 1923), pp. 97-101.

46. Ricardo Flores Magón, *A la mujer* (Oakland: Prensa Sembradora, 1974), pp. 4-5.

47. Flores Magón, *Semilla*, p. 38. This was originally written on February 12, 1916.

48. Martínez Garza, ed. *Antorchas*, pp. 38-39.

49. Myra Ellen Jenkins, "Ricardo Flores Magon and the Mexican Liberal Party" (Unpublished Ph.D. dissertation, University of New Mexico, 1953), p. 254.

50. General Juan F. Azcarate, *Escencia de la revolución* (México: B. Costa-Amic, 1966), p. 80, claimed that only federal soldiers had their families with them and that *soldaderas* were inventions of the film industry. See John Rutherford, *Mexican Society during the Revolution: A Literary Approach* (London: Oxford University Press, 1971), p. 296.

51. J. H. Plenn, "Forgotten Heroines of Mexico: Tales of the Soldaderas, Amazons of War and Revolution," *Travel*, LXVI (April 1936), p. 60. Verna Carleton Millan, *Mexico Reborn* (Boston: Houghton Mifflin Co., 1939), pp. 152-53, contains a description of a *soldadera* giving birth in the field. O'Shaughnessy, *A Diplomat's Wife*, p. 144.

52. O'Shaughnessy, *A Diplomat's Wife*, p. 144; Tito L. Foppa, *La tragedia mexicana* (Barcelona: Buigas Pons y Craj., n.d.), p. 110. "Los que lucharon en la revolución: Heroinas revolucionarias," *El Heraldo Domenical*, November 18, 1934, p. 4, also states that the *soldaderas* were the real heroines of the Revolution.

53. Rutherford, *Mexican Society*, pp. 296-97, quoting Ramírez Plancarte, *La ciudad*, pp. 58-59; John Reed, *Insurgent Mexico* (New York: Simon and Schuster, 1969), p. 106. Reed

devotes an entire chapter to "Elizabetta," a *soldadera* in the state of Chihuahua, traveling with Villa's troops. See ibid., pp. 104-110.
54. Turner, *The Dynamic*, pp. 284-85.
55. Ibid., pp. 199-200; Sáenz Royo, *Historia político*, pp. 33-34.
56. Todd Downing, *The Mexican Earth* (New York: Doubleday, Doran and Co., 1949), p. 248.
57. María Herrera-Sobek, "Mothers, Lovers, and Soldiers: Archetypal Representation of Women in the Corrido" (Unpublished manuscript), pp. 236, 395-97.
58. *New York Times*, May 10, 1911, p. 2, reported that Neri had been a wealthy landowner who joined the Revolution because of excessive taxes. Also, she was said to have commanded one thousand *guerrillas* in the state of Guerrero.
59. This is highly unlikely and may be viewed as an attempt to lessen her stature as a *guerrilla* commander.
60. Downing, *The Mexican Earth*, pp. 230-31, related the story of Neri cutting off ears; *Mexican Herald*, September 2, 1912, p. 1, reported that Neri had Zapatistas under her command.
61. Villarreal G., *Heroinas*, p. 12; Artemisa Sáenz Royo, *Semblanzas; Mujeres mexicanas revolucionarias y guerreras, revolucionarias ideológicas. Por . . . ["Xóchitl"]* (México: Imp. M. León Sánchez, S.C.L., 1960), pp. 22-24.
62. Reed, *Insurgent Mexico*, p. 131. Villa's wife, María de la Luz Corral, was a devoted supporter. Years after Villa's assassination in 1923, she maintained a museum in his honor in her home in Chihuahua. María de los Angeles Mendieta Alatorre, "Las mexicanas en la revolución," *Novedades* (Suplemento "México en la Cultura"), November 6, 1966, p. 6.
63. Lewis Hanke, *Latin America: A Historical Reader* (Boston: Little, Brown, and Co., 1967), p. 582, contains a photograph of Apolinaria Flores.
64. John Womack, Jr., *Zapata and the Mexican Revolution* (New York: Alfred A. Knopf, 1969), p. 170, quoting *La Tribuna*, May 29, June 3 and 4, 1913. Rascón, "La mujer y la lucha social," pp. 156-57, mentions "La China."
65. *Mexican Herald*, June 20, 1913, p. 1.
66. Villarreal G., *Heroinas*, p. 13; Rodríguez Cabo, *La mujer*, pp. 19-20.
67. Rodríguez Cabo, *La mujer*, p. 20; Rascón, "La mujer y la lucha social," p. 156.
68. Sáenz Royo, *Semblanzas*, pp. 29-31; Teodoro Hernández, "Mujeres revolucionarias de los ideales agraristas," in *Antorchas*, ed. by Martínez Garza, pp. 44-45.
69. Antonio Uroz, *Hombres y mujeres de México* (México: Editorial Lic. Antonio Uroz, 1974), p. 258.
70. Rodríguez Cabo, *La mujer*, p. 16; Antonio Barbosa Heldt, *La mujer en las luchas por México* (México: Editora y Distribuidora, S.A., 1972), p. 61.
71. María Antonieta Rascón, "La mujer mexicana como hecho político: La precursora, la militante," *Siempre* (Suplemento, "La Cultura en México"), No. 569, January 3, 1973, p. 1, states that Dolores Jiménez participated in the Plan Político y Social de la Sierra de Guerrero that immediately preceded the Plan de Ayala. Sáenz Royo, *Historia político*, p. 71. Womack, *Zapata*, pp. 393-404, does not mention Jiménez y Muro's participation in the Plan de Ayala.
72. Rodríguez Cabo, *La mujer*, p. 18. *Mujeres mexicanas notables*, pp. 147-49, stated that Jiménez was a brigadier general. Her pension was awarded upon the recommendation of Gildardo Magaña.
73. Rascón, "La mujer y la lucha social," p. 173; *Vésper*, March 15, 1932, p. 1.
74. Pedro Siller, "Testimonios: Juana B. Gutiérrez de Mendoza," *Historia Obrera* 5, II, No. 5 (June 1975), p. 7. Gutiérrez de Mendoza, "Memoirs," notes that Gutiérrez was jailed from September 4, 1913 to July 4, 1914. Juana B. Gutiérrez de Mendoza, "La independencia económica de México y la coalición de militares y civiles revolucionarios," *Vésper*, March 15, 1932, pp. 1, 7.
75. Gutiérrez, "Memoirs." No reference is made to the purpose or the goals of the Labradores Mexicanos Instituto Popular. Laura Mendoza, Juana's elder daughter and her collaborator, died in August 1976 in Cuernavaca.
76. *El Desmonte*, Vol. I, No. 1 (June 15, 1919), pp. 1-2; on p. 4, Elena Torres is mentioned as a collaborator.
77. Gutiérrez, "Memoirs."

78. Gutiérrez adopted two boys (Hesón and Feliciano Pérez Negrete) in Acatlipán, Morelos and raised them to adulthood. Siller, "Testimonios," p. 4, has a photograph. Several years after her husband died, Gutiérrez was the *compañera* of a Zapatista who was killed in combat. Susana Mendoza (Juana's great-niece), interview, Cuernavaca, August 12, 1976.

79. Sáenz Royo, *Semblanzas*, p. 10. Susana Mendoza, interview, Cuernavaca, August 12, 1976, stated that many of her aunt's papers had been burned. When Juana Gutiérrez needed money to keep her press going, she sold beans on the street and used her papers to start the cooking fires.

80. *El Pueblo*, January 25, 1916, p. 3. Two years earlier (November 17, 1914), Obregón had made a plea to the women of Mexico on behalf of the Constitutionalists: "Mothers, wives and daughters!: kneel before the Altar of the Motherland and bring to the ear of your sons, husbands and fathers the sacred call of Duty." Turner, *The Dynamic*, p. 190, quoting Alvaro Obregón, *Ocho mil kilómetros en campaña: Relación de las acciónes de armas electuadas en más de veinte estados de la república durante un período de cuatro años* (México: Librería de la Vda. de Ch. Bouret, 1917), p. 227.

81. Sáenz Royo, *Semblanzas*, p. 49. The author is mistaken when she states that she attended the First Feminist Congress in 1917. Minutes of the meeting show that she attended the Second Feminist Congress in November 1916. Villarreal G., *Heroinas*, pp. 11-12, correctly states that Sáenz Royo attended the Second Feminist Congress in Mérida. Sáenz Royo stated that Hermila Galindo organized the congress under General Alvarado with Carranza's support. Morton, *Woman Suffrage*, p. 3, also notes that Galindo persuaded Alvarado to convene the First Feminist Congress. It does not appear that Galindo was responsible for the congress being held, and the extent of Carranza's support is debatable. For a discussion, see Chapter 3, note 23.

82. Villarreal G., *Heroinas*, pp. 11-12; Sáenz Royo, *Semblanzas*, p. 49.

83. Sáenz Royo, *Semblanzas*, pp. 42-46. Margarita Robles was an admirer of Zapata. Her father owned a hacienda in southwestern Mexico that had been burned and destroyed during the Revolution. Robles wrote a favorable pamphlet about Zapata entitled *El verdadero Zapata*.

84. Mendieta Alatorre, *La mujer*, p. 79.

85. Daniel Muñóz, "Ocho periodistas mexicanas," *El Universal*, October 15, 1954, pp. 3, 28.

86. Ibid.

87. Mendieta Alatorre, *La mujer*, p. 80; Sáenz Royo, *Historia político*, p. 48; Morton, *Woman Suffrage*, p. 5; Hermila Galindo, *La doctrina Carranza y el acercamiento indolatino* (México: n.p., 1919), pp. 160-61.

88. Morton, *Woman Suffrage*, p. 3; Galindo, *La doctrina*, p. 160.

89. Galindo, *La doctrina*, pp. 27-35, 161.

90. *La Voz de la Revolución*, March 15, 1917, p. 1.

91. Muñoz, "Ocho Periodistas," pp. 3, 28; F. Ibarra de Anda, *El periodismo en México*, Vol. II: *Las mexicanas en el periodismo*, 2nd ed. (México: Editorial "Juventa," 1937), p. 67; *New York Times*, March 12, 1917, p. 11; Turner, *The Dynamic*, p. 189.

92. Hermila Galindo, *Un presidenciable. El general don Pablo González* (México: Imprenta Nacional, S.A., 1919), pp. 9-14.

93. Muñóz, "Ocho periodistas," pp. 3, 28; Ibarra de Anda, *El periodismo en México*, p. 67.

94. *Revista de Revistas: El Semanario Nacional*, July 23, 1911, p. 2; Elena Arizmendi y Mejia founded the Cruz Blanca. See Villarreal G., *Heroinas*, p. 11.

95. Villarreal G., *Heroinas*, p. 11; Sáenz Royo, *Historia político*, pp. 30-31.

96. *El Pueblo*, January 25, 1916, pp. 1, 2; Sáenz Royo, *Historia político*, pp. 32-33; Sáenz Royo, *Semblanzas*, pp. 27-28.

97. María Antonieta Rascón, "La mujer mexicana," stated that Flores was in charge of the state of Tepic; Sáenz Royo, *Historia político*, p. 32, stated that Flores had blue eyes and blond hair; Plenn, "Forgotten Heroines," p. 60, described Flores as stout, with red hair, in her early thirties, and dressed in black satin, with a sword at her side.

98. Plenn, "Forgotten Heroines," p. 60; Sáenz Royo, *Historia político*, p. 32; Villarreal G., *Heroinas*, pp. 10-11.

99. Plenn, "Forgotten Heroines," p. 27.

100. Sáenz Royo, *Semblanzas*, p. 36, implied that if Carranza had not been killed, he would have supported Galindo's suffrage efforts and women would have received the vote.

101. *El Desmonte: Por la Tierra y Por la Raza*, Vol. I, No. 1 (June 15, 1919), p. 2; Millan, *Mexico Reborn*, p. 166; Mendieta Alatorre, *La mujer*, p. 137.

102. Millan, *Mexico Reborn*, p. 166.

103. Morton, *Woman Suffrage*, p. 6; Hermila Galindo, *Estudio de la Srita Hermila Galindo con motivo de los temas que han de absolverse en el Segundo Congreso Feminista de Yucatán* (Mérida: Imprenta del Gobierno Constitucionalista, 1916), p. 25.

104. F. V. Niemeyer, Jr., *Revolution at Querétaro: The Mexican Constitutional Convention of 1916-1917* (Austin: University of Texas Press, 1974), pp. 207-208, does not state why Inés Malváez, who had been an active feminist, opposed suffrage, nor whom she represented politically.

105. Morton, *Woman Suffrage*, pp. 5-7, quoting *Diario de los debates del Congreso constituyente de 1916-1917*, 2 vols., II (México: Imprenta de la Cámara de Diputados, 1922), p. 710; Niemeyer, *Revolution at Querétaro*, pp. 66, 108, quoting *Diario de los debates*, II, p. 830.

106. *Diario de los debates*, II, pp. 711-12, 997; Morton, *Woman Suffrage*, p. 1; Félix F. Palavicini, *Historia de la constitución de 1917*, 2 vols., Vol. II (México: República Mexicana, 1938), pp. 95, 98. For the full text of the debate, see *Diario*, pp. 711-19, and Palavicini, *Historia*, pp. 95-104. Niemeyer, *Revolution at Querétaro*, pp. 65, 207-209, suggests that Palavicini thought that Múgica would have offered a fuller explanation than Mónzon. Múgica was known to be a feminist of sorts. He offered scholarships to women while serving as military governor of Tabasco, and he favored granting suffrage to women.

107. Francisco Bulnes, *The Whole Truth about Mexico; President Wilson's Responsibility*, trans. Dora Scott (New York: M. Bulnes Book Co., 1916), pp. 142-48. Bulnes stated also that feminists helped to undermine Limantour because of vengeance, since he had closed the Treasury Department to them.

108. Gruening, *Mexico and Its Heritage*, p. 627.

109. Ibid., p. 630.

110. Lillian Estelle Fisher, "The Influence of the Present Mexican Revolution upon the Status of Mexican Women," *Hispanic American Historical Review*, XXII, No. 1 (1942), p. 214.

111. Ibid.; Victor Alba, *The Mexicans: The Making of a Nation* (New York: Frederick A. Praeger, 1967), p. 138.

112. Morton, *Woman Suffrage*, pp. 8-9.

113. *Mexican Herald*, January 22, 1915, p. 1; Isidro Fabela, ed., *Documentos históricos de la revolución mexicana*, Vol. IV (México: Fondo de Cultura Económica, 1963), pp. 121-22, 132-33. For a copy of the Divorce Law, see *El Nacional*, June 20, 1916, pp. 1, 8.

114. Hermila Galindo, *Estudio*, pp. 18-20.

115. *La Prensa*, February 15, 1915, pp. 1, 6.

116. Eugenia Meyer, historian and director of the Instituto Mora, interview, Mexico City, March 11, 1976, stated that Félix Palavicini, Luis Cabrera, and other male colleagues influenced Carranza to issue the Law of Family Relations because they were separated from their wives, had children with their mistresses, and wanted to marry them. It has also been suggested that Hermila Galindo may have influenced Carranza to issue this law.

117. Ana Macías, "Mexican Women in the Social Revolution, 1910-1920," *The Americas*, xxxvii, No. 2 (1980), p. 12.

118. Fisher, "The Influence," p. 214; Gruening, *Mexico and Its Heritage*, p. 627.

119. G. Sofía Villa de Buentello, *La mujer y la ley* (México: Imprenta Franco-Americana, 1921), pp. 137-47; Gruening, *Mexico and Its Heritage*, p. 627, stated that the law was adopted in 1923.

120. For specifics on the 1917 law, see Fisher, "The Influence," pp. 213-14.

121. Ramón Eduardo Ruiz, *Labor and the Ambivalent Revolutionaries: Mexico, 1911-1923* (Baltimore: The Johns Hopkins University Press, 1976), p. 56.

122. Marjorie Ruth Clark, *Organized Labor in Mexico* (Chapel Hill: University of North Carolina Press, 1934), pp. 27-28, 30-31.

123. "Acrata," *Historia Obrera 5*, II, No. 5 (June 1975), p. 21, quoting Luis Araiza, *Historia de la Casa del Obrera Mundial* (México: Talleres Gráficos del Sindicato de Obreros y Artesanos de la Industria Cervecera y Conexas de la Ciudad de Orizaba, Veracruz, 1963), p. 98, stated that there were four Red Battalions, rather than six.

124. See *Mexican Herald*, November 24, 1911, p. 1, December 9, 1913, p. 3; December 31, 1913, p. 10; and November 1, 1914, p. 1 for descriptions of women's participation in strikes in the Torreón mines and the garment industry in the Federal District.

125. Clark, *Organized Labor*, pp. 41-44; Cockcroft, *Intellectual Precursors*, p. 229.

126. Jean Meyer, "Los obreros en la revolución mexicana: 'Los Batallones Rojos,'" *Historia Mexicana*, XXI, No. 1 (July-September, 1971), pp. 25-26.

127. "Derechos de la mujer campesina," *Derechos de la mujer*, p. 62. Elena Torres and María del Refugio García were leaders in the Communist Party.

128. *New York Times*, November 27, 1910, p. 4.

129. Robert E. Quirk, *The Mexican Revolution and the Catholic Church, 1910-1929* (Bloomington: Indiana University Press, 1973), pp. 17-37; Rodney D. Anderson, *Outcasts in Their Own Land: Mexican Industrial Workers, 1906-1911* (DeKalb: Northern Illinois University Press, 1976), pp. 185-87.

130. Quirk, *The Mexican Revolution*, p. 60.

131. O'Shaughnessy, *A Diplomat's Wife*, pp. 253-54, from a letter to her mother dated April 9, 1914.

132. Quirk, *The Mexican Revolution*, pp. 75-76.

133. Ibid., p. 99.

134. Adelina Zendejas, "La mujer mexicana en el periodismo," *El Gallo Ilustrado*, June 22, 1975, p. 3; Fisher, "The Influence," p. 223.

135. María del Carmen Ruiz Castañeda, "La mujer mexicana en el periódico," *Filosofia y Letras*, XXX, No. 60-61-62 (January-December 1956), p. 215; *La Mujer Moderna*, Año I, No. 7 (October 31, 1915), pp. 3, 9, 14.

136. The best collection of photographs for the period of the Revolution is by Gustavo Casasola, *Historia gráfica de la revolución 1900-1940* (México: Editorial F. Trillas, 1960). However, Casasola rarely identified the women in his photographs.

137. *La Semana Ilustrada*, Año II, No. 62 (January 6, 1911); Año II, No. 81 (May 18, 1911); Año II, No. 83 (June 2, 1911).

138. Ibid., Año II, No. 102 (October 13, 1911). For a photograph of Madero with the Anti-Alcoholic League in Chapultepec, see ibid., Año III, No. 117 (January 24, 1912). Madero was made honorary president of the league; see ibid., Año III, No. 138 (June 19, 1912).

139. Ibid., Año II, No. 88 (July 7, 1911).

140. Ibid., Año IV, No. 189 (June 10, 1913); Año IV, No. 194 (July 15, 1913).

141. Ibid., Año II, No. 97 (September 8, 1911); Año II, No. 100 (September 29, 1911); Año III, No. 150 (September 11, 1912).

142. *Mexican Herald*, September 6, 1912, pp. 2, 3.

143. *El Tiempo Ilustrado*, Año XI, No. 22 (May 28, 1911), p. 383, and Año XI, No. 21 (May 21, 1911), p. 369.

144. Ibid., Año III, No. 133 (November 20, 1919), p. 10.

145. *El Voto*, May 1, 1913, p. 4.

146. Ruiz Castañeda, "La mujer mexicana," p. 216; Rodríguez Cabo, *La mujer*, pp. 18, 20-22; Fisher, "The Influence," p. 223.

CHAPTER 3

1. *La Voz de la Revolución*, March 28, 1917, p. 3; Laureana Wright de Kleinhans, *Mujeres notables mexicanas* (Publicaciones hechas bajo los auspicios de la Secretaría de Instrucción Pública y Bellas Artes; México: Tipográfia Económica, 1910), p. 403. Wright stated that *La Siempreviva* was the first periodical in Mexico published entirely by women.

2. *La Voz de la Revolución*, March 28, 1917, p. 3; Congreso Feminista de Yucatán, *Anales de esa memorable asamblea* (Mérida: Talleres Tipográficos del "Ateneo Peninsular," 1916), p. 29.

3. Antonio Bustillos Carrillo, *Yucatán al servicio de la patria y de la revolución* (México: Casa Ramírez Editores, 1959), p. 186.

4. These theses are located in the Biblioteca Carrillo Ancona in Mérida. For examples, see: Eduardo Cámara Milán, *Derechos de la mujer en Yucatán* (Thesis, Escuela de Jurisprudencia del Estado de Yucatán; Mérida: "Imprenta Universal," 1912); Arturo Escalante Galera, *La mujer en nuestra legislación* (Thesis, Escuela de Jurisprudencia del Estado de Yucatán; Mérida: "La Moderna," 1912); Roberto Castillo Rivas, Jr., *Derechos de la mujer* (Thesis, Escuela de Jurisprudencia del Estado de Yucatán: Mérida: Imprenta Oficial del Gobierno del Estado, 1912); Ricardo Alpuche, *Causas de divorcio* (Thesis, Escuela de Jurisprudencia del Estado de Yucatán; Mérida: La Empresa Editora Yucateca, S.A., 1915).

5. John Kenneth Turner, *Barbarous Mexico*, The Texas Pan American Series (Austin: University of Texas Press, 1969), pp. 12-13.

6. Arnold Channing and Frederick J. Tabor Frost, *The American Egypt: A Record of Travel in Yucatan* (New York: Doubleday, Page, and Co., 1909), pp. 332-45.

7. *Anales de esa memorable asamblea*, p. vii.

8. James Cockcroft, *Intellectual Precursors of the Mexican Revolution, 1900-1913* (Austin: University of Texas Press, 1968), p. 124; Bustillos Carrillo, *Yucatan al servicio*, p. 146.

9. *Anales de esa memorable asamblea*, p. xi.

10. Alvarado even married a local girl, Laura Manzano; *El Universal*, December 27, 1916, p. 8.

11. Alvaro Gamboa Ricalde, *Yucatán desde 1910*, 3 vols., II (Veracruz: Imp. "Standard," 1943-1955), pp. 401-405, 415.

12. *La Voz de la Revolución*, October 28, 1915, p. 1.

13. Anna Macías, "Mexican Women in the Social Revolution" (Revised paper presented at the 86th meeting of the American Historical Association, New York City, December 1971), p. 19, quoting Salvador Alvarado, *Informe que el general Salvador Alvarado rinde al primer jefe del Ejército Constitutionalista C. Venustiano Carranza. Comprende su gestión administrativa desde el 19 de marzo 1915 al 28 de febrero de 1917* (Mérida: Imprenta del Gobierno Constitucionalista, 1917), pp. 38, 52.

14. Charles C. Cumberland, *The Mexican Revolution: The Constitutionalist Years* (Austin: University of Texas Press, 1972), p. 222; Bustillos Carrillo, *Yucatán al servicio*, p. 155; Gamboa Ricalde, *Yucatán*, II, 566-69; Nelson Reed, *The Caste War of Yucatan* (Stanford: Stanford University Press, 1964), p. 260.

15. For a discussion of the congress, see Bustillos Carrillo, *Yucatán al servicio*, p. 169; *La Voz de la Revolución*, September 12, 1915, pp. 1, 2; Santiago Pacheco Cruz, *Recuerdos de la propaganda constitucionalista en Yucatán. Con una semblanza de la vida, actuación i asesinato del gobernador Felipe Carrillo Puerto* (Mérida: Talleres Gráficos y Editorial ZAMNA, 1953), pp. 285, 287.

16. *La Voz de la Revolución*, March 22, 1916, p. 3, quoting statement by Ramírez Garrido in the *Boletín del Departamento de Educación Pública*.

17. *La Voz de la Revolución*, September 10, 1916, p. 1; Rita María Medina de Cetina, "Protección a la infancia yucateca," *Siempre Adelante* (October-November 1974), p. 49. John W. F. Dulles, *Yesterday in Mexico: A Chronicle of the Revolution, 1919-1936* (Austin: University of Texas Press, 1967), p. 139.

18. Rosendo Salazar and José G. Escobedo, *Las pugnas de la gleba, 1907-1922*, 2 vols., II (México: Editorial Avante, 1923), p. 64.

19. Porfiria Avila y C. de Rosado, *Al ilustrado h. segundo congreso feminista en Yucatán: Un recuerdo de su autora* (Mérida: Imp. del Gobierno Constitucionalista, 1916), p. 14.

20. "Codigo del trabajo," in Gamboa Ricalde, *Yucatán*, II, pp. 453-95; *El Universal*, December 12, 1916, p. 6; Bustillos Carrillo: *Yucatán al servicio*, pp. 123-25.

21. Bustillos Carrillo, *Yucatán al servicio*, pp. 154, 159; Gamboa Ricalde, *Yucatán*, II, pp. 370-74.

22. Gamboa Ricalde, *Yucatán*, II, pp. 385-87.

23. J. D. Ramírez Garrido, *Al margen del feminismo* (Mérida: Talleres "Pluma y Lápiz," 1918), p. 44. Ramírez reported that in late October, Yucatán Professor Agustín Franco suggested to him that a feminist congress be held in Yucatán. When Ramírez took that suggestion to General Alvarado, it was adopted immediately. On October 28, 1915, the general

announced that the First Congress would be held in Mérida; order of General Salvador Alvarado quoted in *La Voz de la Revolución*, October 29, 1915, pp. 1, 2.

24. *Anales de esa memorable asamblea*, pp. 36-52; Notices of the congress were printed in *La Voz de la Revolución*. See, for example, November 20, 1915, p. 3; November 21, 1915, p. 3; November 22, 1915, p. 3; November 26, 1915, pp. 1, 5; November 29, 1915, p. 3; December 5, 1915, p. 1; December 13, 1915, p. 3; December 15, 1915, p. 5.

25. *La Voz de la Revolución*, November 16, 1915, p. 1; interview with Consuelo Zavala y Castillo in ibid., December 28, 1915, p. 1.

26. *Anales de esa memorable asamblea*, pp. 65-68.

27. Hermila Galindo, *La mujer en el porvenir* (Mérida: Imprenta y Litografía de "La Voz de la Revolución"), pp. 1-2.

28. The complete text of Hermila Galindo's speech is printed in ibid., pp. 195-202; Artemisa Sáenz Royo ["Xóchitl"], *Historia político-social-cultural del movimiento femenino en México, 1914-1950* (México: M. León Sánchez, 1954), p. 68.

29. *Anales de esa memorable asamblea*, pp. 70, 71, 77, 118. Reactions to Galindo's speech can also be found in *La Voz de la Revolución*, January 14, 1916, pp. 1-3.

30. *Anales de esa memorable asamblea*, p. 72.

31. Ibid., pp. 100-109; *La Voz de la Revolución*, January 14, 1916, pp. 1-3.

32. Alaide Foppa, "The First Feminist Congress in Mexico, 1916," *Signs*, Vol. V, No. 1 (August 1979), pp. 194-95.

33. Ibid., pp. 194-96.

34. *Anales de esa memorable asamblea*, pp. 126-27.

35. Ibid., p. xii.

36. *La Voz de la Revolución*, November 16, 1916, p. 1.

37. Ibid., stated that over two hundred women attended the Second Feminist Congress.

38. Ibid., November 24, 1916, p. 1; *El Universal*, December 9, 1916, p. 4.

39. *La Voz de la Revolución*, November 24, 1916, p. 3.

40. Ibid., November 29, 1916, pp. 1, 3; December 1, 1916, p. 1; December 7, 1916, p. 5. Artemisa Sáenz Royo may have been displeased with the congress, but before leaving Mérida she wrote "Adiós a Mérida," in which she praised Hermila Galindo and Salvador Alvarado for their support of women's issues.

41. Ibid., November 28, 1916, pp. 1, 2.

42. Ibid., November 29, 1916, pp. 1, 3.

43. Ibid., November 30, 1916, pp. 1, 5. Delegates were extremely cautious. Only ninety of the more than two hundred delegates voted on the issue of women holding public office, with only thirty voting in the affirmative.

44. Ibid., December 3, 1916, pp. 1, 2.

45. Ibid., December 3, 1916, p. 2.

46. Hermila Galinda, *Estudio de la Srita. Galindo con motivo de los temas que han de absolverse en el Segundo Congreso Feminista de Yucatán* (Mérida: Imprenta del Gobierno Constitucionalista, 1916), pp. 4, 6, 20-23, 25, 26.

47. *La Voz de la Revolución*, March 29, 1917, p. 3 (italics in original), and April 2, 1917, p. 3.

48. See, for instance, Julio Rodríguez P., *La mujer delicuente* (Thesis, Escuela de Jurisprudencia del Estado de Yucatán; Mérida: n.p., 1917); Antonio Gual García, *La mujer ante el derecho* (Thesis, Escuela de Jurisprudencia del Estado de Yucatán; Mérida: Talleres "Pluma y Lápiz," 1919).

49. Ramírez Garrido, *El margen del feminismo*, pp. 41-42.

50. David Franz, "Bullets and Bolshevists: A History of the Mexican Revolution and Reform in Yucatan, 1910-1924" (Unpublished Ph.D. dissertation, University of New Mexico, 1973), p. 159, quoting *Diario de los debates del congreso constituyente, 1916-1917, comisión nacional para la celebración del sesquicentenario de la proclamación de la independencia nacional y del cincuentenario de la revolución mexicana*, introduction by Hilario Medina, 2 vols., II (México: Talleres Gráficos de la Nación, 1960), p. 1211.

51. Ernest Gruening, "A Maya Idyl: A Study of Felipe Carrillo, Late Governor of Yucatan," *The Century Magazine* (April 1924), pp. 832-36.

52. A. G. B. Hart, *The Pulse of Mexico: Mexico's Monthly Review* (April 1922), pp. 36, 43.

53. Alberto Cámara Patrón and Vicente Ayora Sarlat, *La obra revolucionaria de Carrillo Puerto* (Mérida: University of Yucatán Press, 1974), p. 20; Acrelio Carrillo Puerto, *La familia Carrillo Puerto de Motul, con la revolución mexicana* (n.p., 1959), p. 11.

54. Ernest Gruening, "Felipe Carrillo," *The Nation*, CXVIII (January 16, 1924), p. 61; Cámara Patrón and Ayora Sarlat, *La obra revolucionaria*, pp. 26-27; Hart, *The Pulse*, p. 42. Gruening, "A Maya Idyl," p. 832, stated that Carrillo believed he was descended from Natchi-Cocom, the Mayan king. Hart, *The Pulse*, p. 35, reported that the governor told him that "within my breast there beats an Indian heart."

55. Hart, *The Pulse*, p. 44.

56. Hernán Robleto, "El henequén y el indio," in *El asesinato de Carrillo Puerto* (México: n.p., 1924), p. 109.

57. Bustillos Carrillo, *Yucatán al servicio*, p. 66.

58. Marjorie Ruth Clark, *Organized Labor in Mexico* (Chapel Hill: University of North Carolina Press, 1934), p. 203.

59. Alvaro Gamboa Ricalde, *Yucatán*, II, p. 104; Cámara Patrón and Ayora Sarlat, *La obra revolucionaria*, p. 30.

60. The name of the Partido was changed from the Partido Socialista de Yucatán (PSY) to the Partido Socialista del Sureste (PSS) to reflect the new geographical areas it encompassed. Hereafter, it will be referred to as the PSS.

61. Gamboa Ricalde, *Yucatán*, III, pp. 225, 231-32.

62. Bernardino Mena Brito, *Reestructuración histórica de Yucatán*, 3 vols. (México: Editores Mexicanos Unidos, S.A., 1969), pp. 319-21, 326.

63. Gruening, "Felipe Carrillo," p. 61.

64. Felipe Carrillo Puerto, "New Yucatan," *Survey* LII (May 1, 1924), p. 141.

65. Liga Feminista meetings and activities were given daily coverage. Details on the Pan American Conference of Women held in Baltimore, Maryland were carried in *El Popular*, March 30, 1922, p. 1; April 22, 1922, p. 1; and June 16, 1922, pp. 1, 4. Articles on birth control were printed in *El Popular*, June 6, 1922, p. 1, and *Tierra*, No. 17 (August 19, 1923), p. 13. *Tierra*, No. 15 (August 5, 1923), p. 14, has a translation of Margaret Sanger, *Birth Control Review*. Information on the history of education was printed in *Tierra*, No. 24 (October 7, 1923), p. 9, and No. 21 (September 16, 1923), pp. 20-21. The Divorce Law was discussed in *Tierra*, No. 1 (May 1, 1923), pp. 18, 25, and No. 31 (November 25, 1923), p. 28.

66. *Tierra*, No. 23 (September 30, 1923), pp. 3, 15. In *Tierra*, No. 2 (May 13, 1923), p. 7, there is an article on socialism by Velázquez Bringas. For articles by María del Refugio García, see *Tierra*, No. 8 (June 17, 1923), pp. 6-7; No. 11 (July 8, 1923), p. 10; and No. 13 (July 22, 1923), p. 14. *Tierra*, No. 18 (August 26, 1923), pp. 24-25, and No. 21 (September 16, 1923), pp. 1-2, 13, printed articles by Susana Betancourt. The activities of Elvia Carrillo Puerto were printed daily, and her photograph appeared often. See *Tierra*, No. 18 (August 26, 1923), p. 26, and No. 27 (October 28, 1923), p. 15. In *El Popular*, June 15, 1922, p. 3, Aznar discussed the proper attitude women should have in the social movement.

67. Hart, *The Pulse*, p. 65.

68. Ibid., p. 44.

69. Ibid.; Cámara Patrón and Ayora Sarlat, *La obra revolucionaria*, p. 7. Felipe Carrillo Puerto, *Informe rendido por el gobernador constitucional de Yucatán, C. Felipe Carrillo Puerto, ante la h. XXVII legislatura del estado, El 1 de enero de 1923* (Mérida: Imp. y Lit. Gamboa Guzmán, 1923), p. 76; Rita María Medina de Cetina, "Protección a la infancia yucateca," *Siempre Adelante* (October-November 1974), p. 50; Gamboa Ricalde, *Yucatán*, III, p. 267.

70. *El Popular*, February 23, 1922, p. 3.

71. Felipe Carrillo Puerto, "Programa de preparación social para los maestros," March 7, 1922, in *Diario oficial de gobierno del estado de Yucatán* (Mérida), March 9, 1922, pp. 1-2. Government efforts to promote rationalist education met with considerable resistance. The chief voice of opposition was Carlos R. Menéndez's editorials in *La Revista de Yucatán*. Menéndez argued that few understood the system of rationalist education and that teachers were being forced to accept it; *La Revista de Yucatán*, March 9, 1922, p. 3. The Socialist *El Popular* devoted several pages to combating Menéndez's arguments. See, for example, *El Popular*, March 10, 1922, p. 1.

72. Hart, *The Pulse*, pp. 45-48.
73. Gruening, "A Maya Idyl," p. 836.
74. Congreso Obrero de Motul, *Tierra y libertad; Bases que se discutieron y aprobaron en el congreso obrero celebrado en la ciudad de Motul para todas las ligas de resistencia del partido socialista de Yucatán* (México: Talleres Tipográficos del Gobierno del Estado, 1921), pp. 54-56, 86.
75. Rosa Torres was also referred to as Rosa Torre. In this text she is referred to as Rosa Torres.
76. Congreso Obrero de Izamal, *Segunda gran convención de trabajadores convocado por el partido socialista del sureste de México* (Mérida: Compañía Tipográfica del Sureste, 1922), pp. 165-67, 232; Miguel Cantón, *En tiempo de conquista: Veinte años de acción socialista* (Mérida: "Mayab" S.A., n.d.), pp. 37-38.
77. Florencio Zamarripa M., "Elvia Carrillo Puerto, precursora del voto femenino," *Atisbos* (December 18, 1952), p. 12. Acrelio Carrillo Puerto, interview, Mérida, Yucatán, April 5, 1976. (Acrelio was the only living brother of Elvia and Felipe Carrillo Puerto.) In the *Atisbos* interview, Elvia Carrillo stated that she did not remarry after the death of her husband, but both her brother and sister and many others mentioned a second marriage.
78. Carrillo Puerto, *La familia*, pp. 82-89; Zamarripa M., "Elvia Carrillo Puerto," p. 12.
79. Hart, *The Pulse*, p. 45.
80. See *El Popular*, December 5, 1921, pp. 1, 4; December 17, 1921, p. 4; February 2, 1922, p. 1; February 3, 1922, pp. 1, 4; May 20, 1922, pp. 1, 4; August 8, 1922, p. 2.
81. *Tierra*, No. 26 (October 21, 1923), p. 13, printed an article written by Susana Betancourt supporting Elvia Carrillo's candidacy for the state legislature. The same issue carried an endorsement for Beatrice Peniche de Ponce, who was running for representative to the 28th Legislature; *Tierra*, No. 30 (November 5, 1923), p. 15. The Liga "Rita Cetina Gutiérrez" endorsed Calles for president of Mexico.
82. *El Popular*, December 19, 1921, p. 4. Elvia Carrillo was elected Liga president in mid-December 1921. *El Popular*, February 7, 1922, p. 3; May 4, 1922, p. 3, and July 31, 1922, p. 3. *Tierra*, No. 17 (August 19, 1923), p. 4, and No. 18 (August 26, 1923), p. 12.
83. *Tierra*, No. 15 (August 5, 1923), p. 6.
84. *Feminismo: Organo de la liga feminista "Rita Cetina Gutiérrez,"* No. 2 (May 1, 1923), pp. 28-29, had a poem by local Socialist Beatrice Peniche. Only one copy of *Feminismo* could be located in either the Biblioteca Carrillo Ancona or the Hemeroteca Pino Suárez.
85. Hart, *The Pulse*, p. 44, italics added.
86. Both Elvia Carrillo Puerto and Raquel Dzib lost the nomination in the primary but then changed districts and were elected. Pedro Castro Aguilar, researcher at the Hemeroteca Pino Suárez, interview, Mérida, Yucatán, April 19, 1976; Antonia Jiménez Trava, lawyer and first woman magistrate of the Yucatán Supreme Court, interview, Mérida, Yucatán, April 20, 1976.
87. Gruening, "Felipe Carrillo," p. 62; Gruening, "A Maya Idyl," p. 836.
88. Roque Armando Sosa Ferreyro, *El crimen del miedo* (México: Costa-Amic, Ed., 1969), p. 22; Rosa Lie Johansen, interview, Mexico City, August 8, 1976. Johansen had been Alma Reed's roommate in Mexico City during the last years of Reed's life. Johansen inherited many of Reed's papers, including Felipe Carrillo Puerto's divorce papers.
89. Cámara Patrón and Ayora Sarlat, *La obra revolucionaria*, pp. 24-25; Carrillo Puerto, *La familia*, p. 15; Alma Reed, "Peregrina" (unpublished autobiography), Chapter IX, p. 8. Alma Reed stated that members of the Carrillo Puerto family refused to attend Felipe's wedding because of the cruelties of the bride's brother, Pedro Palma, whom they believed caused the death of their daughter Enriqueta. Felipe persuaded Elvia to attend so that he would have at least one member of his family present.
90. Acrelio Carrillo Puerto, interview, Mérida, Yucatán, April 2, 1976. Angelina Carrillo Puerto de Triay, interview, Mérida, Yucatán, April 5, 1976. Angelina was the only living sister of Elvia and Felipe Carrillo Puerto.
91. Pedro Castro Aguilar, interview, Mérida, Yucatán, April 19, 1976; Margarita P. de Hernández, interview, Mérida, Yucatán, April 16, 1976. Hernández is a writer from Yucatán. Beatrice Peniche de Ponce, interview, Mérida, Yucatán, April 11, 1976. Peniche was the last living feminist from the era of Salvador Alvarado and Felipe Carrillo Puerto.
92. Harry Bercovich, Jr., "Yucatan's Slain Governor Was Savior of His People," *San Francisco Examiner*, March 16, 1924, p. 3. The popular Mexican song "Peregrina" was

written for Alma Reed, at the request of Governor Carrillo. The song expresses both their differences in background (her "pines" and "snow" and his "palms" and "tropical land") and their love for each other. For more information on the song "Peregrina," see Sosa Ferreyro, *El crimen*, pp. 117-20. After Carrillo's death, Reed traveled to Europe and then lived in New York, where she promoted the career of José Clemente Orozco. Eventually, Reed returned to Mexico. She is buried next to Felipe in a Mérida cemetery.

93. For a copy of the Divorce Law, see Sosa Ferreyro, *El crimen*, p. 25 and opposite p. 33; Walter Berry to Consular Bureau, March 14, 1923, U.S. Department of State, Microcopy 274, National Archives, 812.4054/10. Berry noted that the Yucatán law conformed to federal legislation, in that men were eligible for immediate remarriage but women were required to wait for three hundred days. Hereafter all correspondence of the Department of State will be referred to by number.

94. Marsh to Secretary of State, March 26, 1923, 812.4054/1331; Marsh to Secretary of State, March 29, 1923, 812.4054/1332.

95. Hernan C. Vogenitz, American Vice-Consul to Secretary of State, December 6, 1924, 812.4054/1570; Hernan C. Vogenitz to Secretary of State, April 21, 1926, 812.4054/1703.

96. Reed, "Peregrina," Chapter V, p. 22. Reed stated that the governor first became interested in birth control clinics through his acquaintance with Sweden's program. Carrillo maintained contact with Swedish scientists, and they provided advice in developing the Yucatán program.

97. Gruening, "A Maya Idyl," p. 836.

98. Anastasio Manzanilla Domínguez, *El comunismo en México y el archivo de Carrillo Puerto* (México: n.p., 1955); opposite p. 187 is a letter from Mrs. Anne Kennedy to Carrillo about establishing birth control clinics in Yucatán.

99. Margaret Sanger, *La regulación de la natalidad o la brújula del hogar* (Mérida: Imp. "Mayab" S.A., 1922), pp. 3, 26.

100. Esperanza Velázquez Bringas, *La limitación racional de la familia como mejoramiento del proletariado y de la raza* (Mérida: Imp. "Mayab" S.A., 1922), p. 9.

101. *El Popular*, March 10, 1922, pp. 3-4.

102. José Díaz Bolio, interview, Mérida, Yucatán, April 20, 1976. Díaz's sister married Felipe Carrillo's brother Benjamin, who was executed with Felipe in January 1924. Díaz Bolio is a writer. See *El Popular*, March 11, 1922, p. 3; March 14, 1922, p. 3; March 20, 1922, p. 4; March 24, 1922, p. 3; and March 25, 1922, p. 6.

103. Gamboa Ricalde, *Yucatán*, III, pp. 301-302.

104. *El Popular*, August 1, 1922, pp. 1, 4, and July 27, 1922, p. 1.

105. *Tierra*, No. 2 (May 13, 1923), p. 7; *El Popular*, February 24, 1922, p. 3; April 22, 1922, pp. 3-4; April 25, 1922, p. 3; April 26, 1922, p. 3; file on Esperanza Velázquez Bringas in the Bibliographical Collection of the Biblioteca Nacional.

106. *El Popular*, July 6, 1922, p. 1.

107. *La Lucha*, May 19, 1923, pp. 1, 4, and May 9, 1922, p. 3.

108. Ibid., May 22, 1922, pp. 1, 4; July 23, 1923, p. 4; July 7, 1923, p. 4; February 2, 1924, p. 2; May 12, 1923, p. 3.

109. *Pan American Union Bulletin*, LVI, No. 3 (1923), p. 309. Although literate women could vote in San Luis Potosí, the law prohibited women who were members of religious orders (and women who were under their care) from voting and running for office. Walter Boyle to Secretary of State, January 20, 1923, 812.405/121, reported that women were granted suffrage and that a woman was appointed as a substitute magistrate of the state supreme court because of pressure from Governor Rafael Nieto, who wished to appear progressive.

110. Boyle to Secretary of State, November 22, 1924, 812.405, No. 9.

111. Gruening, *Mexico and Its Heritage*, pp. 629-30.

112. Ibid., p. 629.

113. Ibid.; Zamarripa M., "Elvia Carrillo Puerto," p. 12. Apparently Elvia Carrillo's opponents were doing more than trying to frighten her; Carrillo stated that she had been ordered killed.

114. Gruening, *Mexico and Its Heritage*, p. 629. Carrillo won the election by a count of 4,576 to 56 votes. Ward M. Morton, *Woman Suffrage in Mexico* (Gainesville: University of Florida Press, 1962), p. 104; *Excelsior*, July 13, 1926, pp. 1, 7.
115. Carrillo Puerto, *La familia*, p. 85.
116. Artemisa N. Sáenz Royo ["Xóchitl"], "Mujeres revolucionarias: Elvia Carrillo Puerto," *Mujer*, No. 7 (January 1933), p. 15; Fortino Ibarra de Anda, *El periodismo en México*, 2 vols., Vol. II: *Las mexicanas en el periodismo*, 2nd ed. (México: Editorial "Juventa," 1937), p. 139; Carrillo Puerto, *La Familia*, p. 86.
117. Sáenz Royo, "Mujeres revolucionarias," p. 15, wrote in laudatory terms about Elvia Carrillo and her long career as a feminist.
118. Zamarripa M., "Elvia Carrillo Puerto," p. 12.
119. *El Popular*, October 10, 1922, p. 4; February 3, 1922, pp. 1, 4; and May 20, 1922, pp. 1, 4.
120. Leopoldo Aguilar Roca, "Un campeón de la educacion popular," *Revista Yucateca de Pedagogía*, Año I, No. 3 (November 1950), pp. 171-73.
121. Rosa Torre(s) G., *Mi actuación en el h. ayuntamiento de Mérida, Yucatán, México en el año de 1923* (n.p., 1936), pp. 4-13. Rosa Torre was frequently referred to as Rosa Torres, and Rosa Torres is used throughout the text. Fanny Azcuy, "La primera concejal," *Excelsior*, Section C, October 17, 1954, p. 13.
122. Beatrice Peniche de Ponce, interview, Mérida, Yucatán, April 11, 1976.
123. Gamboa Ricalde, *Yucatán*, III, p. 347; Cámara Patrón and Ayora Sarlat, *La obra revolucionaria*, pp. 13-18. Although de la Huerta denied any responsibility for Carrillo's death, Elvia Carrillo blamed him for her brothers' executions. See Sosa Ferreyro, *El crimen*, opposite p. 129 and Zamarripa M., "Elvia Carrillo Puerto," p. 12.
124. Gruening, "Felipe Carrillo," p. 62.
125. General Eugenio Martínez to Obregón, April 30, 1924, Archivo General de la Nación, Papeles Presidenciales, Ramo de Obregón-Calles, 101-R-2-I-1.
126. Elvia Carrillo, in Zamarripa M., "Elvia Carrillo Puerto," p. 12, stated that several Yucatán newspapers announced a reward for her head. Rosa Torre(s) G. in *Mi actuación*, p. 8, noted that after Governor Carrillo's assassination, Elvia Carrillo's home was sacked several times. Elvia Carrillo Puerto to Obregón, September 2, 1924, Archivo General de la Nación, Papeles Presidenciales, Ramo de Obregón-Calles, 428-Y-5.
127. Liga Revolucionaria Feminista "Aurora Abán," *Programa de la acción feminista en Yucatán* (Mérida: n.p., 1930).

CHAPTER 4

1. Dawn Keremitsis, *La industria textil mexicana en el siglo XIX* (México: SepSetentas, 1973), pp. 200-201, noted a downward trend in numbers of women textile workers, which has continued to the present.
2. *Pan American Union Bulletin*, LVII, No. 6 (December 1923), p. 624.
3. Wilfrid Hardy Callcott, *Liberalism in Mexico 1857-1929* (Palo Alto: Stanford University Press, 1931), p. 347.
4. *Pan American Union Bulletin*, LXV, No. 1 (January 1931), p. 105; Lillian Estelle Fisher, "The Influence of the Present Mexican Revolution upon the Status of Mexican Women," *Hispanic American Historical Review*, XXII, No. 1 (February 1942), p. 216.
5. Gabriela Durazo, "La mujer en la historia y en la vida de México," *Pensamiento Político*, XIX, No. 76 (June 1975), p. 209; Ward M. Morton, *Woman Suffrage in Mexico* (Gainesville: University of Florida, 1962), p. 14.
6. Ramón Eduardo Ruiz, "Mexico's Struggle for Rural Education, 1910-50" (Unpublished Ph.D. dissertation, University of California at Berkeley, 1954), p. 67.
7. George F. Kneller, *The Education of the Mexican Nation* (New York: Columbia University Press, 1951), p. 47; Ernest Gruening, *Mexico and Its Heritage* (New York: The Century Co., 1928), p. 518; George I. Sánchez, *The Development of Higher Education in Mexico* (New York: King's Crown Press, 1944), p. 88. Also, an urban cultural mission was created to help train urban teachers.

8. Fisher, "The Influence of the Present Mexican Revolution," pp. 226-27.
9. *Pan American Union Bulletin*, LVII, No. 2 (August 1923), p. 211.
10. *Pan American Union Bulletin*, LVIII, No. 11 (November 1924), p. 1165; Adelina Zendejas, journalist, interview, Mexico City, July 28, 1976.
11. Ernest Gruening, *Mexico*, p. 543, quoting Francisco Bulnes, *El verdadero Díaz y la revolución* (México: n.p., 1920), pp. 422-23.
12. Gruening, *Mexico*, pp. 544-47, quoting the *Boletín del Departamento de Salubridad*, No. 4, 1926, p. 6; Adelina Zendejas, interview, Mexico City, July 28, 1976.
13. Gruening, *Mexico*, p. 547.
14. *El Universal*, June 12, 1934, pp. 1 and 8, and June 19, 1934, p. 8.
15. Fisher, "The Influence of the Present Mexican Revolution," pp. 216, 226; C. J. Velarde, *Under the Mexican Flag, The Mexican Struggle Outlined* (Los Angeles: Southland Pub. House, 1926), p. 305.
16. *Pan American Union Bulletin*, LXII, pt. II (October 1928), p. 1191.
17. Ifigenia M. de Navarrete, *La mujer y los derechos sociales* (México: Ediciones Oasis, 1969), p. 188; Artemisa Sáenz Royo ["Xóchitl"], *Historia político-social-cultural del movimiento femenino en México 1914-50* (México: M. León Sánchez, 1954), pp. 82-83.
18. Adelina Zendejas, "El movimiento femenil mexicano," *El Día*, June 16, 1975, p. 16; "Feminismo," *Enciclopedia de México*, IV, 1970, p. 90; *Pan American Union Bulletin*, LVIII, No. 3 (March 1924), p. 321; LVIII, No. 5 (May 1924), p. 533; LVIII, No. 1 (July 1923), p. 95.
19. *Derechos de la mujer mexicana* (México: XLVII Legislatura del congreso de la unión, 1969), p. 18; Margarita Robles de Mendoza, *La evolución de la mujer en México* (México: Imp. Galas, 1931), p. 19; *El Universal*, February 17, 1922, p. 1; Francesca Miller, "The International Relations of Women of the Americas, 1890-1928," *The Americas*, XLIII, No. 2 (October 1986), pp. 178-80.
20. *Pan American Union Bulletin*, LV, No. 7 (July 1922), p. 48; *El Universal*, May 17, 1923, p. 1; May 23, 1923, p. 1; May 27, 1923, p. 8.
21. *Pan American Union Bulletin*, LVI, No. 6 (June 1923), pp. 630-31; *Derechos de la mujer mexicana*, p. 19; "Feminismo," p. 91, contains a list of delegate demands.
22. F. Ibarra de Anda, *El periodismo en México*, Vol. II: *Las mexicanas en el periodismo*, 2nd ed. (México: Editorial "Juventa," 1937), pp. 131-39. Ana María Zapata served as president of UMA Suriana. For a photograph, with Margarita Robles de Mendoza, see *El Nacional*, September 4, 1936, p. 3. Artemisa Sáenz Royo, *Semblanzas; Mujeres mexicanas revolucionarias y guerreras, revolucionarias ideológicas. Por . . . ["Xóchitl"]* (México: Imp. M. León Sánchez, S.C.L., 1960), pp. 42-46.
23. Robles de Mendoza, *La evolución*, pp. 53, 108.
24. *New York Times*, Section 7, September 26, 1920, p. 6; *Pan American Union Bulletin*, L, No. 1 (January 1920), p. 114.
25. *Women in a Changing World: The Dynamic Story of the International Council of Women since 1888* (London: Routledge and Kegan Paul, 1966), pp. 36-39, 44, 56, 62, 203.
26. María Efraína Rocha, *Semblanzas biográficas de algunas luchadoras mexicanas contemporáneas* (México: Ediciones del Comité Coordinatora Femenino, 1947), p. 27; *Mujeres mexicanas notables* (México: Talleres de la Cámara de Diputados, 1975), pp. 132-33, 240-41.
27. Adelina Zendejas, "Las mujeres de hoy deben rendir público homenaje de reconocimiento a todas ellas," *Mujeres*, No. 67 (August 10, 1961), p. 22; Verna Carleton Millan, *Mexico Reborn* (Boston: Houghton Mifflin Co., 1939), p. 167.
28. Juana Gutiérrez de Mendoza, "El General Calles no ha variado su criterio respecto a los desheredados," *Vésper*, March 15, 1932, p. 2. María Antonieta Rascón, "La mujer y la lucha social," *Imagen y realidad de la mujer*, ed. by Elena Urrutia (México: SepSetentas, 1975), p. 173, dates the founding of the Santiago Orozco Colony as 1919. The colony was probably named after Juana's son-in-law, Santiago Orozco, who collaborated with her in publishing the indigenous newspaper *La Reforma* in 1914. Orozco was a Zapatista general killed in a battle over Indian lands in 1915.
29. Susana Mendoza, interview, Cuernavaca, August 12, 1976; Rascón, "La mujer y la lucha social," p. 173.

30. *Excelsior*, December 18, 1924, p. 1, and January 17, 1925, pp. 1, 6. The president's wife, Natalia Chacón de Calles, was designated honorary president of the congress. *El Universal*, July 6, 1925, p. 1.

31. *El Universal*, July 7, 1925, pp. 1, 8, and July 8, 1925, pp. 1, 3.

32. Ibid., July 10, 1925, pp. 1, 10.

33. Ibid., July 12, 1925, pp. 1, 11; *Mujeres mexicanas notables*, p. 127.

34. *El Universal*, July 13, 1925, pp. 1, 8, and July 16, 1925, p. 10.

35. Ibid., July 15, 1925, p. 3.

36. María Ríos Cárdenas, *La mujer mexicana es ciudadana. Historia con fisonomia de una novela de costumbres, 1930-1940* (México: A. del Bosque, 1942), pp. 26-48, described the first meeting of the National Congress of Women Workers and Peasants, which she attended. *El Universal*, September 28, 1931, p. 1, and October 2, 1931, p. 2. Leticia Barragán and Amanda Rosales, "Congresos nacionales de obreras y campesinas," *Historia Obrera* 5, II, No. 5 (June 1975), pp. 24-44, contains newspaper excerpts from all three congresses. The first meeting is discussed on pp. 24-30.

37. *El Universal*, October 3, 1931, pp. 2, 7. García's speech was printed in Matilde Rodríguez Cabo, *La mujer y la revolución* (México: n.p., 1937), p. 30, and Esperanza Balmaceda de Josefe, "La mujer ante la revolución," December 16, 1936, collection at the office of the Año Internacional de la Mujer in Mexico City.

38. *El Universal*, October 4, 1931, Section 2, pp. 1, 8; *El Nacional*, October 4, 1931, p. 2.

39. María Ríos Cárdenas, "Voto por la mujer," *El Nacional*, October 6, 1931, pp. 1, 2; *El Universal*, October 6, 1931, pp. 1, 8.

40. María Ríos Cárdenas, "Pide al gobierno la reducción de sacerdotes, el congreso nacional de obreras y campesinas," *El Nacional*, October 5, 1931, pp. 1, 2; *Omega*, October 7, 1931, pp. 1, 3.

41. *El Nacional*, Part II, October 8, 1931, pp. 1, 4; *El Universal*, October 1, 1931, p. 1 and October 7, 1931, p. 1.

42. Ríos Cárdenas, *La mujer mexicana*, pp. 49-51.

43. *Excelsior*, November 1, 1933, pp. 3, 10. Barragán and Rosales, "Congresos nacionales," pp. 30-39, contains information on the second meeting. *Excelsior*, Part II, November 27, 1933, p. 1; *El Mundo*, November 28, 1933, p. 1; *El Nacional*, November 28, 1933, p. 5. *Excelsior*, November 28, 1933, p. 5, published a highly critical editorial entitled "Comunismo feminista," which ridiculed the efforts of delegates, especially Uranga, whose comments were called "absurd." The editor concluded that women did not have the faculty or aptitude to address socio-political issues and were merely imitating men.

44. María Ríos Cárdenas, "Emancipación integral de las mujeres," *El Nacional*, November 29, 1933, p. 5; *El Universal*, November 29, 1933, p. 8.

45. *Excelsior*, Part II, November 29, 1933, pp. 1, 6; *El Nacional*, November 24, 1933, pp. 1, 7; *El Mundo*, December 1, 1933, p. 1.

46. Ríos Cárdenas, *La mujer mexicana*, pp. 107-118, stated that more than 400 women attended the Third Congress. *El Universal*, September 18, 1934, p. 1. Barragán and Rosales, "Congresos nacionales," pp. 39-44, discusses the Third Congress. Most of the information was taken from *El Informador* (Guadalajara), September 14, 1934.

47. Morton, *Woman Suffrage*, pp. 9-12.

48. John W. F. Dulles, *Yesterday in Mexico: A Chronicle of the Revolution, 1919-1936* (Austin: University of Texas Press, 1961), p. 619.

49. Morton, *Woman Suffrage*, p. 12; *El Universal*, July 20, 1925, p. 1; July 21, 1925, p. 1; July 22, 1925, p. 1.

50. C. J. Velarde, *Under the Mexican Flag* (Los Angeles: Southland Publishing House, 1926), pp. 303-306.

51. Emilio Portes Gil, interview, Mexico City, August 16, 1976. Portes Gil and Calles were in power when Alexandra Kollontai, Soviet ambassador to Mexico, was serving. She left Mexico in 1928 because the high altitude caused her discomfort.

52. Robles de Mendoza, *La evolución*, pp. 26, 58-61.

53. Robert Quirk, *The Mexican Revolution and the Catholic Church, 1910-1929* (Bloomington: Indiana University Press, 1973), p. 124.

54. Ibid., pp. 126-27.

55. Gruening, *Mexico*, pp. 37, 103, 628.

56. Quirk, *The Mexican Revolution*, pp. 139, 153, 171-72. James A. Magner, *Men of Mexico* (Milwaukee: Bruce Publishing Co., 1942), pp. 533-34, maintained that Calles's attitude toward the church can be understood in terms of his stubborn desire to make himself absolute master of Mexico. Magner noted the contradiction between Calles's words and his personal actions: his second marriage was contracted in the presence of a Catholic priest; some of his daughters were enrolled in Catholic schools in California; and during a serious illness he entered a hospital run by a Catholic sisterhood in Los Angeles.

57. Gruening, *Mexico*, pp. 149, 176, 179.

58. David C. Bailey, *¡Viva Cristo Rey! The Cristero Rebellion and the Church-State Conflict in Mexico* (Austin: University of Texas Press, 1974), p. 303.

59. Brian Kelly, "The Cristero Rebellion—1926-1929: Its Diplomacy and Solution" (Unpublished Ph.D. dissertation, University of New Mexico, 1973), p. 330; William Weber Johnson, *Heroic Mexico: The Violent Emergence of a Modern Nation* (Garden City, New York: Doubleday and Co., 1968), p. 394; Quirk, *The Mexican Revolution*, pp. 190-91; Kneller, *The Education of the Mexican Nation*, pp. 49-51.

60. Bailey, *¡Viva Cristo Rey!*, p. 162, stated that the Brigadas Femeninas were organized by a group of young women from Jalisco, with headquarters in Guadalajara. Bailey noted also that the women obtained ammunition in various ways, including manufacturing it themselves. Jesús Degollado Guízar, *Memorias de Jesús Degollado Guízar* (México: Editorial Jus, 1957), p. 163. Jean Meyer, *Los cristeros*, Vol. III: *La cristada*, 2nd ed. (México: Siglo Veintiuno Ed., S.A., 1974), pp. 24-26, stated that there were 25,000 Brigada members. Kelly, "The Cristero Rebellion," p. 256, quoting J. J. González, *Los cristeros* (México: Impresión privada, 1930), pp. 55-57. Ida Clyde Clarke, *Women of Today* (Chicago: The John Winston Co., 1928), p. 37, noted that on April 12, 1928, *El Universal* reported on Agripina, a rebel leader who conferred the title of colonel upon herself and led 150 men into the field against the government in the district of Colon in Querétaro. After attacking a ranch and seizing thirty horses, she was last seen marching toward Guanajuato. Government troops were rushed in to stop her.

61. Barbara Ann Miller, *The Role of Women in the Mexican Cristero Rebellion: A New Chapter* (Ann Arbor: University Microfilms International, 1981), p. 90.

62. *Excelsior*, August 9, 1926, p. 7; Gruening, *Mexico*, p. 386; Wilfred Parsons, *Mexican Martyrdom* (New York: Macmillan Co., 1936), pp. 77-78, 80-89.

63. Dulles, *Yesterday in Mexico*, p. 363.

64. Ibid., pp. 398-403.

65. Kelly, "The Cristero Rebellion," pp. 260-72; Quirk, *The Mexican Revolution*, pp. 195-234; Parsons, *Mexican Martyrdom*, pp. 69-72; Bailey, *¡Viva Cristo Rey!*, pp. 218-19, 228-29. Madre Conchita published her memoirs in *Hoy*, and later wrote *Una martir de México*.

66. Dulles, *Yesterday in Mexico*, p. 425.

67. Lesley Byrd Simpson, *Many Mexicos* (Berkeley and Los Angeles: University of California Press, 1969), p. 312, stated that the Cristeros believed that they had been betrayed. The provisions of the agreement included: 1) a general amnesty for all Cristeros who laid down their arms, 2) the restoration of priests' and bishops' houses, 3) the civil registration of only those priests who had been appointed by the superior hierarchy, 4) the allowance of religious teaching in public schools, and 5) appropriate guarantees of the above provisions.

68. Bailey, *¡Viva Cristo Rey!*, pp. 39-40.

69. Dulles, *Yesterday in Mexico*, p. 559.

70. Ibid., pp. 562-65.

71. Adelina Zendejas, "La mujer mexicana en el periodismo," *El Gallo Ilustrado* (June 22, 1975), p. 3; *La Mujer*, Año I, No. 1 (December 12, 1926), p. 1; Año 1, No. 6 (June 1, 1927), p. 1; Año II, No. 13 (January 1, 1928), p. 8; Año II, No. 15 (March 1, 1928), p. 8; Año II, No. 14 (February 1, 1928), p. 8. Parts of Esperanza Velázquez Bringas's thesis were published, as well as poetry by Alfonsina Storni. Lola Anderson, "Mexican Women Journalists," *Pan American Union Bulletin*, LXVIII, No. 5 (May 1934), pp. 315-20.

72. Fisher, "The Influence of the Present Mexican Revolution," p. 224; Ibarra de Anda, *Las mexicanas*, pp. 70-72.

73. Zendejas, "La mujer mexicana," p. 3; Fisher, "The Influence of the Present Mexican Revolution," p. 223.

74. Ibarra de Anda, *Las mexicanas*, pp. 60-62; Fisher, "The Influence of the Present Mexican Revolution," p. 223.
75. *El Machete*, February 25, 1928, p. 1; March 24, 1937, pp. 1, 2; April 24, 1937, p. 3; May 29, 1937, pp. 1, 4.
76. Frederick C. Turner, *The Dynamic of Mexican Nationalism* (Chapel Hill: University of North Carolina Press, 1968), p. 12; Juana Gutiérrez de Mendoza, "Comentarios" (unpublished), January 8, 1922.
77. "Acta constitutiva del grupo Indo-América," *América India*, January 12, 1930, p. 6; Juana Gutiérrez de Mendoza, "Tres razones fundamentales del grupo Indo-América," *América India*, December 25, 1929, p. 3.
78. Ibarra de Anda, *Las mexicanas*, pp. 50-54.
79. *La Voz de la Mujer* (June 22, 1932), p. 1; Zendejas, "La mujer mexicana," p. 4.

CHAPTER 5

1. George F. Kneller, *The Education of the Mexican Nation* (New York: Columbia University Press, 1951), pp. 54, 79.
2. Verna Carleton Millan, *Mexico Reborn* (Boston: Houghton Mifflin Co., 1939), pp. 75-79.
3. Nathaniel and Sylvia Weyl, *The Reconquest of Mexico: The Years of Lázaro Cárdenas* (London: Oxford University Press, 1939), pp. 79-80, 138.
4. Betty Kirk, *Covering the Mexican Front: The Battle of Europe versus America* (Norman: University of Oklahoma Press, 1942), p. 45.
5. Kirk, *Covering the Mexican Front*, pp. 75-76.
6. Dawn Keremitsis, "Women and Political Change in the Era of Cárdenas" (unpublished paper, 1976), p. 2.
7. *El Nacional*, December 29, 1936, pp. 3, 7, and February 25, 1938, pp. 1, 4. María Ríos Cárdenas, *La mujer mexicana es ciudadana. Historia con fisonomía de una novela de costumbres, 1930-1940* (México: A. del Bosque, 1942), p. 123. The author was a key participant in the women's rights movement in the 1930s. Archivo General de la Nación, Papeles Presidenciales, Ramo de Cárdenas, Paquete 528, 544/1, #42392.
8. Editorial on alcoholism, *El Nacional*, August 2, 1935, p. 2; October 7, 1935, p. 1; July 5, 1939, pp. 1, 7. Alcoholism was considered a serious social problem, and several conferences on the subject were held. See, for example, Luis G. Franco, *La lucha de la mujer contra el vicio del alcohol* (México: Secretaría de Industria, Comercio y Trabajo, 1930), a fifteen-page pamphlet describing a conference on the subject.
9. *El Nacional*, September 10, 1939, p. 1.
10. Artemisa Sáenz Royo ["Xóchitl"], *Historia político-social-cultural del movimiento femenino en México 1914-50* (México: M. León Sánchez, 1954), pp. 91-92; Lillian Estelle Fisher, "The Influence of the Present Mexican Revolution," *Hispanic American Historical Review*, XXII, No. 1 (February 1942), p. 219; Millan, *Mexico Reborn*, pp. 168-69.
11. Fisher, "The Influence of the Present Mexican Revolution," pp. 217-18; Beatrice Newhall, "Woman Suffrage in the Americas," *Pan American Union Bulletin*, LXX, No. 5 (May 1936), pp. 426-27; Ward M. Morton, *Woman Suffrage in Mexico* (Gainesville: University of Florida Press, 1962), p. 21, quoting José Mijares Palencia, *El gobierno mexicano su organizatión y funcionamiento* (México: Sociedad Mexicana de Publicaciones Editores, 1936), pp. 335-36; Keremitsis, "Women and Political Change," p. 10.
12. Keremitsis, "Women and Political Change," pp. 5-6.
13. *El Nacional*, August 5, 1936, p. 3; Ifigenia M. de Navarrete, *La mujer y los derechos sociales* (México: Ediciones Oasis, 1969), p. 198.
14. de Navarrete, *La mujer*, pp. 192, 203-204; Esperanza de Vázquez Gómez, "Historia y finaldades del Club Internacional de Mujeres," *Mujeres*, No. 68 (August 25, 1961), p. 18; Elena Urrutia, "Elvira Truba," *Fem: Publicación feminista mensual*, Vol. VIII, No. 3 (October-November 1983), p. 17. Amalia Caballero de Castillo Ledón and Julia Nava de Ruisánchez were among the charter members of the Club Internacional de Mujeres.
15. *Pan American Union Bulletin*, LXXI, No. 9 (September 1937), p. 729; LXXII, No. 7 (July 1938), p. 434; LXXIV, No. 5 (May 1940), pp. 415-16; de Navarrete, *La mujer*, p. 204.

16. Millan, *Mexico Reborn*, p. 168.

17. *Pan American Union Bulletin*, LXIV, No. 10, pt. II (October 1930), p. 1078.

18. Millan, *Mexico Reborn*, p. 167. Morton, *Woman Suffrage*, p. 15, reported that García accused Calles and Ortiz Rubio of withdrawing support for women's suffrage. Sáenz Royo, *Historica político*, pp. 90-91.

19. *El Nacional*, January 28, 1932, pp. 1, 2, 8.

20. Millan, *Mexico Reborn*, p. 166; Emilio Portes Gil, *Quince años de política mexicana*, 2nd ed. (México: Ediciones Botas, 1941), p. 514. See John W. F. Dulles, *Yesterday in Mexico: A Chronicle of the Revolution, 1919-1936* (Austin: University of Texas Press, 1961), pp. 640-49, for a brief account of the conflict between Múgica and Portes Gil.

21. Adelina Zendejas, "El movimiento femenil mexicano," *El Día* (June 16, 1975), p. 15. Millan, *Mexico Reborn*, pp. 164-66, reported that when she visited Frente headquarters, many women in the office were non-Spanish-speaking Indians. Esperanza Tuñon, "El frente unico pro derechos de la mujer 1935-1938," *Fem: Publicación feminista*, Vol. VIII, No. 30 (October-November 1983), p. 19.

22. Newhall, "Woman Suffrage," p. 427; Morton, *Woman Suffrage*, p. 22.

23. Portes Gil, *Quince años*, p. 528; Millan, *Mexico Reborn*, pp. 106-107; Morton, *Woman Suffrage*, p. 27. Among the papers of Juana B. Gutiérrez de Mendoza was a twenty-seven-page pamphlet called *Estatutos del grupo "Acción Femenina" centro nacional director pro-Múgica* (México, n.p., 1939). *Estatutos* outlined General Múgica's support for women's issues and his supportive activities at the 1917 constitutional meeting. Gutiérrez's feelings on Múgica's candidacy are unclear. Adelina Zendejas, interview, Mexico City, July 21, 1976, stated that Múgica was not a feminist in his personal life. During this period Múgica was married to Matilde Rodríguez Cabo, but they later divorced.

24. Charles C. Cumberland, *Mexico: The Struggle for Modernity* (New York: Oxford University Press, 1968), pp. 288-89.

25. *El Informador de Guadalajara*, September 10, 1934, p. 1.

26. Weyl, *The Reconquest of Mexico*, p. 322. See pp. 166-67 for an account of an attack against teachers in Ciudad González, Guanajuato, where eighteen teachers were killed and thirty injured.

27. *El Nacional*, January 21, 1936, pp. 1, 7; April 25, 1936, pp. 1, 4; and September 10, 1936, pp. 3, 4.

28. Morton, *Woman Suffrage*, p. 28, quoting Joseph Freeman, Luis Chávez Orozco, and Enrique Gutmann, *Lázaro Cárdenas visto por 3 hombres* (México: Editorial Masas, 1937), p. 21. Capitalization was used in the original document.

29. *New York Times*, April 4, 1937, p. 5, and April 12, 1937, p. 9. More than 10,000 women voted in Mexico City. Millan, *Mexico Reborn*, p. 167; María Antonieta Rascón, "La mujer y la lucha social," *Imagen y realidad de la mujer*, ed. by Elena Urrutia, SepSetentas, No. 172 (México: Secretaría de Educación Pública, 1975), pp. 169-70.

30. *El Universal*, April 29, 1937, pp. 1, 12; April 30, 1937, pp. 1, 8; August 27, 1937, pp. 1, 4; *New York Times*, Part VI, September 12, 1937, p. 7; and August 28, 1937, p. 5.

31. Archivo General de la Nación, Papeles Presidenciales, Ramo de Cárdenas, Paquete 528, 544/1, #41938, Elvia Carrillo Puerto to Cárdenas, August 27, 1937; #9905, María del Refugio García, Lucinda Villarreal, and Margarita Robles de Mendoza to Cárdenas, March 1, 1937. The women wanted to meet with the president to discuss suffrage. #49946, M. Rodríguez Cabo to Cárdenas, August 28, 1937; #42272, Hermila Galindo to Cárdenas, August 30, 1937.

32. Archivo General de la Nación, Papeles Presidenciales, Ramo de Cárdenas, Paquete 528, 544/1; Anna Kelton Wiley, "Woman Suffrage in Mexico," *Equal Rights*, Vol. 23, No. 11 (June 15, 1937), pp. 84, 88, 102-104.

33. *El Universal*, December 17, 1937, pp. 1, 6; CTM pledged its full support for the amendment, December 22, 1937, pp. 1, 11; and December 23, 1937, pp. 1, 10.

34. Morton, *Woman Suffrage*, p. 34, quoting William P. Tucker, *The Mexican Government Today* (Minneapolis: University of Minnesota Press, 1957), pp. 43, 49-50, 58.

35. *El Nacional*, April 11, 1938, pp. 1, 6; April 12, 1938, pp. 1, 5; April 13, 1938, pp. 1, 6; April 14, 1938, p. 1.

36. *El Nacional*, July 7, 1938, p. 1; *New York Times*, July 8, 1938, p. 8.

37. Morton, *Woman Suffrage*, p. 36; William Cameron Townsend, *Lázaro Cárdenas: Mexican Democrat* (Ann Arbor: George Wahr Publishing Co., 1952), p. 335.

38. *El Nacional*, September 23, 1938, pp. 1, 6; October 4, 1938, p. 8; *New York Times*, May 28, 1939, p. 15.

39. Lesley Byrd Simpson, *Many Mexicos* (Berkeley and Los Angeles: University of California Press, 1969), pp. 335-38. David C. Bailey, *¡Viva Cristo Rey! The Cristero Rebellion and the Church-State Conflict in Mexico* (Austin: University of Texas Press, 1974), pp. 297-98, stated that Camacho headed the Colima campaign against the Cristeros. On December 2, 1940, his second day in office, Camacho released Madre Conchita from prison.

40. Morton, *Woman Suffrage*, p. 39.

41. *El Nacional*, May 18, 1939, pp. 1, 7; May 25, 1939, pp. 1, 8; Morton, *Woman Suffrage*, pp. 40-41.

42. Townsend, *Lázaro Cárdenas*, pp. 334-35.

43. *New York Times*, March 25, 1950, p. 5.

44. Adelina Zendejas, "La mujer mexicana en el periodismo," *El Gallo Ilustrado* (June 22, 1975), p. 4. Mexican women's magazines during the 1940s, 1950s, and 1960s, such as *Ideas: Revista de Mujeres de México* and *Mujeres*, are packed with information on the women's struggle. *Ideas* published articles by some of Mexico's most talented women writers: Patricia Cox, Eulalia Guzmán, Leonor Llach, Julia Nava de Ruisánchez, María Luisa Ocampo, Enriqueta de Parodi, Elena Sodi de Pallares, Elena Torres, Luz Vera, and Artemisa Sáenz Royo. *Mujeres*, a monthly still being published, ran several features on Mexican women from the time of the Aztec empire to the present. Sáenz Royo, Adelina Zendejas, Palma Guillén, and María Elvira Bermúdez contributed articles on women to *Mujeres*.

45. Zendejas, "La mujer mexicana," p. 4; *Mujeres*, No. 22 (September 20, 1959), pp. 12-13.

46. Susana Mendoza, interview, Cuernavaca, August 12, 1976.

47. *Alma Mexicana*, November 1, 1935, p. 1, and November 15, 1935, pp. 5-8; María de los Angeles Mendieta Alatorre, *La mujer en la revolución mexicana* (México: Talleres Gráficos de la Nación, 1961), p. 33.

48. *El Heraldo de México*, October 8, 1930, pp. 1, 4; December 3, 1930, pp. 1, 3; April 29, 1931, p. 1.

49. Gutiérrez's intense dislike of Spaniards surfaced in her work *Los tres problemas nacionales*.

50. The Amigas del Pueblo was a continuation of the original 1909 Club. Founders were Manuela Peláez, Laura Mendoza, Rosa G. Vda. de Maciel (Juana's sister), and Juana Gutiérrez.

51. Esperanza Tuñon, "El frente unico pro derechos de la mujer 1935-1938," *Fem*, Vol. VIII, No. 30 (October-November 1983), pp. 21-23.

52. Juana B. Gutiérrez de Mendoza, unpublished papers.

53. María Efraína Rocha, *Semblanzas biográficas de algunas luchadoras mexicanas contemporáneas* (México: Ediciones del Comité Coordinador Femenino, 1947), pp. 6-7, 17; Rosalie D'Chumacero, *Perfil y pensamiento de la mujer mexicana*, 3 vols., Vol. I (México: Edicion de la Autora, 1961), pp. 180-82; *Mujeres mexicanas notables* (México: Talleres de la Cámara de Diputados, 1975), pp. 189-95.

54. *Mujeres mexicanas notables*, pp. 218-20; Rocha, *Semblanzas*, pp. 15-16, 19; C. Frerot, "Contribución de la Dra. Esther Chapa a la liberación femenina," *Excelsior*, January 31, 1976, pp. 1, 2, 6. It is interesting to note that Esther Chapa and Laura Mendoza (Juana's daughter) had been married to the same man. After Lorenzo Rosendo Gómez (a Communist) divorced Mendoza, he married Chapa. Rosendo was Chapa's second husband. Her first was Ismael Cosío Villegas, brother of historian Daniel Cosío Villegas. Dr. Virginia Chapa (Esther Chapa's sister), interview, Mexico City, July 19, 1976; Susana Mendoza, interview, Cuernavaca, August 12, 1976.

55. D'Chumacero, *Perfil y pensamiento*, pp. 31-34; Sáenz Royo, *Historia político*, pp. 28-30; *Mujeres mexicanas notables*, pp. 123, 127; Morton, *Woman Suffrage*, pp. 57, 79, 88, 133.

56. *Mujeres mexicanas notables*, pp. 133-34, 156; Rocha, *Semblanzas*, p. 28.

57. Rocha, *Semblanzas*, pp. 22-23, 28-30.

58. María de los Angeles Mendieta Alatorre, *Carmen Serdán* (México: Editorial Bohemia Poblana, 1971), pp. 155, 206. In 1971, Carmen Serdán was the subject of both a biography and a play written by historian Mendieta Alatorre. Carmen Serdán was honored nationally on November 18, 1967 at a ceremony held in Puebla.

59. *Derechos de la mujer mexicana* (México: XLVII Legislatura del Congreso de la Unión, 1969), p. 114.

60. Sáenz Royo, *Semblanzas*, pp. 29-31; Teodoro Hernandez, "Mujeres revolucionarias de los ideales agraristas," in *Antorchas de la revolución*, ed. by Aurora Martínez Garza Vda. de Hernández (México: Gráficos Galeza, 1964), pp. 44-45.

61. Julio Scherer García, "María de Pino Suárez compañera olvidada," *Excelsior*, November 18, 1960, pp. 1, 9. María de Pino Suárez explained her concern that the amount provided by the revolutionary pension was inadequate. Always poor, she asked every president's wife for aid in raising pensions but was unsuccessful.

62. Adelina Zendejas, interview, Mexico City, July 21, 1976, stated that García became separated from her colleagues. While working as a servant for a young woman (who had no idea of García's revolutionary background), García became ill and died. Rascón, "La mujer," p. 143, stated that the Gutiérrez de Mendoza family had to sell Gutiérrez's typewriter to pay for her internment, but members of her family did not mention this. Gutiérrez was poor, and many of her papers were destroyed when she was forced to use them to build fires to heat the food she sold on the streets. Susana Mendoza, interview, Cuernavaca, August 12, 1976. Elisa Acuña y Rossetti was no longer active after the violent phase of the Revolution, and Dolores Jiménez y Muro died on October 15, 1925.

63. Adelina Zendejas, interview, Mexico City, July 21, 1976. Millan, *Mexico Reborn*, pp. 160-61, stated that "man is the Mexican woman's worst enemy."

Glossary

Americas—Western Hemisphere nations

campesino/a—man/woman peasant

Carrancista—supporter of Venustiano Carranza in 1913-1917 civil war and as president, 1917-1920

científicos—Social Darwinists; advisors of Díaz, 1877-1910

compañero/a—man/woman companion, mate

coronela—woman colonel

corregidora—wife of the corregidor, or mayor

corridos—ballads

Cristeros—Catholic guerrillas fighting against the state during the Cristero Rebellion, 1926-1929

curandera—female healer

ejido—communal land

Federal District—greater Mexico City

federales—Díaz's federal troops

guerrillo/a—man/woman who engages in unconventional warfare

hacendado—ranch owner; large estate owner

hacienda—ranch or large estate

henequen—drought-resistant perennial whose leaves produce elastic fibers used principally for making twine

henequenero—owner of henequen plantation

hispanidad—cultural, historical, religious, and linguistic unity of the Spanish world

Huertista—supporter of Victoriano Huerta, 1913-1914

Liberal clubs—political groups formed to oppose Díaz, the resurgence of clericalism, and the loss of political freedoms, 1900-1903

machismo—extreme male dominance

Maderista—supporter of Francisco Madero, 1909-1913

mestizo/a—man/woman of mixed European and American Indian ancestry

mujer—woman

mujeres de la raza—literally "women of the race"; used in the context of the 1925 Congress of "Mujeres de la Raza" and the Cooperative Union "Mujeres de la Raza" to refer to white, Spanish-speaking women

mutualista—mutual benefit society

norteño/a—man/woman from northern Mexico

Obregonista—supporter of Alvaro Obregón during the 1913-1917 civil war and as president, 1920-1924

obrero/a—male/female worker

Porfiriato—presidency of Porfirio Díaz, 1877-1910

Porfirista—supporter of Porfirio Díaz, 1877-1910

rurales—Díaz's rural police force

soldadera—female soldier

Sonoran Triangle—leaders from Sonora: Adolfo de la Huerta, Alvaro Obregón, and Plutarco Calles

Teresitas—anti-Díaz followers of Teresa Urrea

vale—pay certificate redeemable at company store

Veracruzana—woman from the state of Veracruz

Villista—supporter of Francisco (Pancho) Villa, 1911-1916

Yucateco/a—man/woman from the state of Yucatán

Zapatista—supporter of Emiliano Zapata, 1910-1919

Bibliography

ARCHIVES, LIBRARIES, AND DOCUMENT COLLECTIONS

Archivo General de la Nación. Papeles Presidenciales. Ramos de Obregón, Calles, and Cárdenas. Mexico City.

Biblioteca Carrillo Ancona. Mérida, Yucatán.

Biblioteca de la Oficina del Año Internacional de la Mujer. Mexico City.

Biblioteca Nacional. Biographical Collection. Mexico City.

Hemeroteca Nacional de México. Periodical Collection. Mexico City.

Hemeroteca Pino Suárez. Periodical Collection. Mérida, Yucatán.

Latin American Collection. University of Texas. Austin, Texas.

U.S. Department of State. *Records of the Department of State Relating to the Internal Affairs of Mexico, 1910-1929.* University of New Mexico, Coronado Room. Albuquerque, New Mexico.

PERIODICALS

Newspapers

Alma Mexicana: Por la Tierra y Por la Raza, Mexico City and Morelia.

América India: Por la Unión Indoamericana, Mexico City.

El Día, Mexico City.

El Diario del Hogar, Mexico City.

Excelsior, Mexico City.

El Gráfico, Mexico City.

El Heraldo de México, Mexico City.

El Informador, Guadalajara.

El Machete, Mexico City.

Mexican Herald, Mexico City.

El Mundo, Mexico City.

El Nacional, Organo Oficial del Partido de la Revolución, Mexico City.

New York Times, New York.

Novedades, Mexico City.

El Popular, Mexico City.

El Pueblo, Mexico City.

La Revista de Yucatán, Mérida.

El Sol de Puebla, Puebla.

El Universal, Mexico City.

Vésper: Justicia y Libertad, Guanajuato.

El Voto, Mexico City.

La Voz de la Revolución, Mérida.

Magazines

Arte y Letras, Mexico City.

Diario Oficial del Gobierno del Estado de Yucatán, Mérida.

El Hogar, Mexico City.

La Mujer Moderna, Mexico City.

Pan American Union Bulletin, Washington, D.C.

La Revista de Revistas: El Semanario Nacional, Mexico City.

La Semana de las Señoritas Mejicanas, Mexico City.

La Semana Ilustrada, Mexico City.

El Semanario de las Señoritas Mejicanas, Mexico City.

Siempre, Mexico City.

El Tiempo Ilustrado, Mexico City.

Tierra, Mérida.

Todo, Mexico City.

El Universal Ilustrado, Mexico City.

BOOKS

Primary Sources

Bases que se discutieron y aprobaron en el congreso obrero. México: Ligas de Resistencia, 1921.

Bulnes, Francisco. *El verdadero Díaz y la revolución.* México: n.p., 1920.

Bulnes, Francisco. *The Whole Truth about Mexico: President Wilson's Responsibility.* Translated by Dora Scott. New York: M. Bulnes Book Co., 1916.

Cantón, Miguel. *En tiempos de conquista: Veinte años de acción socialista.* Mérida: "Mayab" S.A., n.d.

Carrillo Puerto, Acrelio. *La familia Carrillo Puerto de Motul, con la revolución mexicana.* N.p., 1959.

Carrillo Puerto, Acrelio. *Lo que no se olvida, Felipe Carrillo Puerto.* Mérida: Imprenta "29 de Junio," 1964.

Carrillo Puerto, Felipe. *Informe rendido por el gobernador constitucional de Yucatán, C. Felipe Carrillo Puerto, ante la h. XXVII legislatura del estado, el 1 de enero de 1923.* Mérida: Imp. y. Lit. Gamboa Guzmán, 1923.

Channing, Arnold, and Frost, Frederick J. Tabor. *The American Egypt: A Record of Travel in Yucatan.* New York: Doubleday, Page, and Co., 1909.

Congreso Feminista de Yucatán. *Anales de esa memorable asamblea.* Mérida: Talleres Tipográficos del 'Ateneo Peninsular,' 1916.

Congreso Obrero de Izamal. *Segunda gran convención de trabajadores convocado por el Partido Socialista del Sureste de México.* Mérida: Compañía Tipográfica del Sureste, 1922.

Congreso Obrero de Motul. *Tierra y libertad; Bases que se discutieron y aprobaron en el congreso obrero celebrado en la ciudad de Motul para todas las ligas de resistencia del Partido Socialista Yucatán.* México: Talleres Tipográficos del Gobierno del Estado, 1921.

Degallado Guízar, Jesús. *Memorias de Jesús Degollado Guízar.* México: Editorial Jus, 1957.

Diario de los debates del congreso constituyente: 1916-1917. Comisión nacional para la celebración del sesquicentenario de la proclamación de la independencia nacional y del cincuentenario de la revolución mexicana. Introduction by Hilario Medina. 2 vols. México: Los Talleres Gráficos de la Nación, 1960.

Evans, Rosalie. *The Rosalie Evans Letters from Mexico.* Edited by Daisy Caden Pettus. Indianapolis: The Bobbs Merrill Co., 1926.

Flores Magón, Ricardo. *A la mujer.* Oakland: Prensa Sembradora, 1974.

Flores Magón, Ricardo. *Semilla libertaria.* 3 vols., II. México: Ediciones del Grupo Cultural "Ricardo Flores Magón," 1923.

Fornaro, Carlo de. *Diaz Czar of Mexico.* New York: The International Publishing Co., 1909.

Galindo, Hermila. *La doctrina Carranza y el acercamiento indolatino.* México: n.p., 1919.

Galindo, Hermila. *Un presidenciable. El general don Pablo González.* México: Imprenta Nacional, S.A., 1919.

Gamboa, Ignacio. *La mujer moderna.* Hoctun, Yucatán: Imprenta "Gamboa Guzmán," 1906.

García, Génaro. *Apuntes sobre la condición de la mujer.* México: Compañía Limit. de Tipógrafos, 1891.

King, Rosa E. *Tempest Over Mexico: A Personal Chronicle.* Boston: Little, Brown, and Co., 1938.

Lara y Pardo, Luis. *La prostitución en México.* México: Librería de la Vda. de Ch. Bouret, 1908.

Martínez Garza Vda. de Hernández, Aurora, ed. *Antorchas de la revolución.* México: Gráficos Galeza, 1964.

O'Shaughnessy, Edith. *Diplomatic Days.* New York: Harper and Bros., 1917.

O'Shaughnessy, Edith. *A Diplomat's Wife in Mexico.* New York: Arno Press, 1970.

Palavicini, Felix F. *Historia de la constitución de 1917.* 2 vols. México: Republica Mexicana, 1938.

Portes Gil, Emilio. *Quince años de la política mexicana.* 2ª edición. México: Ediciones Botas, 1941.

Ramírez Garrido, José Domingo. *Al margen del feminismo.* Mérida: Talleres "Pluma y Lápiz," 1918.

Reed, John. *Insurgent Mexico.* New York: Simon and Schuster, 1969.

Ríos Cárdenas, María. *La mujer mexicana es ciudadana. Historia con fisonomía de una novela de costumbres, 1930-1940.* México: A. de Bosque, 1942.

Robles de Mendoza, Margarita. *La evolución de la mujer en México*. México: Imp. Galas, 1931.

Rocha, María Efraína. *Semblanzas biográficas de algunas luchadoras mexicanas contemporáneas*. México: Ediciones del Comité Coordinador Femenino, 1947.

Rodríguez Cabo, Matilde. *La mujer y la revolución*. México: n.p., 1937.

Sáenz Royo, Artemisa ["Xóchitl"]. *Historia político-social-cultural del movimiento femenino en México, 1914-1950*. México: M. León Sánchez, 1954.

Sáenz Royo, Artemisa ["Xóchitl"]. *Semblanzas; mujeres mexicanas revolucionarias y guerreras, revolucionarias ideologicas, Por . . . ["Xóchitl"]*. México: Imp. M. León Sánchez, 1960.

Turner, Ethel Duffy. *Revolution in Baja California: Ricardo Flores Magon's High Noon*. Edited and annotated by Rey Davis. Detroit: Blaine Ethridge, 1981.

Turner, Ethel Duffy. *Ricardo Flores Magón y el partido liberal mexicano*. Translated by Eduardo Limón G. Morelia: Editorial "Erandi" del Gobierno del Estado, 1960.

Turner, John Kenneth. *Barbarous Mexico*. The Texas Pan American Series. Austin: University of Texas Press, 1969.

Turner, Timothy. *Bullets, Bottles and Gardenias*. Dallas: South-west Press, 1935.

Tweedie, E. Alec. *Mexico As I Saw It*. London: Thomas Nelson and Sons, 1911.

Urrea, Blas [Luis Cabrera]. *Obras políticas del Lic. Blas Urrea . . . .* México: Imprenta Nacional, S.A., 1921.

Villa de Buentello, G. Sofía. *La mujer y la ley*. México: Imprenta Franco-Americana, 1921.

Wright de Kleinhans, Laureana. *Mujeres notables mexicanas*. México: Tipografía Económica, 1910.

Secondary Sources

Alba, Victor. *Historia de la mujer*. México: Editorial Patria, S.A., 1953.

Alba, Victor. *The Mexicans. The Making of a Nation*. New York: Frederick A. Praeger, 1967.

Anderson, Rodney D. *Outcasts in Their Own Land: Mexican Industrial Workers, 1906-1911*. DeKalb: Northern Illinois University Press, 1976.

Bailey, David C. *¡Viva Cristo Rey! The Cristero Rebellion and the Church-State Conflict in Mexico*. Austin: University of Texas Press, 1974.

Barbosa Heldt, Antonio. *La mujer en las luchas por México*. México: Editora y Distribuidora, S.A., 1972.

Bustillos Carrillo, Antonio. *Yucatán al servicio de la patria y de la revolución*. México: "Casa Ramírez Editores," 1959.

Cámara Patrón, Alberto, and Ayora Sarlat, Vicente. *La obra revolucionaria de Carrillo Puerto*. Mérida: Prensa de la Universidad de Yucatán, 1974.

Casasola, Gustavo. *Historia gráfica de la revolución mexicana: 1900-1960*. 4 vols. México: Editorial F. Trillas, 1960.

Chaney, Elsa. *Supremadre: Women in Politics in Latin America*. Austin: University of Texas Press, 1979.

Clark, Marjorie Ruth. *Organized Labor in Mexico*. Chapel Hill: University of North Carolina Press, 1934.

Clarke, Ida Clyde. *Women of Today*. Chicago: The John C. Winston Co., 1928.

Cockcroft, James. *Intellectual Precursors of the Mexican Revolution: 1900-1913*. Austin: University of Texas Press, 1966.

Cosío Villegas, Daniel. *Historia moderna de México*. 9 vols. México: Editorial Hermes, 1955-1973.

Bibliography • 179

Downing, Todd. *The Mexican Earth*. New York: Doubleday, Doran and Co., 1940.

Dulles, John W. F. *Yesterday in Mexico: A Chronicle of the Revolution, 1919-1936*. Austin: University of Texas Press, 1961.

Fernández y Fernández, Aurora. *Mujeres que honran a la patria*. México: n.p., 1958.

Galván, Luz Elena. *La educación superior de la mujer en México: 1876-1940*. No. 109. México: Cuadernos de la Casa Chata, 1985.

Gamboa Ricalde, Alvaro. *Yucatán desde 1910*. 3 vols. Veracruz: Imp. "Standard," 1943-1955.

Gómez-Quiñones, Juan. *Sembradores, Ricardo Flores Magón y el Partido Liberal Mexicano: A Eulogy and Critique*. Los Angeles: Aztlán Publications, University of California, 1973.

González Navarro, Moisés. *El porfiriato: La vida social*. Vol. IV of *Historia moderna de México*. Edited by Daniel Cosío Villegas. 9 vols. México: Editorial Hermes, 1957.

Gruening, Ernest. *Mexico and Its Heritage*. New York: The Century Co., 1928.

Hanke, Lewis. *History of Latin American Civilization: Sources and Interpretations*. Vol. 2, *The Modern Age*. 2nd ed. Boston: Little, Brown, and Co., 1973.

Hart, John M. *Anarchism and the Mexican Working Class, 1860-1931*. Austin: University of Texas Press, 1978.

Henderson, Peter V. N. *Mexican Exiles in the Borderlands, 1910-1913*. Southwestern Studies Monograph no. 58. El Paso, Texas: Texas Western Press, 1979.

Hernández, Ana María. *La mujer mexicana en la industria textil*. México: Tipografía Mod., 1940.

Holden, William Curry. *Teresita*. Owings Mills, Maryland: Stemmer House Pub., 1978.

Ibarra de Anda, Fortino. *El periodismo en México*. 2 vols. Vol. II, *Las mexicanas en el periodismo*. 2nd ed. México: Imprenta Mundial, 1937.

Iturriaga, José E. *La estructura social y cultural de México*. México: Fondo de Cultura Económica, 1951.

Keremitsis, Dawn. *The Cotton Textile Industry in Porfiriato, Mexico 1870-1910*. New York: Garland Publishing Co., 1987.

Keremitsis, Dawn. *La industria textil mexicana en el siglo XIX*. México: SepSetentas, 1973.

Kirk, Betty. *Covering the Mexican Front: The Battle of Europe versus America*. Norman: University of Oklahoma Press, 1942.

Langham, Thomas C. *Border Trials: Ricardo Flores Magon and the Mexican Liberals*. Southwestern Studies Monograph, no. 65. El Paso, Texas: Texas Western Press, 1981.

Lenero, Estela. *El hueso y el sexo (la mujer obrera en dos industrias de Tlaxcala)*. No. 106. México: Cuadernos de la Casa Chata, 1984.

Lepidus, Henry. *The History of Mexican Journalism*. Journalism Series, no. 49, edited by Robert S. Mann. University of Missouri Bulletin, vol. 29, no. 4. Columbia, Missouri: University of Missouri Press, 1928.

Macías, Anna. *Against All Odds: The Feminist Movement in Mexico to 1940*. Westport, Connecticut: Greenwood Press, 1982.

Manzanilla Domínguez, Anastasio. *El comunismo en México y el archivo de Carrillo Puerto*. México: n.p., 1955.

Martínez, Pablo L. *A History of Lower California*. Translated by Ethel Duffy Turner. Mexico City: Editorial Baja California, 1960.

Mendieta Alatorre, María de los Angeles. *Carmen Serdán*. México: Editorial Bohemia Poblana, 1971.

Mendieta Alatorre, María de los Angeles. *Juana Belén Gutiérrez de Mendoza (1875-1942): Extraordinario precursora de la revolución mexicana*. México: María de los Angeles Mendieta Alatorre, 1983.

Mendieta Alatorre, María de los Angeles. *La mujer en la revolución mexicana*. México: Talleres Gráficos de la Nación, 1961.

Meyer, Jean. *Los cristeros*. 3 vols. Vol. III: *La cristada*. 2nd ed. México: Siglo Veintiuno Ed., S.A., 1974.

Millan, María del Carmen. *Diccionario de escritores mexicanos*. México: U.N.A.M.-Centro de Estudios Literarios, 1967.

Millan, Verna Carleton. *Mexico Reborn*. Boston: Houghton Mifflin Co., 1939.

Miller, Barbara Ann. *The Role of Women in the Mexican Cristero Rebellion: A New Chapter*. Ann Arbor, Michigan: University Microfilms International, 1981.

Morton, Ward M. *Woman Suffrage in Mexico*. Gainesville: University of Florida Press, 1962.

Niemeyer, E. V., Jr. *Revolution at Queretaro: The Mexican Constitutional Convention of 1916-1917*. Austin: University of Texas Press, 1974.

Pacheco Cruz, Santiago. *Recuerdos de la propaganda constitutionalista en Yucatán. Con una semblanza de la vida, actuación, asesinato del Governador Felipe Carrillo Puerto*. Mérida: Talleres Gráficos y Editorial ZAMNA, 1953.

Parsons, Wilfred. *Mexican Martyrdom*. New York: Macmillan Co., 1936.

Peña Samaniego, Heriberto. *Río Blanco*. México: Centro de Estudios Historicos del Movimiento Obrero Mexicano, 1975.

Quirk, Robert. *The Mexican Revolution and the Catholic Church 1910-1929*. Bloomington: Indiana University Press, 1973.

Raat, W. Dirk. *Revoltosos: Mexico's Rebels in the United States, 1903-1923*. College Station: Texas A & M University Press, 1981.

Ruiz, Ramón Eduardo. *Labor and the Ambivalent Revolutionaries: Mexico, 1911-1923*. Baltimore: The Johns Hopkins University Press, 1976.

Rutherford, John. *Mexican Society during the Revolution: A Literary Approach*. London: Oxford University Press, 1971.

Sosa Ferreyro, Roque Armando. *El crimen del miedo*. México: Costa-Amic, Ed., 1969.

Soto, Shirlene Ann. *The Mexican Woman: A Study of Her Participation in the Revolution, 1910-1940*. San Francisco: R & E Research Associates, 1979.

Townsend, William Cameron. *Lázaro Cárdenas: Mexican Democrat*. Ann Arbor, Michigan: George Wahr Publishing Co., 1952.

Turner, Frederick C. *The Dynamic of Mexican Nationalism*. Chapel Hill: University of North Carolina Press, 1968.

Uroz, Antonio. *Hombres y mujeres de México*. México: Editorial Lic. Antonio Uroz, 1974.

Vaughan, Mary Kay. *The State, Education, and Social Class in Mexico, 1880-1928*. DeKalb: Northern Illinois University Press, 1982.

Velarde, C. J. *Under the Mexican Flag, The Mexican Struggle Outlined*. Los Angeles: Southland Pub. House, 1926.

Womack, John, Jr. *Zapata and the Mexican Revolution*. New York: Alfred A. Knopf, 1969.

Women in a Changing World: The Dynamic Story of the International Council of Women since 1888. London: Routledge and Kegan Paul, 1966.

ARTICLES

Primary Sources

"Acta constitutiva del grupo Indo-América." *América India: Por la Unión Indoamericana* (January 12, 1930).

"Ahora o nunca." *Crónica Ilustrada Revolución Mexicana* LVIII (1967-68): 9.

Carrillo Puerto, Felipe. "New Yucatan." *Survey* LII (May 1, 1924): 138-42.

Carrillo Puerto, Felipe. "Programa de preparación social para los maestros." *Diario Oficial del Gobierno del Estado de Yucatán* (March 1, 1922): 1-2.

Flores Magón, Enrique. "Profa Elisa Acuña y Rosete." *El Nacional* (November 27, 1946).

Gutiérrez de Mendoza, Juana B. "Acta constitutiva del grupo Indo-América," *América India: Por la Unión Indoamericana* (January 12, 1930).

Gutiérrez de Mendoza, Juana B. "El General Calles no ha variado su criterio respecto a los desheredados." *Vésper* (March 15, 1932).

Gutiérrez de Mendoza, Juana B. "La independencia económica de México y la coalición de militares y civiles revolucionarios." *Vésper* (March 15, 1932).

Gutiérrez de Mendoza, Juana B. "Tres razones fundamentales del grupo 'Indo-America'," *América India: Por la Unión Indoamericana* (December 25, 1929).

Hart, A.G.B. *The Pulse of Mexico: Mexico's Monthly Review* (April 1922): 33-70.

Hernández, Teodoro. "Hay que hacer justicia a las mujeres revolucionarias de principios del siglo." *El Nacional* (November 30, 1958).

"La instrucción nocturna para obreras." *La Convención Radical Obrera*, a. 12, no. 531 (January 16, 1898): 1.

Llach, Leonor. "Tres escritoras mexicanas." *El Libro y el Pueblo* XII, no. 4 (April 1934): 165-74.

Ríos Cárdenas, María. "Emancipación integral de las mujeres." *El Nacional* (November 29, 1933).

Ríos Cárdenas, María. "Pide al gobierno la reducción de sacerdotes, el Congreso Nacional de Obreras y Campesinas." *El Nacional* (October 5, 1931).

Ríos Cárdenas, María. "Voto por la mujer." *El Nacional* (October 6, 1931).

Sáenz Royo, Artemisa N. ["Xóchitl"]. "Mujeres revolucionarias: Elvia Carrillo Puerto." *Mujer*, no. 7 (January 1933): 16.

Wiley, Anna Kelton. "Woman Suffrage in Mexico." *Equal Rights* XXIII, no. 11 (June 15, 1937): 84-104.

"Yucatan Schools Seek Our Help." *Survey* XXXVII (March 10, 1917): 659-60.

Zamarripa M., Florencio. "Elvia Carrillo Puerto, precursora del voto femenino." *Atisbos*, año III, no. 310 (December 18, 1952): 12.

Secondary Sources

"Acceso a la educación en todos los niveles." In *Derechos de la mujer mexicana*, 69-78. México: XLVII Legislatura del Congreso de la Unión, 1969.

Aguilar Roca, Leopoldo. "Un campeón de la educación popular." *Revista Yucateca Pedagogía*, año I, no. 3 (November 1950): 171-73.

Anderson, Lola. "Mexican Woman Journalists." *Pan American Union Bulletin* LXVIII, no. 5 (May 1934): 315-20.

Axelrod, Bernard. "St. Louis and the Mexican Revolutionaries, 1905-06." *The Bulletin of the Missouri Historical Society* 28 (January 1972): 94-108.

Barrágan, Leticia, and Rosales, Amanda. "Congreso nacionales de obreras y campesinas." *Historia Obrera 5*, II, no. 5 (June 1975): 24-44.

Bercovich, Harry, Jr. "Yucatan's Slain Governor Was Savior of His People." *San Francisco Examiner* (March 16, 1924).

Bermúdez, María Elvira. "La familia." In *México: Cincuenta años de revolución*. 4 vols. Vol. II: *La vida social*, edited by José Iturriaga, Humberto Romero, and Génaro Vázquez Colmenares, 81-112. México: Fondo de Cultura Económica, 1960-62.

Chacón, Ramón D. "Rural Educational Reform in Yucatan: From the Porfiriato to the Era of Salvador Alvarado, 1910-1918." *The Americas* XLII, no. 2 (October 1985): 207-228.

de Isoldi, Gerardo. "'Las Adelitas' de la revolución: Las mujeres mexicanas contribuyen valerosamente y con gran espiritu de lucha, al triunfo de la causa iniciada en 1910." *Hoy*, no. 405 (November 25, 1944): 22-26.

Fem: Publicación feminista. "Feminismo en México: Antecedentes" VIII, no. 30 (October-November 1983).

Fem: Publicación feminista trimestral. "La mujer en la historia de México" III, no. 11 (November-December 1979).

"Feminismo." *Enciclopedia de México.* 1970. Vol. IV.

Fernández Ponte, Fausto. "Mary Petre, correo de Madero." *Excelsior* (December 7, 1966).

Fisher, Lillian Estelle. "The Influence of the Present Mexican Revolution upon the Status of Women." *Hispanic American Historical Review* XXII, no. 1 (February 1942): 211-28.

Flores, Ana María. "La mujer en la sociedad." In *México: Cincuenta años de revolución.* 4 vols. Vol. II: *La vida social,* edited by José Iturriaga, Humberto Romero, and Génaro Vázquez Colmenares, 329-49. México: Fondo de Cultura Económica, 1960-62.

Gill, Mario. "Teresa Urrea. La Santa de Cabora." *Historia Mexicana* VI, no. 4 (April-June 1957): 626-44.

González Navarro, Moisés. "La huelga de Río Blanco." *Historia Mexicana* VI, no. 4 (April-June 1957): 510-33.

Gruening, Ernest. "Felipe Carrillo." *The Nation* CXVIII (January 16, 1924): 61-62.

Gruening, Ernest. "A Maya Idyl: A Study of Felipe Carrillo, Late Governor of Yucatan." *The Century Magazine* (April 1924): 832-36.

Herrick, Jane. "Periodicals for Women in Mexico during the Nineteenth Century." *The Americas* XIV, no. 3 (October 1957): 135-44.

Macías, Anna. "Felipe Carrillo Puerto and Women's Liberation in Mexico." In *Latin American Women.* Contributions in Women's Studies, edited by Asunción Lavrin, no. 3. Westport, Connecticut: Greenwood Press, 1978.

Macías, Anna. "Women and the Mexican Revolution 1910-1920." *The Americas* XXXVII, no. 2 (1980): 53-82.

Medina de Cetina, Rita María. "Protección a la infancia yucateca." *Siempre Adelante* (October-November 1974): 49-51.

Mendieta Alatorre, María de los Angeles. "Las mexicanas en la revolución." *Novedades.* Suplemento "México en la Cultura." (November 6, 1966).

Meyer, Jean. "Los obreros en la revolución mexicana: 'Los Batallones Rojos.'" *Historia Mexicana* XXI, no. 1 (July-September 1971): 1-37.

Miller, Barbara. "Women and Revolution: The Brigadas Femeninas and the Mexican Cristero Rebellion, 1926-29." In *Women and Politics in Twentieth Century Latin America.* Studies in Third World Societies, edited by Sandra F. McGee, vol. 15. Williamsburg, Virginia: The Editors, 1981.

Miller, Francesca. "The International Relations of Women of the Americas." *The Americas* XLIII, no. 2 (October 1986): 171-82.

"La mujer en la vida sindical y el Articulo 123." In *Derechos de la mujer mexicana,* 62-68. México: XLVII Legislatura del Congreso de la Unión, 1969.

Newhall, Beatrice. "Woman Suffrage in the Americas." *Pan American Union Bulletin* LXX, no. 5 (May 1936): 424-28.

Plenn, J. H. "Forgotten Heroines of Mexico: Tales of the Soldaderas, Amazons of War and Revolution." *Travel* LXVII (April 1936): 24-27, 60.

Putnam, Frank Bishop. "Teresa Urrea, The Santa de Cabora." *Southern California Quarterly* XLV, no. 3 (September 1963): 245-64.

Rascón, María Antonieta. "La mujer mexicana como hecho político: La precursora, la militante." *Siempre*. Suplemento "La Cultura en México," no. 569 (January 3, 1973).

Rascón, María Antonieta. "La mujer y la lucha social." In *Imagen y realidad de la mujer*, edited by Elena Urrutia, SepSetentas, no. 172. 139-74. Mexico: Secretaría de Educación Pública, 1975.

Rip-Rip [Rafael Martínez]. "Las mujeres en la revolución." *El Gráfico* (September 8, 1930).

Robleto, Hernan. "El henequén y el indio." In *El asesinato de Carrillo Puerto*, 107-110. México: n.p., 1924.

Ruiz Castañeda, María del Carmen. "La mujer mexicana en el periodico." *Filosofía y Letras* XXX, no. 60-61-62 (January-December 1956): 207-221.

Salgado, Eva. "Fragmentos de historia popular II. Las mujeres de la revolución." *Secuencia: Revista Americana de Ciencias Sociales*, vol. III (September/December 1985): 206-214.

Scherer García, Julio. "María de Pino Suárez, compañera olvidada." *Excelsior* (November 18, 1960).

Siller, Pedro. "Testimonios: Juana B. Gutiérrez de Mendoza." *Historia Obrera 5*, II, no. 5 (June 1975): 4-12.

Soto, Shirlene. "Three Historical Models of Chicana Feminism." *El Mirlo: A National Chicano Studies Newsletter*, vol. 10, no. 3, Summer 1983.

Soto, Shirlene. "Women in Mexico." In *Twentieth-Century Mexico*, W. Dirk Raat and William Beezley, eds., 17-28. Lincoln: University of Nebraska Press, 1986.

Soto, Shirlene. "Yucatan's Leadership in the Women's Movement: The First and Second Feminist Congresses, 1916." In *Between Borders: Essays on Mexicana/Chicana History*, edited by Adelaida R. Del Castillo, 483-91. Encino, CA: Floricanto Press, 1990.

Tuñon, Esperanza. "El Frente Unico Pro Derechos de la Mujer 1935-1938." *Fem: Publicación feminista* VIII, no. 30 (October-November 1983): 19-23.

Turner, Frederick C. "Los efectos de la participación femenina en la revolución de 1910." *Historia Mexicana* LXIV, no. 4 (April-June 1967): 603-620.

Vázquez Gómez, Esperanza de. "Historia y finalidades del Club Internacional de Mujeres." *Mujeres*, no. 68 (August 25, 1961): 18.

Zamora, Emilio, Jr. "Sara Estela Ramírez: Una Rosa Roja en el Movimiento." In *Mexican Women in the United States: Struggles Past and Present*, Magdalena Mora and Adelaida R. del Castillo, eds., 163-70. Occasional Paper No. 2. Los Angeles: UCLA Chicano Studies Research Center Publication, 1980.

Zendejas, Adelina. "El Movimiento Femenil Mexicano." *El Día* (June 16, 1975): 16.

Zendejas, Adelina. "La mujer mexicana en el periodismo." *El Gallo Ilustrado* (June 22, 1975): 3.

PAMPHLETS

Galindo, Hermila. *Estudio de la Srita. Hermila Galindo con motivo de los temas que han de absolverse en el Segundo Congreso Feminista de Yucatán*. Mérida: Imprenta del Gobierno Constitucionalista, 1916.

Liga Revolucionaria Feminista "Aurora Abán." *Programa de la acción feminista en Yucatán*. Mérida: n.p., 1930.

Sanger, Margaret. *La regulación de la natalidad o la brujula del hogar*. Mérida: Imp. "Mayab" S.A., 1922.

Torre(s) G., Rosa. *Mi actuación en el h. ayuntamiento de Mérida, Yucatán, México en el año de 1923*. N.p., 1936.

Velázquez Bringas, Esperanza. *La limitación racional de la familia como mejoramiento del proletariado y de la raza*. Mérida: Imp. "Mayab" S.A., 1922.

UNPUBLISHED SOURCES

Gutiérrez de Mendoza, Juana B. Unpublished papers. Cuernavaca, Mexico.

Herrera-Sobek, María. "Mothers, Lovers, and Soldiers: Archetypal Representation of Women in the Corrido." Unpublished manuscript, 1986.

Keremitsis, Dawn. "Women and Political Change in the Era of Cardenas." Unpublished paper, 1976.

Reed, Alma. "Peregrina." Unpublished autobiography, n.d.

DISSERTATIONS/THESES

Franz, David. "Bullets and Bolshevists: A History of the Mexican Revolution and Reform in Yucatan, 1910-1924." Ph.D. dissertation, University of New Mexico, 1973.

Hernández Tovar, Inés. "Sara Estela Ramírez: The Early Twentieth Century Texas-Mexican Poet." Ph.D. dissertation, University of Houston, 1984.

Jenkins, Myra Ellen. "Ricardo Flores Magon and the Mexican Liberal Party." Ph.D. dissertation, University of New Mexico, 1953.

Kelly, Brian. "The Cristero Rebellion—1926-1929: Its Diplomacy and Solution." Ph.D. dissertation, University of New Mexico, 1973.

Lau Jaiven, Ana. "Conciencia y acción de lucha. Aproximación a una historia del movimiento feminista en México, 1970-1976." Thesis, Universidad Nacional Autónoma de México, 1983.

Ochoa Flores, María del Carmen. "Desarrollo social de la mujer mexicana." Thesis, Universidad Nacional Autónoma de México, 1968.

Salas, Elizabeth. "Soldaderas in the Mexican Military: Myth and History." Ph.D. dissertation, University of California, Los Angeles, 1987.

Soto, Shirlene Ann. *The Mexican Woman: A Study of Her Participation in the Revolution, 1910-1940.* Ann Arbor: University Microfilms International, 1979.

Tanabe Velasco, Yolando. "La mujer y la profesión de contador público en México." Thesis, Universidad Nacional Autónoma de México, 1962.

Tuñon Pablos, Esperanza. "La lucha de las mujeres en el cardenismo." Thesis, Universidad Nacional Autónoma de México, 1986.

Vallens, Vivian M. "Working Women in Mexico during the Porfiriato, 1880-1910." Master's thesis, California State University, Long Beach, 1975.

INTERVIEWS

Bermúdez, María Elvira (lawyer, writer, and feminist). Mexico City. July 25, 1976.

Carrillo Puerto, Acrelio (author, brother of Elvia Carrillo Puerto). Mérida. April 2, 1976.

Carrillo Puerto de Triay, Angelina (sister of Elvia Carrillo Puerto). Mérida. April 5, 1976.

Castro Aguilar, Pedro (researcher at Hemeroteca Pino Suárez). Mérida. April 19, 1976.

Chapa, Virginia (dentist, sister of Esther Chapa). Mexico City. July 19, 1976.

Díaz Bolio, José (author, former brother-in-law of Elvia Carrillo Puerto). Mérida. April 20, 1976.

Hernández, Margarita P. de (journalist). Mérida. April 16, 1976.

Jiménez Trava, Antonia (lawyer, author). Mérida. April 15, 1976.

Johansen, Rosa Lie (artist, former roommate of Alma Reed). Mexico City. March 10, July 14, and August 4, 1976.

Mendieta Alatorre, María de los Angeles (professor and author). Mexico City. March 12 and July 16, 1976.

Mendoza, Susana (great-niece of Juana Gutiérrez de Mendoza). Cuernavaca. August 12 and 13, 1976.

Meyer, Eugenia (historian at Programa de Historia Oral). Mexico City. March 11, 1976.

Peniche de Ponce, Beatrice (author and feminist). Mérida. April 11, 1976.

Portes Gil, Emilio (former president of Mexico). Mexico City. August 16, 1976.

Ruz Menéndez, Rudolfo (Director, University of Yucatán Library, author). Mérida. April 6, 14, and 16, 1976.

Zendejas, Adelina (author and feminist). Mexico City. July 21, 1976.

Index